THE VINCE LOMBARDI SCRAPBOOK

THE VINCE LOMBARDI SCRAPBOOK

by George L. Flynn

GROSSET & DUNLAP   PUBLISHERS

A Filmways Company

NEW YORK

To Bill Heinz, a great writer and dear friend;
to Joe Lombardi, the nicest Lombardi of them all;
and to Will Mangas, editor and friend, whose help
I sorely missed during this project.

Published simultaneously in Canada

Library of Congress Catalog card number: 76-556
ISBN 0-448-12401-7 (hardcover)
ISBN 0-448-12405-X (paperback)

First printing
Printed in the United States of America

Acknowledgment

Many thanks are due the people who helped put this book together: to Chuck Lane, for his help in Green Bay; to Robert Markel, of Grosset & Dunlap, who decided to publish the book; and to Jane Toonkel, my editor, who made sure the book was finished on time. A special thanks to Marilyn Mangas, Will Mangas's widow, for her typing and encouragement. And to Bill Broad, for letting me use his brand new Selectric so all my typing mistakes could easily be corrected. Thanks to Mike Manuche for allowing me to use his restaurant as my New York office. And, of course, it is impossible to do a book about Vince Lombardi and his Packers without the help and friendship and pictures of Vernon J. Biever.

A very special thanks to my wife, Jill, for all her help and patience during the course of this project.

Contents

1 / Introduction   9

2 / Dinner Conversation with Vince Lombardi   14

3 / The Early Years — *Joe Lombardi, Betty Lombardi,*
     and Fr. Guy McPartland   27

4 / The Formative Years — *Wellington Mara, Joe Cahill,*
     and Frank Gifford   50

5 / The Green Bay Years — *Tom Miller, Tony Canadeo, Forrest*
     Gregg, Bart Starr, Willie Davis, and the Bilotti brothers   67

6 / Run to Daylight! — *W. C. Heinz*   130

7 / The Media and Vince Lombardi — *Chuck Lane, Ray Scott,*
     and Jerry Izenberg   138

8 / Three in a Row — *Chuck Mercein*   182

9 / Washington — *Vince Promuto*   204

10 / September 3, 1970   216

1
Introduction

H E HAD a funny way of smiling at you, and the first time you met him, you didn't know if he had had something bad for lunch or if he was just suspicious of your motives. Later, after he trusted you, the smile was warm and beautiful, and it made you feel good all over. I first met Vince Lombardi in New York at the Football Hall of Fame dinner. John Kennedy was the featured speaker. He was just completing his first year as president. It was December 1961. Later that month Lombardi's Packers would cream the Giants, and football's most spectacular dynasty would be launched.

Lombardi stood in the center of the suite *Sports Illustrated* had rented at the Waldorf Astoria. I had called him in Green Bay, asking to see him about a publishing venture for my company, Prentice-Hall. He said he'd be in New York to receive the *SI* Twenty-fifth Silver Anniversary Award and asked me to meet him at the suite. I didn't have an invitation, but I rented a tux and just walked in. Somebody came up to me and started to ask what I was doing there, but I spotted the Coach and headed for him. I guess he was the guy checking credentials, and thinking I knew Lombardi, he decided I was invited.

I introduced myself and Lombardi drew a blank, looking at me with that half-smile and giving me the eye. I mentioned Prentice-Hall and the phone conversation, and he still looked right through me. Finally, I said the magic name, Red Smith, and he smiled for real and shook my hand with that powerful grip. He was very pleasant for a second or two and told me to meet him after the NFL title game at the league meetings in Miami in January. Then he excused himself and went to greet a friend. I retired to the bar and watched him from a distance. It was *SI*'s party and the place was loaded with celebrities, but he was the center of attention. He still had to beat a great Giant team later that month but he was already the man of the hour. Later that night, when introduced to the thousand plus in the Grand Ballroom, he got the longest and warmest ovation of the evening. It must have felt wonderful, the boy from Brooklyn receiving the biggest ovation in the grandest of hotels.

But after the championship, when I saw him in Miami, he did not remember me.

Red Smith had been the magic name because Smith had agreed to help me launch a special new series of sports books, cleverly called the "Red Smith Sports Series." We wanted Lombardi to do the book on pro football, and Red had written Vince about our plans. Lombardi, a great friend and fan of Smith, agreed to be part of the series. The purpose of the meeting in Miami was to explain the concept of the series to Lombardi and to set up further meetings. Thus began the making of one of the classic books of sports literature, *Run to Daylight!*

Probably no coach or athlete has had as much written about him as has Lombardi. He has been the subject of countless books, articles, films, and documentaries. There are schools named after him, roads and rest areas, arenas and clinics. Little league coaches who know nothing about coaching think that by hollering at youngsters they become another Lombardi. Social scientists, psychologists, and others use his desire for achievement as an example in criticism of sports and the competitive American system. Businessmen and leaders of all walks of life use Lombardi as their "patron saint" for success; he signifies the sacrifices they demand of themselves to be successful. All leaders are compared to him, and many wrap the "Lombardi Credo" around themselves whenever talking about their own commitment to discipline, sacrifice, and hard work. But if any of them, especially on the political level, ever were as committed and worked as hard as Lombardi, there would be a lot fewer ills in this country.

For all that has been written, for all that has been said, for all the incantations to the Lombardi spirit, very few people really knew and understood this highly intelligent, completely dedicated man. It is hoped that *The Vince Lombardi Scrapbook* will help bring a clearer and more accurate understanding of this man.

We have tried in this book to get away from the well-known stories that have been repeated ad nauseum. Also, the illustrations include some never before seen. Of course, there really are not any secrets to expose here. Rather, this is a fresh look at the man by people who, by and large, knew him in a way different than those who have previously reported about him. The section on the media and Lombardi includes material from people who covered him — some who were close, others who weren't. Indeed, how so many top professionals read the man differently makes for fascinating reading.

Many of the people interviewed are famous in their own right. You can't do a book about someone as well-known as Lombardi without including the stars and celebrities. But mostly there are those who worked with him day by day: those who learned from him when he was just beginning, those who played for him before he was famous, and those who were with him in the glory days at Green Bay.

It is no accident that the explosion of pro football into our number-one sport and the emergence of Vince Lombardi as its high priest came at the same time. Lombardi was from New York and had been an assistant with the Giants when they began their championship years. And as the Giants took hold of the city and became the darlings of the writers and broadcasters, television found the people in advertising agencies and big corporations with the money to sponsor pro football. With this money came greater exposure, and a game so perfectly suited for television viewing soon captured the public's attention. In 1958, when the Colts beat the Giants in that great overtime game for the NFL title, the drama and excitement captured the entire country. The combination of pro football and television began their fantastic climb in popularity. But it is even money, had the Colts played the Pittsburgh Steelers in that game and had the game gone into overtime, no matter how successful and exciting, the advertisers and money people would not have been so turned on. It was the Giants and New York's love affair with them that meant the money for TV.

Then in 1959 Lombardi went to Green Bay to take over the Packers. The year before, the NFL had thought of dropping the franchise because the team was so bad (won 1, lost 10, and tied 1); the Packers never drew any fans on the road or even in Wisconsin. So the man from New York went to the town that helped found pro football at a time when New York was wild over the sport. No playwright worth his pencil could ever write the story that followed: Lombardi, the New York boy, takes the smallest town and worst team in football and in three years they are champions. And who did they beat? The New York Giants. Well, at least it was a New Yorker that beat us, said the Giants fans, and soon the Packers were the city's second-favorite team. And you couldn't get seats on the few flights to Green Bay because the writers from New York and points west were all on their way to see the "Wonderman" and his team. There had not been a writer from another town covering the Packers since the Ice Age, but now the bars and motels were filled with them, and countless readers across the country began learning about Taylor and Hornung and Starr and the rest.

So the Giants got Madison Avenue excited about pro football; television handled its newly found gold mine properly; and Vince Lombardi and the Packers became the national team. Wherever they played, they sold out; they became the second team on the television doubleheader, so that throughout the country, all the fans could see Green Bay play. It became such a good thing that others decided they wanted a piece of the action, and in the good old American way, a new league set up shop. That meant more television, newer stadiums, higher salaries, and higher advertising rates. The sport of the masses became pro football.

Without question, Lombardi was the most famous sports personality of the sixties. He transcended that limited area of sports as no man before him had done. He began to speak to business organizations and make inspirational films, and through it all, he won as no coach before him had done in such a very short time.

When he arrived in Green Bay, he told the press and the fans that he was "no miracle maker." And after watching the films of the team he inherited, he knew he had not overstated the case. The Packers were dreadful. No veterans wanted to be traded to "Siberia," and rookies hoped they would not be drafted by Green Bay. Looking back with perfect twenty-twenty hindsight, we can all see the Taylors, Kramers, Greggs, and Starrs, just ready to bloom into greatness. But in 1959, no coach in football would have traded any player on his team for any on the Packers, with the exception of Forrest Gregg. After months of studying the films, Lombardi summed it up by saying to his assistants: "Gentlemen, we have one professional on our team, Gregg." But you don't win championships with one professional player, especially when the professional is an offensive tackle. What began in those winter months of study and analysis carried over into the summer camp, and those Packers who survived Vince Lombardi's first camp became the foundation on which he built the empire.

Bart Starr described the camp as "vicious." Others were less kind. But when it was over, the Coach had them ready to play professional football. He had asked for a five-year contract because he thought it would take that long to make the Packers respectable. In three years, they had won it all. To those players who had been in Green Bay, playing on losing teams and having the townspeople vilify them and their families, the suffering of Lombardi's camp and the practice sessions were small hurts forgotten in the happiness of victory.

Lombardi lost the NFL title game in his second year, and he always blamed himself for that defeat. But he remembered, and he made his players remember how very close they were when they lost; and they never again lost a playoff or championship game under him. Winning the first championship was especially dear to Lombardi, and beating the Giants for it made it doubly wonderful. Not that Lombardi had anything against New York — after all, the Giants had helped him into pro football. But he had hoped to be their coach after the 1958 season. He had actually been promised the job, but when Jim Lee Howell stayed on for another year, he took the Green Bay job.

The fourth year, Green Bay again played for the title in New York, and in one of the most brutally fought football games ever played, the Packers won again.

Winning a championship is quite an achievement. Repeating it, year after year, is the mark of greatness. Lombardi's Packers, in seven years, won five NFL titles and the first two Super Bowls. If there had been Super Bowl games before that, they'd have won those too. For the players, these were golden times. The salaries were up, the endorsements came flowing in, the press was there for the quick statement, the fans were adoring, and the playoff money took care of the creditors. For the Coach, however, it became something else.

To Lombardi, winning and making the effort to win again were what life was all about. He had no understanding of those who questioned why winning was so important and why winning all the time was such a goal. To him, it was not winning for winning's sake but the constant struggle to improve oneself, to work to the limits of one's ability and then go a little beyond that, that made his quest for success so important. To him, the basic fundamental was to use the talent God gave you to the fullest. And in sports, or any endeavor, winning is the sign that you have done just that. As he so often told his team, "The spirit, the will to win, and the will to excel — these are the important things that transcend the game itself."

Lombardi put heavy pressure on his players, especially in practice. In fact, he made practice so difficult and demanding that the games often seemed easy in comparison. He told the players one day that if they could not stand the pressure he was putting on them, how would they stand up against 70,000 screaming fans with time running out? But with each winning season, the tension and pressure began to take its toll on him. Lombardi was never one to sit down with writers and small talk about football and the players. His press conferences were marked with tension, and most of the reporters covering the game were afraid to question him too closely. Certainly, he was not beyond telling a writer his question was stupid if he thought it was. Articles critical of him and his philosophy of winning, spartanism, and dedication were soon present in the press, but not in Green Bay's.

He was called tyrannical, vindictive, cruel, moody, short-tempered, a martinet, and an S.O.B. He also was termed tender, understanding, compassionate, friendly, warm, dynamic, considerate, and a saint. And he was actually all of these to those who really knew him. He chewed out everybody that had ever been close to him except his parents and Earl Blaik. He also was warm and considerate to all these same people. Player or friend, writer or a fan, nobody ever knew exactly which face Lombardi would wear at any specific time. Indeed, his mood could change in a second. At times, especially in the later days in Green Bay, his anger would only surface when he was really upset or when he wanted to turn it on to shake up the team. People close to him say he was like a Shakespearean actor, using his moods and his language to move the team at his will.

As Red Smith put it, "Vince Lombardi is neither sadist or saint. He happens to be a decent man who is extremely capable at doing his job."

With all the stories about Lombardi, most often forgotten is the uniquely American one, that of the man from immigrant parents who struggled for years to become a success in his chosen field. Most forget that Vince Lombardi was forty-six years old before he got his first head coaching job in pro football. The only other head coaching job he had held was at St. Cecilia's High School in New Jersey in the early forties. Most of us would have thrown in the towel and semiretired if we were not a corporate vice-president by forty. Lombardi got discouraged, but he never quit; and when he got his shot, nothing could keep him from his goal.

This Vince Lombardi scrapbook will introduce you to some of the people who were with Lombardi as he struggled through the years of frustration on the way to Green Bay. There are those at St. Cecilia's who played for him; those who knew him at Fordham; and the cadets at West Point, where he began the disciplined coaching that took him to the Giants and finally to the glory years in Green Bay and to the rebuilding of the Redskins. Through these people, there comes a new picture of Lombardi. Vince Lombardi was a man of intense dedication, intelligence, and strong will power; and he had a great love for football, country, his players, and God.

Hopefully, after reading *The Vince Lombardi Scrapbook*, you will have a greater understanding and appreciation of what a unique human being this great man really was.

2

Dinner Conversation with Vince Lombardi

IT WAS October 1968. The Packers had played four or five games, and it was clear that they were not going to win their fourth National Football League title in a row or go back to Miami do defend their Super Bowl crown. Vince Lombardi had retired as the Packer head coach in February of that year. He was still the general manager.

We had made a date to have dinner the next time I was in Green Bay when I had seen him in New York. That was in the springtime, and he was in for the league meetings. He looked great and had been playing a lot of golf. After he retired as Packer coach, he and Marie and friends had done a lot of traveling, and he looked rested and happy.

So I was in Green Bay when the Packers came to the opening of their first training camp without Lombardi. And I saw him and forgot about having dinner with him. He was miserable. The happy, relaxed, laughing general manager of the springtime was as mean as a grizzly bear and just as communicative. I stayed around anyway for a few days to visit with the players, and they seemed very confident about the coming season. After all, it was basically the same team that had won an unprecedented three NFL titles in a row. And, on good authority, the players were ready to show the world who was responsible for all that winning.

We finally got together and met at the Bilotti's Forum. We sat in the Lombardi room; it was closed off so we could have some privacy and he could relax. I guess we talked for about four or five hours. The dinner was fine and the drinks were plentiful. He seemed much more at home with being a general manager, but it still was a subject I stayed away from. I tried not to dwell on the team as it was playing then, nor to recount the great wins of the past.

Obviously, when you spend that amount of time with the greatest coach in the history of football, you're going to talk about football. But before I got to that, we talked about many things, especially politics. It was Nixon against Humphrey, and I knew that Vince had helped Jack Kennedy in the

1960 Wisconsin primary and had a very warm spot for Bobby. Vince did not exactly go out and knock on doors for Jack Kennedy, but he let it be known to the press whom he supported in that primary and it may have helped.

When I mentioned that, a few weeks before coming out, I had read somewhere that his name had been mentioned by the Nixon people as a possible vice-presidential running mate, he was most amused. Vince was a life-long Democrat and had little regard for Nixon. Not that he was wild about Hubert Humphrey either. And later when he was in Washington and Nixon was president, I don't think Vince's feelings changed.

There really was no special reason for our dinner. We had gone out many other times in the past, but this time I told him I'd just like to sit and talk and tape it. He said fine, as long as he could hear the tapes. But, until I was asked to put this book together, I never gave another thought to them. After listening to them, I thought they might give a better look at the man. These are his words.

DINNER CONVERSATION WITH VINCE LOMBARDI: FALL OF 1968

Flynn: When you were coaching in high school, how did you teach young players to overcome their natural fears and stick their nose in there?

Lombardi: First of all, you never force a boy to put his head down and tackle. You can expose him to injury too easily. Of course, if we get a man up here in the pros who won't stick his nose in there, then we get rid of him right away. But these are men. But at the high school level, he may not do it for a number of reasons. But you continue to expose him to it and he watches the other players. And you explain to him what he must do, but you never try to force him to go in there. But that's it. If he does not do it, you ignore it. He learns by example and explanation. Quiet explanation. It takes a great deal to be a high school coach, a great deal of understanding of youth. The boys are not physically mature enough, except for a few, and that's what you must be careful of.

Flynn: You film everything these days, the practice, the games, etc., and run them over and over. When did you, as a coach, begin using films?

Lombardi: You won't believe this, but I first started using film to study from when I was at West Point in 1949. That was when TV first started and we took TV pictures. Actually, we took moving pictures of a game being played on television. And you almost went nuts because of the strobe, or whatever, that caused a line in the film. That was a long time ago and nobody ever did that. We also were the first ones to use closed-circuit television on the sidelines during a game. It was a huge unit, about fifty times the size of the ones out today. Only West Point could afford it.

Flynn: Do you use closed circuit on the sidelines today?

Lombardi: No. They outlawed it. They thought I was getting an advantage.

Flynn: Were you?

Lombardi: Yes. But anybody else could get the same advantage, but nobody else understood what the hell they were doing so they said, "The hell with it. Nobody can use it." Great world. At West Point, I distinctly remember seeing Pittsburgh, Michigan, all the rest of them on that old machine. We beat Michigan in those years, and they had great college teams.

Flynn: You hear so much about the "psychology" of pro football today. What does that mean to you?

Lombardi: You simplify it when you say "psychology." It's a lot more complicated than that. All the teams are relatively equal in talent. To me it's a mental attitude more than anything else. I don't think there is too much psychology to it. You can say what you want about psychology. People say the reason the Packers win is Vince Lombardi's psychology. That's not true. I just think it is the mental attitude of the players now. You appeal to that mental attitude. You appeal to their pride; you appeal to their desire. You appeal to things like that, you see, more than anything else. But I don't think it's psychology. I don't know of anyone, with the possible exception of Rockne, who deliberately tried to "psyche" his football team. The present-day players are much too sophisticated for that. You have to be honest with them really, to start with.

Flynn: How did you each week come up with the right thing to motivate the team?

Lombardi: I think you have to study that. You have to know what to say. If the team you're playing that week is not as good as you and if you and the players know it, maybe that's the week you don't say too much. There are only so many times that you feel you can get your team up, you see. How many that is depends. Maybe six or seven or eight times. Other times they get themselves up, right? And there are certain weeks when you feel you are the better football team, and if they just go out and play their game, you'll win. And that's the week you say very little, saving what you would have said for another time.

Flynn: Bart Starr said he's heard all your talks, but the one that moved him the most was the one before the Rams game in Milwaukee in 1967 for the Western Conference title. What do you remember about it?

Lombardi: Yes, but I could no more repeat what I said than I could fly to the moon. I don't know what I said at the time. I think the conditions have to dictate what you say. You know, like how the team is playing, what the other team is doing, what position you are in the standings, how many people are hurt on your team. That particular time, before that Rams game, I don't know what I said. I couldn't attempt to repeat what I said. I know we had done a great deal of winning and I probably did what I did all that year: said something about winning, as I always did, what the game meant, not only right now but to the future. I think I said that all of the glamour, all of the noise, all of the excitement, all the color, they linger only in the memory; but the spirit, the will to excel, the will to win, they go on forever, you see. This is probably what I tried to tell them about. In other words, if they could win, what this great record they had would mean. As far as what this meant to each one of them personally, I told them they were part of a team that won three National Football League titles in a row, something that no team had ever done.

Flynn: In 1959 you left New York to take over the worst team and franchise in pro football. In *Daylight* you told of the defeatism you found here. How did you dispel that?

Lombardi: Yes, there was defeatism here, a feeling that we had to dispel. And how do you dispel that feeling? I could no more tell you that now than remember my Rams speech. I don't know how. I think you grab it by the ears and throw it out. What you have to present to your team is a feeling of confidence. You defeat defeatism with confidence. And that confidence comes from the man who leads. They pick that up from the person that leads. I really don't have the words to explain how you do it, but it's something you have and feel. You just have it. It's nothing you get. You have it right here in your belly. That's where it is. You have to have confidence in what you can do. You also have to be a realist. I did not just come in here and say we're going to be a winner here because I've never been on a loser. I know I said that, but I also knew I had some of the things here that make a winner.

Flynn: You told Bill Heinz that because the coach becomes so closely involved with the quarterback, he becomes an extension of the coach's personality on the field. So with the team. Are there any other players like that?

Lombardi: In addition to your quarterback, there is your defensive quarterback, the middle linebacker. Actually, your defensive signals can be called from the sideline. You can more or less anticipate a team's offense. That's why it's so easy to defense teams. In certain situations, you may not be able to call the exact play but can almost anticipate what they will do. You do this by studying their past history. They don't change. People don't change what has been working for them.

I don't say they are going to run left or to the right, but you generally know where they're going to run or who they are going to throw to, if they're going to throw a pass. It depends upon the down and the distance and the situation in the game. This is what the defensive quarterback is supposed to know.

Flynn: Your defensive quarterback was Ray Nitschke, maybe the best that ever played.

Lombardi: Yes, he is, but we call our defenses from the sideline. There is too much of a burden for him to carry all that information and still execute, and we are much more aware of down and distance and tendencies so we take the burden off him.

Defense is much more of an emotional game than is the offense. So if you start a boy thinking on defense, he's not going to do the job for you. Even if you have just one boy calling all the defensive signals, thinking of all that has to be remembered on each play, he's not going to do the job for you. He may do a great job calling the signals, but he won't do his job itself.

An offensive player is much more of a technical player. He plays almost without emotion. Not completely. He has to. He has to be highly skilled, highly technical. He can't overreact. The defense can overreact a little bit. The offensive player cannot overreact. He has to be thinking all the time with all the defensive changes and quarterback audibles, and he has to be a thinking man really. Defense is a game of reaction. You react to what the offense does. It's more of a natural thing to play defense rather than offense.

Flynn: If the offensive players are to be that technical and skilled and disciplined not to overreact, how do you develop that discipline?

Lombardi: Discipline is a part of the will really. A disciplined person is one who follows the will of the one who gives the orders. Also, you teach discipline by doing it over and over, by repetition and rote. Especially in a game like football where you have very little time to decide what you are going to do. So what you do is react almost instinctively, naturally. You have done it so many times, over and over and over again, don't you see?

Flynn: Rookie offensive linemen always have trouble with pass blocking. Why?

Lombardi: It is a very difficult technique, and it is something which they are not accustomed to. Today, that does not seem to be as true, however, as it was a few years ago. They seem to have better fundamentals in pass blocking, because they are using more drop back passers in college. Also, they are taught to block aggressively to protect their quarterback, because most of the plays are play pass-action plays where they fire out at the defense. So this is something we have to break them of before they can pass block at this level.

Flynn: What is it that makes a quarterback great?

Lombardi: Well, first of all, he has to have the ability to throw the ball. Next, he has to have the ability to anticipate the break of the receiver into the pattern. If he can't throw, forget about him. He can be the most intelligent player in the world, a great ball-handler but if he can't throw, forget him. He has to have the arm to throw the ball, he has to have the quick release, and he has to be able to anticipate the receiver. That's the number one thing. Anything you find after that is a plus. No matter what else he has — running ability, brains, Phi Beta Kappa, personality, six-foot four, and strength — if he can't do that you just say, "Son, you'll have to play some other position."

Flynn: And after passing ability, then what?

Lombardi: There are many things. He has to have height so he can see over the pass rushers. If he can run, pull the ball down, and take off, so much the better. These are the natural things. If he is intelligent, that's a great plus. That's about it.

Flynn: If your man has all that, now what?

Lombardi: Well, that's an easy job.

Flynn: What's the toughest position to fill on the team, besides quarterback?

Lombardi: I'd say the tight end. He has to be a receiver. He has to have speed. He's got to block like an offensive tackle. He's got to be able to get into the passing lanes, catch the ball, run, and also handle the blocking assignments, usually against a tough linebacker or on the defensive end. There haven't been very many that fit all of that. I had one, Ron Kramer. He was a good one. He could do everything.

Flynn: What was your best team?

Lombardi: '61 and '62 were great teams, but the '63 team was probably the best team of all time. And we didn't win it that year either. Had we won then, we would have had the three in a row that we got later. That was a great football team. The Bears won the title, but we lost to them twice that year, our only losses. And both times, Bart Starr was out with injuries.

Flynn: When did you first know you wanted to be a coach?

Lombardi: I was going to Fordham Law School, and I wanted to get married. My father, being Italian, said you're not going to get married until you can support yourself. So I took a job over in Englewood, New Jersey, teaching school and coaching in order to get married. From then on, that's what I was, a football coach. I coached at St. Cecilia's for eight years. We won six state championships, went undefeated three or four times, and I remember we had a winning streak of thirty-six games in a row.

Flynn: What have you put into the game today?

Lombardi: I get a big kick out of watching the other teams today because we put a lot of stuff into this league. The Sweep, Do-Dad blocking, the passing game, the idea of reading the defense; a lot of teams are using our passing game. And some of them have beaten us with it. Anybody that coached here has picked it up and carried it on. We have the best passing game in the business, I think. It takes an intelligent quarterback in order to do it.

Flynn: How did you put this passing game together?

Lombardi: I think that it just came over the years. Putting in this and that, and then putting up a defense against it and seeing how it looked. And when we put in the passing game in the old days, we'd wind up with about sixty pass plays, which was impossible. Once they started putting in the multiple defenses, it became even more difficult, and the pass plays multiplied.

For instance, let's say we'd have ten plays to go against the man-to-man defense, six plays against the zone, five plays against the combination man-to-man and zone, four plays against a frank defense, and so forth.

Hell, we'd wind up with twenty-five, thirty, or forty pass plays. Well, there is no way you're going to use them all, and there is no way for the quarterback to anticipate the defense when he calls the play in the huddle. So it became a guessing game.

So we had to come up with some sort of a system whereby one pass play could be used to defeat three or four defenses. Or just take two of the defenses. A team will use, for example, on say sixty-five defensive plays, a major defense twenty-five times, a secondary defense maybe fifteen times, another defense maybe fifteen times, and another defense once in a while. The one that is used once in a while you just say, "Hell, I can't get ready for everything, so just throw that out." If you tried to get ready for everything in this game, all possibilities, you'd never be ready.

When Lombardi put in the Power Sweep, one of its options was the Halfback Option. Here Paul Hornung, #5, gets ready to throw off the "Sweep" to Boyd Dowler, #86. (*Vernon J. Biever*)

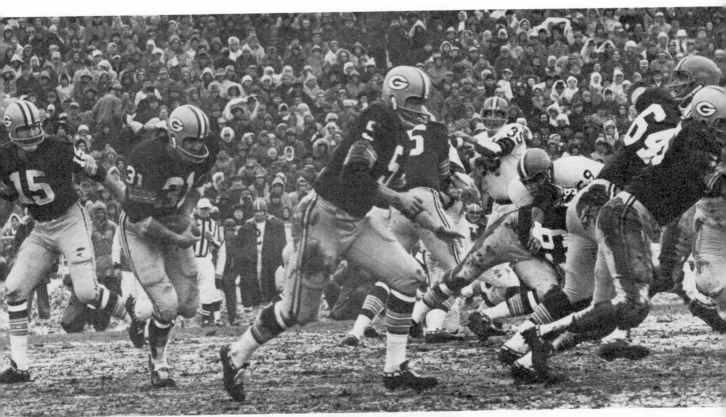

The "Sweep" worked with either the halfback carrying or the fullback. Here Jimmy Taylor has the handoff from Bart Starr and follows Paul Hornung around the defense to make a long gain. *(Vernon J. Biever)*

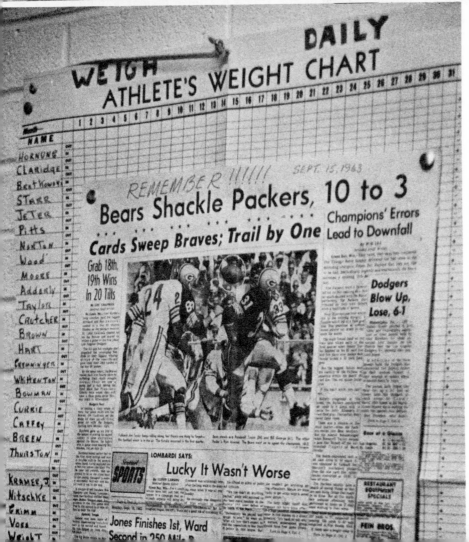

These headlines tell all about what happened to the Packers in the 1963 season: they lost to the Bears twice and that was it. *(Vernon J. Biever)*

So what you try to do is to defeat what they do best. Just like I try to do what I do best, and you try to stop it. So you try to come up with maybe ten pass plays that the quarterback can use, and you give him the "keys" that he must read to make the play work against those three defenses. On one pass, the key to the defense might be the middle linebacker; on another, the key might be the strong-side safety; on another, the weak-side safety; and so on.

In other words, the quarterback calls the pass play in the huddle, and as he comes away from the line of scrimmage, he keys that defensive man. If the middle linebacker goes strong, he will throw to the weak side. If the middle linebacker happened to go to the weak side, he would throw strong. Also, the receivers have to "key." Those same receivers who are going out there will also key the middle linebacker. So if the middle linebacker comes toward them, they know what to do in order to clear it for the receiver on the other side.

So everybody has the same key. You may have three or four passes that go against that key. And you'll have three or four passes in which the key will be the strong-side safety. When the strong-side safety comes up to force, or when the strong-side safety goes back to cover deep, and so forth and so on, then the reaction is such and such and the quarterback either throws to it or away from it.

Everybody reads. That's why it's a coordinated type of offense. And we were the first ones to do that, really, to any great extent in the league. Brodie has never done it. Maybe he's doing it now; I don't know. They have a new coach there. And he's a great passer. Unitas has never done it, and he's a great passer. They just throw to the people, regardless, do you see? And they are good enough — have good enough talent, good enough arms, and good enough receivers — to get away with it.

Flynn: Your passing game is now being copied throughout the league?

Lombardi: Yes, and it's very simple. It is a very simple thing to do, and a very simple thing to put in.

Flynn: The old passing game was built on a great passer throwing to a great receiver, but today's defenses are so complicated that they probably would not work, right?

Lombardi: That's correct.

Flynn: And yet nobody has won as much as you and Starr.

Lombardi: Well, Starr is by far the best quarterback that the league has ever seen, from all aspects that we have discussed.

Flynn: You put all of this in, the keying and reading by the quarterback and the receivers. How?

Lombardi: It is simply a matter of teaching them to recognize the defenses and of coordinating their recognition.

But you can't teach the anticipation and the instinct on when to throw and when to hold. You get a real strong arm thrower, he may be able to anticipate a little later than others, for instance like Starr. Starr does not have a real strong arm, a bullet or rifle type of arm. Starr throws a good, strong pass but it's a different type of pass. Jurgenson, for instance, he has a rifle, you see. He can put the ball in that big a crack, about an inch wide between the defender and receiver, and he'd try to. Starr would never do that, you see.

Flynn: When do you think you knew that coaching was for you?

Lombardi: I don't know. Football had always been a great part of my life, and even when I was going to law school, though I did not realize it at the time, I think I was already headed for coaching. You know, the Lord has a funny way of putting you in the right place.

Flynn: Football to you is more than a game, is that not true?

Lombardi: Football is a way of life. Really. It really is. Now I think that anybody who has ever been a part of it has to think that way. I think that football is the symbol, really, of a lot of things. It's a symbol of courage. It's a symbol of stamina. I think football is a symbol of teamwork, of efficiency. I think it is all of these things. And if you look and analyze what I just said, these are three areas that you would have to say made the United States, made America great. Courage, stamina, and teamwork — or coordinated efficiency, or whatever you want to call it.

I think football has become a symbol of these qualities. It is also, I think, many other things. I think it is a game of leaders, for one thing. I don't mean to say that everybody that plays football eventually becomes a leader, because I think that leadership is not only ability but also commitment. And most people will not commit themselves.

I don't know of any other game, by itself, because of the controlled violence that is football that demands a personal discipline which I don't think is found in any other sport.

Of all the years that I've been in football, never have there ever been any racial or social problems on my team. All things are equal, racially and socially on that team. There are no barriers. There just aren't any, in spite of what has been written in some magazines recently. And I've been close enough to it to know. I'm talking about my football, the people I know and have had with me and as opponents. I've had people from all over this country, and everybody is accepted, regardless of your race, regardless of your social or religious status and beliefs. There are not any barriers.

I think these are important things. I don't know of another sport where there is so much fun when you win. And yet it requires so much determination when you lose at football. Football requires everything that is required to succeed in life.

There is a great deal of selflessness in football. Really, the only personal satisfaction that a person receives in football is being part of the successful whole. You can be the greatest football player in America, and if your team doesn't win, you're a nothing. So the only satisfaction you receive is being part of a winner.

I call it a "spartan" game. And I like that word. I'm always telling that to the team. It takes "spartanlike" qualities in order to play football. It takes sacrifice to play it, and it takes self-denial, which are two of the great spartan qualities. It takes all of those things to be a part of it, not just for players but for everyone who is part of the group.

Flynn: This summer, for the first time, the players went on strike. It did not last more than two weeks but do you think it hurt the game?

Lombardi: I think we had a terrible setback here as far as professional football is concerned with the union business. I think it has hurt the game, miserably. I don't know whether it will be overcome or not. I think the game itself may defeat it really. It may defeat that feeling.

But there is that feeling. I know I felt it; that feeling of frustration and helplessness.

It's not the kind of game that you can understand being unionized. How the hell can you unionize a football player? It's getting away from the realm of being a disciplined game, you see what I mean. At least the way I think about it.

There is one other thing, too. Football teaches mental toughness. That's the most important phase of the game to me. And that's a lot of things. That's spartanism, right? Mental toughness is humility, really, it is. Mental toughness is a disciplined will above anything else. What I mean by that is that disciplined will is your own character in action.

Flynn: What you're talking about, the disciplined will, in your case with the Packers is that all members subjugate their individuality to your will for the good of the team.

Lombardi: That's right. That is what we don't have in America today. There is too much individualism. No one wants to do away with a man's individualism, don't misunderstand me. But we have gone completely beyond the feeling of selflessness really. We don't have that now. We have more of an ego type of society today.

Flynn: Do you believe that this selflessness that you teach and your players practice carries over into life after football?

Lombardi: Yes, sir. I don't think there is any question about it. I can't believe that a man can be trained, if you want to call it that, or be a part of the game of football for any time and lose it in later years. I don't believe that. I can't say every man will have that, but I'll say that the majority of them will turn out pretty damn well.

One of the great problems today, I think, is that the rights of the individual have been put way above the rights of society. Which is not right, I think.

The rights of the group, I'm talking about. Everybody's rights are above the group, today, instead of the group determining what is right and wrong. Each individual today is trying to determine what is right and wrong and then going off and acting on what he wants. You can't live that way. Nobody can live in a society like that.

Flynn: What about the high school coach of today with this apparent lack of discipline?

Lombardi: Well, he's probably the only man in the school that can do anything about discipline. And to do that, the first thing I would tell that coach is to be himself. He must get across to the team or the youngsters he's teaching what he is. That's the first thing I did here and in any place I've been, whether it was St. Cecilia's, Fordham, West Point, the Giants, or the Green Bay Packers.

The first thing you have to do is, and I hate to use this term, to sell yourself. That's the number-one objective you must have. You have to sell yourself to them, to the group. And in order to sell yourself to the group, there is no way you can be dishonest about it. Therefore, what you sell has to come from the heart, and it has to be something that you really believe in. That belief can be anything. It can be just the plain belief in the game of football, right? That belief can be in the United States of America as a great democracy. That belief can be in the school itself that you represent.

Whatever it may be, you've got to get across to the players that feeling of truth, that feeling of honesty, that feeling of selflessness, do you see? You've got to get that across to each player that you have there.

Jesus, you've really got me going now, coach. I'm going to have to listen to all this. I'm not sure it's going to come out right! Let's order dinner, or I'll be here all night.

The championship team of 1961. It may have been the greatest team in the history of Pro Football. *(Lefebvre Photos)*

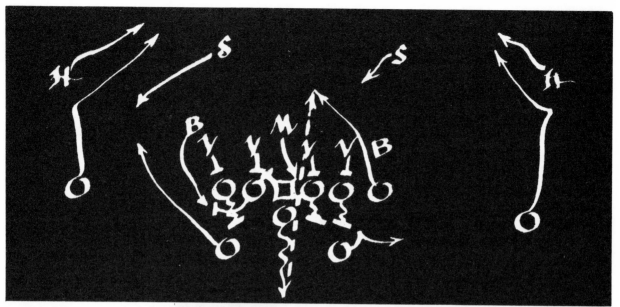

"Backs Divide": This was one of Coach Lombardi's favorite pass plays and illustrates how simple and clear his passing game was. On this play, if the middle linebacker blitzes, as shown, the quarterback simply dumps the ball off the tight end, who is also reading the middle linebacker and knows that on a blitz, he'll be getting the ball right away. If there is no blitz, the quarterback will usually throw to the wide receiver, who will curl back under the defensive halfback. (George Flynn)

Ron Kramer was the best tight end in football during his Green Bay days. He was so strong it often took two or three men to bring him down. (Vernon J. Biever)

3

The Early Years

THERE ARE probably smaller schools in New Jersey than Englewood's St. Cecilia High School; there certainly are many that are many times larger. But no school has a more glamorous football tradition than "Saint's." And Vince Lombardi is the reason. St. Cecilia's had about 100 boys and 400 girls when he was coaching there, and they played the biggest and best schools in the Metropolitan area. Not only in Bergen County, but everywhere in New Jersey, as well as in Brooklyn, the Bronx, Westchester, Long Island, and Manhattan. As has been said, the 400 girls gave him the best cheering section in the area. And the 100 boys gave him the talent he needed to win.

Lombardi took over the football team in 1942. He couldn't go to war, even though he tried, because his eyesight was too bad. The team lost its first game to Englewood, the big public school that is its great rival. From that first game in 1942 until the St. Cecilia–Englewood game in 1945, Vince Lombardi and the "Saints" didn't lose a football game. They scored 679 points to the oppositions' 79 during that time. In fact, Vince was the school's basketball coach before he was the head football coach. And even though he had never played the game, he coached them to winning seasons and, in 1945, to the state championship.

But it was as a teacher that most of the students at St. Cecilia's remember him. And he was a fine teacher. Chemistry, physics, and math were his subjects, and he'd also pick up anything else whenever they needed help. Betty Costanza was a student under Vince Lombardi and later became his sister-in-law. She remembers him in a special way.

Fr. Guy McPartland played for Vince Lombardi at St. Cecilia's. So did Joe Lombardi, who was the youngest of Harry and Matilda Lombardi's children. He also worked with his brother in the sporting goods business. And of course, he saw Vince Lombardi in a very special way.

JOE LOMBARDI

Marie gave me the championship ring about two months after Vince's death. The ring, as beautiful as it is, is nothing compared to the note that Marie gave me along with it. In this little note she said, "In our book you're number one, and this is the number-one ring." The ring says "Lombardi" on one side and "NFL" on the other; then it has the score, "Green Bay Packers 37, New York Giants 0." I think the real meaning of the ring is on the inside. It has the inscription of the Sacred Heart and the Blessed Virgin and, of course, Vince's name, "Vince Lombardi, Coach and General Manager."

What we didn't know about Vince then was that he had the same inscription of the Sacred Heart and the Blessed Virgin in all of his rings, even his wedding band. As far as my getting the ring, it came as a complete surprise. I never expected it. I never even realized that there were so many rings. I'm prejudiced, but looking at all the rings Vince had received for championships, this one has a special meaning. It's "number one" and I think, by far, the best looking of all the rings.

We saw so little of each other over those Green Bay years. It was always just a drink or a cup of coffee at Mom's when he came to New York. We never really talked about the Packers or anything other than just seeing each other and really well-wishing. We had a close relationship, and not much had to be said.

You must remember that there was an age difference between Vince and me of seventeen years. I remember Vince more than anything in the Fordham–NYU game. They were supposed to go to the Rose Bowl that year. I think they ended up with a loss to NYU of 7–6. Of course, they never got the bid to go to the Rose Bowl.

Vince would come home, and he was an idol; a superstar, really, is the only way you can put it. We all had to take castor oil or some kind of tonic in those years, and my mother was always after me. I remember Vince's coming home on a weekend and walking up to the corner drugstore and making sure I took castor oil with sarsaparilla. I took it because Vince told me to take it, and *he* got sick! As I took it, Vince got sick watching me take it.

Going back to those years, I remember Vince coming home . . . it was Coach Jim Crowley, Alex Wojohowicz, Leo Paquin, and a number of the Seven Blocks of Granite . . . for one of Mom's great Italian dinners. Of course, we weren't allowed to be there, but I remember sitting on the top of the steps and listening to all this and not remembering anything, but looking at all these great football players who are heroes to me still today. Looking back on those dinners and looking with awe at that whole group of football heroes, it was always a question of who was more meaningful, my father or my brother.

I remember that Vince graduated from Fordham. I don't remember much about the graduation, but I do remember Vince's getting a job at Manhattan Beach as a lifeguard. I remember that because we all belonged to Manhattan Beach. After that he went back to Fordham to get his law degree and his CPA. From then on, I remember Vince not being able to get a job.

He went to St. Cecilia High School and worked with Andy Palau as assistant football coach. He went there because he couldn't get a job to make decent money, and he wanted to get married to Marie. To my knowledge, he wanted to finish Fordham with his law degree and go on to be a tax lawyer. And to my knowledge he did finish, but he never practiced law because he fell in love with being a football coach. Andy Palau got a job as a head coach somewhere else or went in the service, so Vince went on to be head coach at St. Cecilia High School.

Of course, he tried to get in the service as well, but with his eyes as they were, they just wouldn't accept him. From that point on he became very, very successful as a coach. He lost very few games. When I graduated from grammar school, I went to St. Cecilia's and played ball for Vince. Mom and Dad decided they were going to follow Vince and move to New Jersey. We moved to Englewood, and I entered as a freshman at St. Cecilia High School. Vince was now planning his wedding. The whole family was moving to Englewood — Madeline, Harold, and Clair. The family, now, for the first time in a number of years, was all together again.

Vince got married and was living near the high school, and we lived in a home on Knickerbocker Road. It was a colonial home and a "fun" house. I have so many good memories from there . . . Vince coming with Father Tim and the other priests and all playing cards on Saturday afternoons. Whether there was one or twenty coming for dinner, my mother would have enough there to feed an army, it would seem. I don't know how she did it. The football games were played on Sunday and, if we won, I can remember everyone coming back to our home because Vince was there for Sunday dinner. After the game the students would come and cheer because we seemed to be well on our way to a state championship, which we had won for the last three years.

Sunday dinner was always after the football game, because it was kind of a big thing in our lives at that time for my mother, dad, sisters, brothers, Vince and Marie, and the priests. Sunday dinner was a real get-together. It was a big time. The family was happy, but only if we won. If we didn't win, no one spoke.

Vince sat in an easy chair, and it was like pulling teeth even to get him to acknowledge that anyone else was there. We never knew what it was going to be with twenty to twenty-five people being there for dinner. Some of the people we didn't even know, just that they were friends of the priests or came to our home because they wanted to see Vince and sit with him and talk to him. His young children were always on stage because their dad was such a great coach and was always the king of this particular game every Sunday.

Vince was really a quiet man, I would have to say. In fact, we would be upset because Vince wouldn't acknowledge or talk to us because of a particular thing that happened that afternoon. As far as my mother and father were concerned, he was an idol. He could do no wrong. Particularly, I remember my dad's place of business where there were newspaper clippings of Vince on the wall of his office and pictures of him going back to the days of the Seven Blocks of Granite and the days of St. Cecilia High School — pictures of Vince all over his office wall.

Joe Lombardi

Vince now had the acclaim of being "the" coach in North Jersey and the Metropolitan area because of winning the games that he had and being the first to win three state championships, being the first coach to bring the T-formation into high school football, being the president of the Bergen County Coaches' Association. All this had a great effect on our family. They considered it a normal thing to have a brother like Vin.

Going back to my freshman year at St. Cecilia's, coming into high school and having a brother as the head football coach as well — I thought I was a fair athlete, and I found out that I was just another guy on the football field. I knew I had something to prove because my brother was a tough taskmaster. I watched Vince put this whole football club together and then said to myself that I had something to prove to him; it was not so much that I had to prove to myself the fact that I was a good football player. I had to prove to my *brother* that I was a good football player. And I not only had to convince Vince that I was good, but I also had to convince my teammates that I earned this job on the starting football team.

Football, at this point in my life, was such a big thing. Football in the Lombardi family was such a big thing. Playing for Vince was a very special time in my life. I remember getting dressed for practice and going out on the football field and being the first one to block against Vince. Of course, we had no blocking sleds or any kind of machine we could hit. We hit Vince.

Vince would say, "Hit me on three." On two he would smack me. And this went on for four years! In my fourth year I finally hit him and he said, "It's about time!"

When I say smack me I meant I was in a blocking position, and Vince was in a defensive stance. It was one-on-one. Vince, being the coach, took the position he took on every ball player on a given afternoon. Of course, he had on just a T-shirt and a pair of football pants. I'll say this, he was tough.

I remember one incident with Vince. I'm not sure now whether this was my junior year or my senior year. I had just come off a season of being All Metropolitan, All State, All County. Of course, this went to my head a little bit. I was the finest, or at least, I thought I was. I'm in a scrimmage now and Vince called a particular play. Well, there was a halfback coming off my right side, and I missed the block. And then I missed the block again, and then Vince stood back in the huddle and said, "Play T 16," and I missed the block a third time. This went on for about six times, his calling this particular play. And finally we got back to the huddle, and he said, "Somebody's missing that block. I wonder who the hell it is!" And I wouldn't answer him. The next thing I know I was on my back, and I had a bloody nose!

Going back to my blocking with Vince head on. I was the first one to hit him every day, and as I said, it took me four years to realize what he was trying to do to me. I can still remember that one particular afternoon when we were at a football camp at Hacketstown, New Jersey. I came out that day to block against Vince. He said, "Okay, hit me on three." I felt that I'd had enough of this after three years, and I hit him on one and a half. From that point on he never bothered me.

Vince wasn't only my high school football coach, he was my brother, and adding on to that, my best man at my wedding. He also taught me in school. He was my teacher.

Vince taught physics, which I took. He also taught Latin and math. I was a sophomore. We had something like 123 boys and 400 girls. At the end of the school year, we'd go to the auditorium and Vince would read our report cards. He went through the seniors. He went through the juniors. He went through the sophomores, passed over me, and went through the freshmen. Being the young, very innocent brother, I thought maybe I was going to get a special reward, which I did get. He said, "Now I have the report card of Joseph Lombardi," and he called me up there. Vince looked at me and the principal, Sister Baptista, was sitting behind him, as well as Father Tim and the athletic director. The whole faculty was up there on that stage, and he took one look at me and never read my report card. He just hit me and knocked me right off the stage. I ran right out the door with him after me. When I did get home, my father hit me again. Needless to say, my junior and senior years were much different. I did pass, and I did considerably better.

Vince was a unique teacher. He would stand behind us in class with a pointer and a handful of chalk. If we didn't answer the question the way he wanted it answered, we either got hit with the pointer or we got a piece of chalk on the back of our heads. I remember one particular afternoon in physics when he was doing an experiment. He had everyone around his desk and he liked that. He liked to put on a show and have all the students around his desk. He called me up there and said, "Stand right in front of me." And he did this experiment, and it blew up right in my eye and in my face. And the next thing I knew he got mad at me, slugged me, because I was too close to the experiment!

Vince never patted me on the back during the four years of high school. It was a very private thing with him. It was a personal thing. He did tell me that I was doing a good job, and he did tell me that I was a good athlete, but it was done in the privacy of our home or in his office at school. As often as we kid about his scolding someone, he never really belittled anyone in front of anyone else. It was a very private thing with him. I think this was really what Vince Lombardi was all about. He could yell at us and tell us how wrong we were, but never once got very personal with anyone, except maybe me.

There comes a time in everyone's life where you have a big brother and it's a little bit too much. Vince was a Fordham graduate and so was my brother Harold. Really, I would say it was a family school. Of course, I was expected to go on to Fordham. I played under Vince for four years at high school, and at this time Vince had resigned from St. Cecilia High School and had taken a job at Fordham University as freshman football coach. I had a scholarship to Fordham, but I wasn't about to take that scholarship to play four more years under Vince Lombardi! I'd had it. I went to St. Bonaventure's. St. Bonnie's was then a small school but was kind of a power. Vince wanted me to go on to Fordham. I think he was upset that I didn't at that time. When Vince went on to the varsity football team, I left St. Bonnie's and came down to Fordham. At that time Vince went on to West Point. My leaving St. Bonnie's wasn't a matter of choice. It was, as a matter of fact, that I went there on a full football scholarship and didn't make it. I had a half scholarship, and I felt that I was a better athlete than that. I came down to Fordham because I felt I wanted a full football scholarship. I didn't play under Vince that one year that he was there because I was red-shirted.

There was a lot of talk about Vince being head football coach at Fordham, and it was one of Fordham's better years. Ed Danowski was head coach and had a great season. Vince left because he couldn't be head coach, and he went on to West Point with Colonel Blaik into some of the greatest years at West Point. Vince left St. Cecilia High School to take the job at Fordham with the understanding that he would be freshman coach one year, assistant coach the second year, and head coach the third year. With the success that Fordham had, public feeling was that they couldn't get rid of Ed Danowski that year. Of course Vince, being the man that he was, felt that he had to leave and go on to another school. I guess this was his greatest opportunity, because he went to West Point and coached under Colonel Blaik. Vince always said that he was one of his greatest teachers.

Pop had a meat market. He was a wholesale butcher in New York on West Twelfth Street. Dad's partner was my godfather, Uncle Eddie. They did very well with it. Of course, we were all eventually to go into this business. Vince didn't like it, my brother Harold didn't like it, and I didn't like it. At this time I had finished school, and my father had a heart attack. The hours that he kept at the meat market were terrible — four in the morning until three in the afternoon — and he decided that he wanted to go into a different business. Even though he kept the meat market, he bought a sporting goods store in Englewood, New Jersey. We called it the Englewood Sports Shop. My dad was treasurer, of course; Vince was president; I was vice-president; and my brother Harold was secretary. We kind of called ourselves the Lombardi Brothers also.

One of the reasons we got into this was that Vince was a coach, and we felt that he could really help us because at this time he was at West Point. It was kind of prestigious to sell to the Military Academy, which we did.

I can remember going up to call on Vin. Actually, I wasn't calling on Vin; I was calling on Colonel Blaik. I went to West Point once a week to handle the account and to have dinner with Vin and Marie. Along about this time the love bug bit me, and I decided to get married. In everyone's life the wedding is the most important thing. Vince was at West Point, and the wedding was to be in Leonia, New Jersey. In those days it was a pretty good drive to come down and Vince never made a rehearsal. The first time I'd seen Vince after all those rehearsals we had was at the wedding. He was standing with me at the altar, and Betty was coming down the aisle with her dad. As Betty got closer — she was now twenty feet away — Vince turns to me and says, "Are you sure you're doing the right thing?" This was a normal whisper of Vince's, which was a stage whisper, and everyone in the church heard it! And now, twenty-four years later, I know I did do the right thing.

I'm minding the sports shop, calling on West Point and most of the high schools in Bergen County. We are really fairly successful with the sports shop. Vince comes in periodically, not so much to help in the store as to make an appearance there, because he is sort of the "favorite son" of Englewood. Just about this time — what is that saying, "How do you make a fire"? — we had a fire and lost the sports shop.

Maybe it was a blessing in disguise that we lost it. I now don't have a job. Vince is coaching. He goes from West Point to the Giants. I think, all things being equal, that this has helped me too, because I finally get a job with the United States Rubber Company as, of all things, a golf ball salesman!

Vince takes the job at the New York Football Giants as the offensive coach under Jim Lee Howell. At this point, through Jim Lee Howell, I become the ticket agent for the Giants in Englewood, New Jersey, which was really a great plus for the sports shop. Vince, having taken the job with the Giants, buys a home in Oradell, New Jersey. Betty and I had been living in Oradell. Of course, we see each other quite often during this period. But when I take the job with United States Rubber, we see very little of each other because I'm starting to do a considerable amount of traveling and he is working late hours with the Giants. I do see Marie and the children, and I know that Vince is becoming very, very frustrated. The fact is that he wants to be a head coach and he knows that he's capable of being a head coach, but the jobs aren't really there for him.

Vince moved from Oradell to Fair Haven, New Jersey, and one day when I was on a sales trip, I stopped by to see him and Marie and the children. Vince wasn't home yet, so I had a cup of coffee with Marie. We were sitting in the kitchen, and Vince comes in and very casually tells us he has taken the job at Green Bay.

I knew he had been interviewing for head coaching jobs, but I thought he was happy with the Giants. Those other head coaching jobs were in colleges and the only other pro job I knew he had looked at was Philadelphia, and that was the year earlier. He had interviewed at Southern Cal and for the new Air Force Academy job and had come in second. It had happened many times to him, and he was very frustrated.

I couldn't understand why he wasn't going to stay with the Giants. We talked about it in the kitchen, and he told me that though he had been promised the head coaching job with the Giants, Jim Lee Howell wanted to stay on another year and they — the Maras — had asked Vince to wait again. They also gave their blessing to talk to Green Bay, and Vince felt that the Packer job was for real and the Giants' job was a maybe. As it turned out, it was the right decision.

When Vince took the Packer job and moved to the wilds of Wisconsin, Mom and Dad were a little hurt, even though they were very proud of Vince in his new job. Dad was very happy for Vince. And Vince, being the only celebrity in the family, made Dad and all of us happy for him and yet sad that he was leaving. Mom was most upset because the closeness of the family was being broken up since Vince was moving west.

Of course, Dad knew how successful Vince was going to be. They were very much alike; both strong-willed people, strict disciplinarians, completely dedicated to success. My dad was a very successful butcher and worked very hard. He was a good businessman, and a lot of that rubbed off on Vince. My father was a beautiful man. He was hard on us but very warm and loving. He

Joe Lombardi   **33**

was also very direct and called a spade a spade. There was no room for bull. My father walked to church every day and was a daily communicant, just like Vince was. He was a very basic man. There was only right and wrong, and he believed that you only did the right thing all the time. When I was growing up, I never remember sitting down and discussing anything of importance with my father, other than asking to borrow the car.

My father never discussed anything with me until years after Vince was in Green Bay. Betty and I had moved to upstate New York and then back to New Jersey. Mom and Dad moved back to Brooklyn, just a block from where Vince and I were born. Suddenly, Dad and I became very close. I'm not the baby anymore in his eyes, as I was all those years. So, he started to talk to me about many things, but almost always it is about Vince and his love of what Vince's life has meant to him. And you can almost see him living this life in his later years.

The scrapbooks on Vince would fill a bookcase. The walls in the house have pictures of Vince everywhere. I always teased my mother and father about not having my picture on the wall. And one day when I walked in their house, there it was, my picture in the middle of all of Vince's. I was very proud and moved, even though I had been teasing them.

Vince had a great influence on my life and my career as a sporting goods salesman. One time, I walked into Solomon's Sporting Goods Store in Elizabeth, New Jersey, and Mars Solomon, the owner, greeted me, talked about Vince, about how proud Mom and Dad must be, about what a great guy Vince was, and about how great the Packers were, and all the time he was walking me toward the door. When we got outside he said, "Joe, next time you're in town, stop by and we'll have another chat." With that, he went back in and that showed me how helpful having a famous brother can be in selling sporting goods!

Recalling the years at Green Bay, the "Lombardi Era," I felt Vince had kind of gone on and gotten what was important, or at least what I thought was important. The closest that Vince and I were then was a phone call out of the blue one evening. It was just "How are you? How are you doing? How is Betty? How are the children?" I was not doing as well as I wanted to do at the time. My wife was in the hospital. Vince wanted to know what he could do for me. I said that there wasn't really anything. Three days later I received a blank check in the mail and a note saying, "Do what you have to do. Hope this helps." We rarely see each other at this time. He's at Green Bay and I'm in Syracuse. I called him at Christmas and wished him and Marie a very merry Christmas. It was a close but strange relationship. I don't know how to explain it other than that the love was there, the feeling was there, but we just didn't see each other.

Everyone wanted to talk about Vince Lombardi. I was very well accepted as a salesman, but I had to make a decision that I either talk about Vince and his career and be a good-will man for him or become a good salesman, which I did do. I said, "If you want to talk about Vince, let's talk about him after I write your order." This all happened about 1961 — his first championship. They lost the first championship to the Eagles and then came back and beat the Giants. This was when all this happened. Because my brother was such a great celebrity, I became a celebrity. I kind of enjoyed every minute of it, but I didn't know how to handle it. It's always difficult to put yourself aside and say that there's someone else in your family who has made your name outstanding. We don't like to believe that, I guess, as individuals. I can remember the time when I wanted to change my name from Lombardi to any name you want to think of. But I also realized that I couldn't hide from my face — I look so much like Vince. We had dinner with Vince before the Baltimore game, and after the game, Vince, Marie, and the club went back to Green Bay, and Betty and I and a few of our friends went into a little restaurant in Baltimore. A drunk, I guess I would have to say, came up and said, "Can I have your autograph, coach?" This was still a new thing to me and I said, "I think you've made a mistake. I'm not Vince Lombardi." And then he wanted to take a swing at me.

I realized then that there was no way I could change my name to anything else! How do I say that I'm a Lombardi and really mean it rather than saying I'm a Lombardi with a very meak voice? Or, I'm Vince Lombardi's brother, and this took me a long time to say. Fame is a great thing for the individual who's receiving it. But fame is a very, very tough thing for an individual's family, whether it's his children or his brothers or sisters. I think the only ones who can enjoy fame of that type is the man who's receiving it or his mother and father.

I don't know when I started to accept the fact that I was Vince Lombardi's brother. I would think sometimes that someday I might become president of the United States, and I can see on the day of my inauguration being announced as the president of the United States, Vince Lombardi's brother, Joe! My children gloried in this before I could. My son Billy was looking at a color photograph of Vince. I said, "Billy, do you know who this is?" And he said, "Yes, that's God."

I don't know when I accepted it, but I do know that I finally did, and I realized that my acceptance made me a better person. It made me realize that Vince not only did something for himself and for his immediate family, but he did something for all who were around him, even his friends. It seemed like he had a Midas touch, because whoever he was with seemed to glory in the fact that they were a part of Vince Lombardi.

Vince's success was sometimes a drain on the family. A Sunday afternoon wasn't a Sunday afternoon at the Lombardi house. A Sunday afternoon during the football season was a pressure pot. We invited people to our home to watch the football game and to have cocktails with us. But no one was allowed to talk. If they wanted a drink, they had to go into the other room to make it, because the ice cubes going into the glass bothered me.

My father was an amazing guy. If they lost, the referee was wrong because they lost. Vince was never wrong. The club was never wrong. I don't know how we handled it. We were annoyed. If they won and they didn't win the right way, we were annoyed because someone said something was wrong with the Green Bay Packers. If they won and they won the way I thought they should have won, it still wasn't right, because we built such a dynasty in our minds of Green Bay and of Lombardi that everything he did had to be super, super right. There wasn't a Sunday that went by that we couldn't find a Green

Bay game on TV. We saw local football. I lived in Syracuse at the time. We saw a lot of Cleveland because of Jimmy Brown. But right after that Cleveland game was over, we saw Green Bay. Super years, super teams, super times really — and very, very trying times.

Every week, in fact every season, the pressure seemed to build. It went on from that particular week into the season and then on to the following year, and there's no way of trying to explain what this meant to me. It was a very special time in my life to live with this. To walk out on Monday morning and say, "I know my brother did it. We knew he was going to win." But also, that Sunday afternoon, during those few hours, how terrible it was, the fact that he may lose. Vince never won big. They won most of their games very close. He never believed in ridiculing the other coach.

I remember watching the first Super Bowl. The Kansas City Chiefs built up the fact of what they were going to do to the Green Bay Packers — the terrible Kansas City Chiefs, the big, tough football team from the other league. I knew Vince and how he instructed his Packers to just keep quiet and not say a word. But the pressure got there. The pressure got to the point where I doubted that the Green Bay Packers were going to win that game before it started. And then, finally, it did start. That first quarter, even going into the first half, I wondered whether the Packers were going to win that game. And then all hell broke loose! They got rid of the hammer, and they got rid of the butterflies that they possibly had and went on to win 35 to 10. I had that feeling of nausea in my stomach saying, "Are they going to do it?"

And then, watching Vince after the game when he still had that feeling, he said, "They're a good team, but they don't belong in our league!" And he gloried in the fact that he'd said it.

Today I look at that and say maybe he was wrong, but I loved every minute of the day that he said it. It's a very tough thing to explain. I don't know that anyone else has experienced this type of thing — how close you are to something like this. I think the fan, the Green Bay fan, the pro football fan, can understand what I'm saying. No way do you follow a team or be part of a team or be part of a family and not experience the fact that, damnit, you just want to die if they don't win.

We have all seen something written by Vin or something that someone else has written for Vince or said about Vince — about love — love of his team, love of his God, love of his job. But the one thing that most of us don't realize, as tough as he was, where he had an uncontrollable temper in his earlier years, he had that same love. He had that love of his family, love of his brothers and sisters. When people talk about this, they talk about it starting only when he got to Green Bay and after he had received the fame that went with his success. But it was there much, much before that. As I mentioned earlier, when Vince sent me that blank check — that was love.

Actually, it was a great influence. Walking in and saying, "I'm Joe Lombardi," and the Packers have just won another big game didn't hurt. It really did help, and I was able to get in to see buyers because of the name more often than not. Of course, I had to have the merchandise and be able to make the sale, but being Vince's brother was a great help to me in my career in business.

When I was with Rawlings Sporting Goods Company, Vince was on our advisory staff. They were always asking me to get them into the NFL to sell their football equipment and to get the NFL to use our football. Well, Vince bought a lot of the Packer equipment from us; not because of me, however. And because we sold to the Packers and they are the most successful team in sports, this helps us all across the country at all levels.

One of the things about Vince was that he never missed a chance to give his players an edge. Talking about uniforms reminds me of the way he would dress the Packers for practice. The jerseys were all old ones with the numbers half torn off, and they had more holes in them than Swiss cheese. For a championship team, they looked terrible. But come Sunday and the team would arrive in the locker room, there would be those beautiful green and gold uniforms, sparkling new and clean and pressed, and each player could just feel himself getting a lift. It was a small thing but important. They looked like champions.

I remember him doing that to us in high school. Our practice uniforms were torn, the pants held together with tape and often the jersey you wore was something you brought from home. But come Sunday, according to whom we were playing, he might give us new jerseys and a few weeks later, new pants, if the game was a tough one. Of course, the school never had the money to buy new uniforms each year, so he had to really work to get us new jerseys and pants. I think most of the sporting goods people in the area helped out for free. And this gave us a big lift for the key games.

After winning Super Bowl II, Vince retired from the Packers as head coach. I was very surprised. I knew he had been under a terrible strain winning that third title in a row and the second Super Bowl. I also knew he was upset at the way the press was getting on him about all the winning he did. But still, he was only in his middle fifties and was just not the kind of man to resign and get out of coaching.

That winter, after he quits coaching, Vince, it seems, is always in New York getting some award. We see a lot of each other, and he seems really happy and relaxed and sure he's done the right thing. And then the next season begins and the players report for practice, and all he has to do is play golf and be general manager of the Packers. For another man being general manager would be a full-time job. For Vince, it's nothing.

The next time I see him is in the city where he's attending a league meeting. We meet for a drink one evening, and he is no longer the happy brother I saw in the Spring. The Packers are not winning, and he now knows that he made a great mistake giving up coaching. It's not their losing that hurts him so much but his frustration of not being able to go down there and do something about it. It's obvious to me that somehow he'll be back into coaching.

One good thing that came out of his not coaching was that we became very close. I start to see more of him, and we go to banquets and dinners together. Now we are more like brothers, and it's a great time for me.

Though he never confided in me, I'm delighted when I hear that he's taking over the Redskins. Now he'll be back in football and closer to the family. Mom and Dad are both very happy that Vince and Marie will be so close and Dad's delighted that his son is back into coaching.

I really thought that Vince was coming back to New York to take over the New York Jets. As I said, he never confided in me, but his friends Eddie Breslin, Mike Manuche, and his attorney Peter Campbell Brown would see me in town and tell me what Vince was doing. The strongest rumor had him taking over the Jets. I know that the Eagles were also talking. I didn't know that the Redskins had the inside line, but there were a number of stories that he was headed there.

I think the Jets thing never happened because of Vince's feeling toward the Maras and the Giants. Remember, in those days the Jets had just won the Super Bowl in the great upset of the Colts, and they were the talk of New York. It was no secret that the Jet owners wanted Vince, but I think he never would have taken the job because of what it would have meant to the Maras.

Even though the two leagues had finally merged, there was still a great deal of bitterness between the owners, especially in New York. It would have been a blow to the old league, the NFL, to have their champion, Vince Lombardi, take over a team from the new league, especially one that beat them in the Super Bowl. Of course, we all hoped that the Jets rumor was going to become fact. It would have brought Vin back to New York, and it would have been wonderful for the family and for the city.

Why the New York Giants didn't go after Vince, I'll never know. They knew he wanted to get back into coaching. They needed a new man because the Giants had fallen on bad times, and they needed a big move to get the press away from the Jets. What a coup that would have been if, after the Jets won the Super Bowl, the Giants stole their thunder with the announcement that Vince Lombardi was coming back to the New York Giants. But they never did ask him.

One of the more memorable stories about those days, after the Jets' win in Super Bowl III, took place the next day in New York. Vince and Marie had been in Miami on Sunday at the Super Bowl and flew up to New York right after the game. The next day Vince was to become a Knight of Malta in the Catholic Church. This is a very high honor and may be the most important honor the Church can bestow on a lay person.

So Monday morning I go to St. Patrick's with Betty, and we attend the mass and induction of Vince and others into the Knights of Malta. After the mass, we go to his suite in the Waldorf, where he and Marie are throwing a brunch for close friends. When we get there he's still in the black cape with the red and white heart on the left side and the plumed hat with the beautiful sword by his side. And around his neck was the medallion. He was so proud and happy and grinning from ear to ear.

Nobody is there yet of the guests that had been invited, so we get a chance to talk. He takes off the finery, and we have a drink at the small bar set up in the room. After congratulating him I bring up the Super Bowl and the Jets' win.

Well, he changes from the happy "Knight" to an angry coach. "How could they do that?" he shouts. "How could they lose *my* game?" Now he is rolling and I don't say anything. He takes the Colts apart, talks about how he's won the thing for the NFL the past two years and keeps saying, "How could they lose *my* game," as if the Super Bowl was his and not any other team's. And he meant it.

Marie also joined in saying that the Colts had always called the Packers lucky, and when they get their chance, they blow it to, of all people, the Jets. The mass and the honor of Malta are forgotten as Vince lets loose on the Colts, and there is no question that as far as he is concerned, if he had been coaching, it would have been three in a row. Thank goodness the rest of the guests arrive and he models his "Knights" clothing and the Super Bowl is put aside. But he always felt that the Super Bowl was his game, and he'd be very happy to know that the trophy is now the "Vince Lombardi" trophy.

Even though Vince and Marie move to Washington, I don't see too much of him. Of course, I follow every game in the papers and watch them whenever they play on television. Because Lombardi is now with the Skins more of their games are shown in New York. And, of course, I'm delighted when they beat the Giants that year.

A couple of months go by and Vince is in town with Marie to receive the Tim Mara award from the CYO. His son, Vince, Jr., and his son's wife, Jill, are also in town on business, and the next night after the banquet we all meet at Manuche's for dinner. We have a great time, and after dinner we walk over to P.J. Clarke's. It's a beautiful Spring evening, and when we get to P.J.'s, the place is filled. There are people everywhere, and there isn't a table for us. However, Frankie, the head man gets us a table and the girls sit down, but Vince wants to visit all the friends there. And everyone in P.J.'s is Vince's friend.

Finally, about three in the morning, we leave and stand outside waiting for a cab. Now, it's early Sunday morning, Mother's Day. There is a little old lady who has been on the corner of P.J.'s for years and she sells flowers. Vince walks over and buys three bouquets of violets and comes back and gives one each to Marie, Betty, and Jill, kisses them and wishes them happy Mother's Day. It was a great evening, a family evening, and it was the last time I saw Vince before his illness.

It is late in June that the rumors that I've been hearing about Vince being ill are confirmed. I call Marie, and she asks me to come down to Maryland because Vince wants to see me. He has already had the first operation and it was a pretty well-kept secret from the public. I see Vince at his home and we visit for a long, long time. He looks fit and feels that the operation has arrested the cancer. In fact, he's planning the opening week of practice, and there seems to be no doubt that he'll be coaching the 'Skins that year.

We go outside for a walk around the grounds, and he tires very quickly. But that's to be expected since he's just been operated on. But for some reason, I'm troubled. He's planning for the future and he seems well, but with cancer, one never knows.

There is a players' strike that year — a short one — and Vince goes to New York for the owners' meeting. He tires so easily that he only attends one meeting, where he makes a brief but impassioned speech about the owners maintaining the integrity of their game.

A few weeks later, Marie calls and says that Vince is back in the hospital. She wants me to come down. So I go see them at Georgetown University Hospital. Neither one would let on that the cancer is as serious as it is, and I'm not sure they even know how serious it was. He doesn't get up when I go into his room, but he seems fine and looks good. We visit for an hour, and then I leave and visit with Marie. By now, many of his former players and old friends are coming to see him, and the hospital waiting room is a *Who's Who* of sports.

I return the next week for another visit, and Vince looks worse. But as usual, he has something quick to say when I walk in. He looks at me and says, "Don't you ever work?" After that, I'm coming down two or three times a week.

We all know now how serious this is. Vince has asked me to take care of Mom and Dad and to keep them informed as to how he is doing. But he doesn't want me to let them know how bad he is, and he won't let them come down to visit him. With the newspapers and television reporting on his condition, this is really hard for me to do. But Cousin Dorothy and Uncle

The "Fighting Saints" of St. Cecilia High School. In 1944, this team won 10, lost none, and tied one. (*H. Tarr, Inc.*)

The brothers Lombardi. (*Bill Greene*)

Pete bring Mom and Dad down, and they see Vince and find out how bad it is.

On September 2nd, I have to go to Alabama for a job interview. I have dinner with the people that night, and the next morning I turn on the television in the motel room and hear that Vince Lombardi is dead.

I return to Washington and go to be with Marie and the children. Then that night I return to New York and go to see Mom and Dad and try to console them. It is really tough. They don't understand why nobody would tell them and how it could happen so fast. I never really answered them, because there was nothing I could say.

People were just beautiful. From all over the country people want to help and send their sympathy. More than anything, this outpouring of sympathy and love for Vince helped Mom and Dad. They were old, but they were proud of him and so pleased with the way the people reacted. For me, it was the most difficult period of my life because I had to handle most of the details. I was too busy to feel the loss and grief as deeply as I did after the funeral was over and everyone had left. Then I knew he was gone.

Joe Lombardi, #91, as a member of the New York World Telegram All Metropolitan football team. Joe was a junior on that team in 1945. *(Bill Greene)*

BETTY LOMBARDI

I was taking my final physics test in my senior year at St. Cecilia's. Vince had been our teacher, but the test was to be proctored by one of the nuns. Knowing that, I had made a "crib" sheet to help me pass. As the tests were passed out, I felt confident. But as soon as everyone had their papers, Sister left and in walked Vince. And he catches me cribbing. He would walk up and down the aisles singing "I'm Forever Blowing Bubbles," or picking up your paper and making some comment like, "Not bad, but not good" or something to distract you. So he comes to my desk and picks up my paper and my "crib" sheet falls on the floor. He just looks at me and says, "Get out." So I leave, and I must have cried for three hours.

Finally, I know I have to apologize to him, so I go to his office, knock, and walk in. As soon as I see him I start to cry. Finally, I stop, and he says he'll give me a chance to pass if I will write the whole physics textbook word for word and have it in his hands in one week. Well, I do a great deal of writing, but by the end of the week I'm nowhere near finished. But he takes what I've done, and as I remember, he gave me a pretty good grade.

My strongest impression of Vince when I was a student was that all the students were afraid of him, myself included. And so were most of the faculty. When Vince spoke everybody jumped — nuns, lay teachers, priests, it didn't matter who. But also everybody loved him, if you can imagine this love/fear relationship. It was a crazy kind of thing.

And, of course, his success with the football team was so unbelievable. Because of Vince we had probably the most school spirit of any school, any high school, I've ever known. After all, we had really nothing else in the school, and we were so small compared to the other schools, public as well as parochial. So the football success gave us stature and importance. We would go to the locker rooms after the games and wait outside for the guys, and anybody that wanted to would go over to Vince's mother and father's place, and Vin and Marie would be there and all the kids would be outside. Vin and Marie and Mom and Pop would come outside and all the kids would be yelling. It was fantastic! I've never known any school that had that kind of feeling, and I do believe it was because of Vin.

Joe and I were friends in high school and he sat behind me for most of my classes through our four years. We were not dating or anything then. We were just friends.

Well, when the report cards came out that one time the whole school just knew that something was going to happen. Nobody wanted to leave the auditorium, but you had to leave as you got your report card and walked off the stage. So by the time Joe was to get his there was really hardly anybody in the hall, but Joe's teammates had placed themselves at strategic points in the hallway and by the doors of the auditorium. They, as well as the rest of us, knew something was going to happen. And the rest of us were watching!

Vin read the marks off and Joe had flunked a couple of things. Now Joe was standing right in front of Vince on the stage, and as Vin read off Joe's marks he got madder and madder and reached out to hit Joe. He knocked Joe off the stage and Joe ran like hell. Hooks Cerotti, a teammate, was at the auditorium door where Joe was headed, and he opened it when he saw Vin coming after Joe. He slammed the door in Vin's face, and everybody took off, running in all directions. It was mad! We were all scared to go to school the next week, but nothing happened.

It took years before I was comfortable around Vincent because I was always, always scared to death of him. The first time I was ever invited to Joe's house for dinner, they sat me next to Vincent. And all he did was grin at me through the whole dinner. He'd just look at me and smile. And he did that dumb little laugh he had and said, "Miss Costanza, you were stupid!"

And the Lombardi's didn't eat a normal twenty-five minute meal. You had to sit there three hours! Well, I heard this for three hours from him. By the time I got through with that dinner, I went home and threw up. I was such a wreck, I couldn't stand it.

Joe and I got engaged, and Vince did not say too much about it. Finally, we set the wedding date, and Joe asked Vin to be the best man. He never made a rehearsal. He didn't know from beans about anything that was going on. All he ever did was get measured for his wedding tux.

I walked down the aisle with my father, and Joe and Vin walked out from the side of the altar. Vin looked at me and then he looked at Joe, and he said to Joe, "Are you sure you're doing the right thing?" Now Joe was ready to throw himself on the altar and say, "No, I don't want to get married!" Can you imagine! Just before the wedding mass! I just couldn't believe it; I couldn't believe it!

After we had Beth Ann, he would come over to the house, he would play with Beth Ann and toss her in the air and talk to her in baby talk. Joe and I couldn't believe it. We would just get hysterical listening to him talk baby talk, but I think it was because he missed doing it with his own kids. He was always working — coaching, teaching, officiating — doing all those things you have to do to get established and get known. So he never really took the time to do those things with his children, and he enjoyed the chance to do them with ours.

In my opinion, I think he was always afraid that people would think he was soft. So he didn't do those things at home.

I am amazed at the success Vince had. I was so happy for him because he worked so hard for it, but I'm still amazed at what he achieved and that it's still going on today. He certainly was deserving of all this, because he made such a contribution to football. But I'm still surprised that it's still going on. There was something in him that you just don't find in people today, and I guess that's why the admiration and respect are still there. He was such a deeply moral man, so dedicated and so strong. And, also, so kind.

I guess I never thought of Vincent as being "great," truly "great," until he died. You know, I'd read about him and seen him on television and knew all the things his teams were doing, but it never really made that much of an impact on me when it was happening. And then he died, and I saw all those people coming to pay their respects. I'll never forget it. They didn't know him, had never met him or spoken to him, but they had to be there. I'll just never forget it. It was unbelievable to me that so many people, and millions more across the country, found something in him that they wanted to thank him for.

And I think today he is probably greater in the eyes of the people than he was when he was alive.

Basketball coach Vince Lombardi and his team. He won a State Championship in 1945. *(Courtesy, Joe Lombardi)*

The teacher. Students who studied under Vince Lombardi learned and understood their subject. Or else. *(Courtesy, Joe Lombardi)*

FR. GUY McPARTLAND

I went to St. Cecilia's High School, and I played under Vince Lombardi in the seasons of '44, '45, and '46. I was his fullback and during those years, his brother Joe was playing also. He was the guard on the team. I remember his relationship with his brother was no different than his relationship with any other of the ball players. He was hard on Joe just as he was hard on all of us. I remember one particular week we were scrimmaging in preparation for the Englewood game, and it was Vince's custom to call each of the offensive plays from the huddle; one particular play he called was the fullback up the middle, a trap play, and Joe had to do the trapping and I was the fullback running the play. It just involved a little duck step that the fullback took, and then he took the ball going straight up the middle. Joe had to make the trap, but the defensive guard wasn't coming across. So they ran the play once, this guard was right in the middle in the hole there and he wracked me up something good.

We came back to the huddle and Vince was a little disturbed. You could see he was blinking a little more rapidly, and he was puffing on his cigarette a little more and he said "run it again." So we ran it again and the guard still didn't come across, and Joe, of course, couldn't make the trap and I was wracked up again. I came back to the huddle and again this time he said it — he said it out loud — "run it again," and I got wracked up for the third time.

Joe came back and he was a little shook about the whole thing, that he couldn't make the trap, and Vince tore into him and said "Joe, you're All-County — that's what people tell me, you're a good guard! You stink, Joe. You stink!" He really blasted him that day. So we went up to the line of scrimmage; he said, "run it again," and we ran it and this time the guard came across, because somebody in the line told him he'd better come across, and he came across and Joe made the trap and it went fine.

We had a very inexpensive athletic program. We were a small school, and the athletic program didn't rate a great deal of equipment. We had no blocking sled — we had these beat-up dummies — a few of those — but most of the blocking was done on Vince. Vince was the blocking sled. I remember practice after practice, just watching those linemen pair off with him, because this was the way he conducted his practices. We would do some laps and some calisthenics, and the linemen would go over there and he would go over to the linemen. He had an assistant that usually went with the backs and ran us through some plays.

We used to peek over and watch those linemen go through their paces blocking Vince. It was something to watch because he would take each guy — each individual guard, tackle, center, and end — and he would get down with them and the boy would have to get down there and come out of his stance and hit. He hit Vince, and Vince would be using his hands, hitting and pushing him, telling him, "Drive!" "Drive!," "Drive!" "Block!" "Block!" "Block!" till the kid went for two or three minutes and he pretty much collapsed. We would just run our plays, and we would be watching it and thanking God that we were backs and not linemen. I don't know whether we could have taken that.

He was the first one to put that five–four defense in — everything was six–two in those days; six–two, two–one, that was traditional, but he put this five–four — he put in the pro defense. It was something new — this was back in the middle forties. He put the five–four in; we worked on it; we used it against Englewood the first time. I don't think anybody in the whole area used five–four.

On the sidelines, he was a mass of nerves, walking up and down. He blinked and smoked incessantly. I remember my first game starting as fullback. The plan was that the first play would be a pitch out to the fullback, and we had just received the kickoff and on the first play, Billy White, the quarterback who was killed in Korea — God rest him — threw the ball out to me and I fumbled. We called it again, I fumbled it again. We called it a third time and I fumbled it again. Finally, Vince pulled me out of the game.

He pulled me out of the game, and I went running over to the sidelines. I was sure to stay away from him, because I didn't want to en- counter him after fumbling three times in a row in the first three plays of the game. There he was, making his way down to the end of the team, blinking and puffing on his cigarette. He came up to me with a big grin, hit me up the side of the head, and said, "What's wrong with you? What's wrong with you? Put some rosin on your hand and go back in there." So I put some rosin on my hand, went back in there, and my nervousness was over and we went on from there to win.

I remember once in the locker room during the half — we were hav- ing a pretty hard game — and Vince was a little disturbed that the quarter- back wasn't being hit on every play, and he started yelling at the linemen for not hitting the quarterback. One kid made the mistake of saying, "I didn't hit him coach because I didn't want to draw a penalty," and Vince blew up.

"You didn't want to draw a penalty? You hit that quarterback. You hit him on every play. I'll take the penalty — I'll worry about the penalty! Hit him! Hit him! Hit him!"

I remember a scrimmage where he was walking around watching the backs run through their plays, and the linemen were working with one another — pairing off with one another — and he walked back among the linemen and he noticed his first-team tackle's nose bleeding — Reggie Parkey — and he spotted him and said, "Your nose bleeding?" Reggie said yeah, and Vince started walking up and down among the linemen and said "Who did that? Who did that? Who made his nose bleed?" It happened to be that my brother, Frank, was a tackle at that time, and he was playing second team and my brother said, "I did." "Good, good, I like to see that!"

I think Vince's characteristics — his traits — that made him what he was and what he is were these: he was a perfectionist, he was a fundamen- talist, and he was a father to his ball players. He had the will of a perfectionist, the mind of a fundamentalist, and the heart of a father. And it was this combination of traits that made him the great man that he was and the great coach that he was.

To give you an example, as far as his perfectionism was concerned, you've heard the expression: "Winning isn't a big thing; it's the only thing." Well, this is the way he was. He didn't change much in his technique and his approach to football from the time he left St. Cecilia's to the time he went to Washington or to Green Bay. Fundamentally he was the same.

I was surprised when I went to Washington and the training camp. Sitting in the skull drill with the Washington Redskins and finding out that what he was saying to them, he was saying to us twenty-five years before. Winning is the only thing. He used to say, "Anybody can lose, and I'm not here to teach you how to be a good loser. Anybody can be a good loser. I'm teaching you how to be a good winner. There is no substitute for winning. You have to be a bad loser — a hard loser."

Fundamentalism came out in that he always said, "The team that blocks and tackles the best will win the ball game." He wasn't much for razzle-dazzle plays; he had very few tricky plays. For him what mattered was that we block and tackle better than the other team. We'd have to do that in order to win.

The heart of the father. I say that was the key characteristic, because he related to the team not only as a father and coach, but to every individual on the team. Each kid felt toward him something special. This was their father, their leader, their teacher and this was why I think he was such a great football coach. He was a great teacher — he was a great teacher in the classroom — I had him for physics and chemistry. He knew the textbook backward and forward, and he didn't have to refer to the textbook when he gave his classes. I think because of his great ability as a teacher, it made him so successful in the coaching field. I don't think that he was a great man because he happened to be successful in football. He was successful at football because he was a great man and he had those characteristics. He had the will of a perfectionist, the mind of a fundamentalist, and the heart of a father, and it was this unique combination that's found in very few coaches — very few men — that made him so successful.

I remember him as a strong man with a grin — a smile that made you feel that he took a deep and personal interest in you and that he had an affection for you. You weren't just a ball player — you were a man, a human being, a brother. I remember him standing as he did; he had a beautiful build — big and strong — but I remember that grin. That's what I remember most about him. The grin stood for toughness — he was mentally tough — and that was one of the qualities he thought every man should have and should be developed in his ball players. I don't think even the times when that grin turned to a scowl, when he was yelling at you, that you feared him — you were in awe of him.

I was never physically afraid of him. I was afraid that I wasn't living up to his expectations of me. This is what hurt you the most, what you feared most — not living up to what he expected of you. When he was disappointed with you, he showed it physically in his face; and when he was pleased with you, he gave you that toothy grin, which meant an awful lot to us.

This is the genius of the man. The man could evoke from you the best you had, and he was always striving to evoke more from you when you thought you had given everything you had or were capable of according to

Fr. Guy McPartland

your own capacities and talents. He wouldn't settle for that; he wanted to evoke even more from you, and when you did something and you thought you were doing even better and he approved of it with his wide grin, that gave you a tremendous amount of satisfaction.

We didn't reflect on his greatness, we just knew that he was awesome — he inspired awe. There was no relationship to him like a big brother. There was your leader. There was somebody there to teach you more than just football, but not only to teach you how to be great on the football field, also how to be great in life.

When I read in the newspapers when he died where some of them said he was one of the greatest, if not the greatest football coach, he knew how to win, how to win the big ones, but this was one game he couldn't win or that time ran out.

I thought to myself, that isn't true — that's the one game he won going away — that was a rout — he won life by a rout. He may have lost a few ball games in his coaching career and time may have run out on some of his games, but in the game of life he won by such a big score that it wasn't even close.

That's Paul Horning wearing #45 and Henry Jordon with #57 on. This was to confuse the spies that may have been watching from the stands. *(Vernon J. Biever)*

Vince at brother Joe's wedding. *(Courtesy, Joe Lombardi)*

Bergen County Coaches' Association

"OLD TIMERS NIGHT"

Tuesday, May 9, 1967

Vince Lombardi was feted many times in his career, but this one was one of his favorites.

4

The Formative Years

ONE TIME a scout from another NFL team was sitting in the press box in Green Bay watching the Packers play. He had his stack of paper with the football field lined out on the pages and his pencils were all in a neat row, with each color of each pencil representing some secret code known only to him and the team he worked for. He had his trusty binoculars, without which no scout would be caught dead. And he had his program with all the names and numbers of all the players. And he just sat there.

It was a good game, too. Finally, speaking to no one in particular and everyone in general, he sighed and said, "How in the hell do you scout blocking and tackling?"

That was Lombardi football: As fundamental as blocking and tackling and about as pure as the game could be played. And there was no question but that this football was as close to perfection as the game has ever seen. It said all that had to be said about Vince Lombardi as a coach. And if you looked a little closer you could see that it all began as a player at Fordham, at West Point, where Lombardi learned under Earl Blaik, and with the Giants, where he was shaped for professional football.

Look at his background and you'll understand him. Like all of us, Vince Lombardi was the total of the experiences he had lived with. His education was classical: parochial grammar and high school, Jesuit university. His football, as a player, was fundamental: the Fordham teams blocked and tackled, and if they sometimes threw a pass, it was the exception.

And when he left Fordham, he began his career in a small Catholic high school, teaching the sciences and Latin. The nation was at war, and it was a great time for patriotism. He contributed by making sure that any young man who left that school and his team would be ready for the armed forces, physically, mentally, and morally.

When he left the high school, he went back to his alma mater. Again, it was the classical environment, the Jesuit education and students, and the Church.

From there, he went to that citadel of fundamentalism and discipline, the United States Military Academy. Those gray buildings, that tradition, that spirit, and the Corps made it easy for Vince Lombardi to be at home. For it was the same as Fordham, the Jesuits, the Catholic Church; the ordered life continued and he was comfortable because there was no time for doubts or questions. There was the Army way, and he agreed with it. After all, it was the way he believed and had been raised.

And when he finally knew that in order to get ahead in his field he must break free of the institutional life he had led, he joined the perfect organization for his personality, the New York Giants. The Mara family was from Fordham. They were hard-working and church-going Catholics. The Giants were a New York institution, and they were a family. There was loyalty to the family, demanded and expected from the players and everyone in the organization. And with his intelligence, his drive, and his organizational ability, Vince Lombardi was very much at home with the Giants and the Mara family. Even though it was pro football, it was still New York and he ran the offense. He knew who he was responsible to and what was expected of him. And he applied all these years of study and learning and experimentation in football to the Giants. Here he tested his concepts, his theories, and his ability against professionals. And he made the team a winner.

His whole preparation for Green Bay began in an ordered existence of parochial education, Jesuit discipline and logic, West Point organization, promptness and esprit de corps, and finally in the family of the Maras and the Giants. Nowhere in this world do you see the shadings of gray. It is all black and white. These years are the "formative years" that he will use to build his Packers on. And his Packers are a reflection of the nuns and priests and cadets and high school players and the "blocks of granite" and his family and the Giants. And they reflected proudly.

Wellington Mara is the president of the New York Giants. He was one of Vince Lombardi's closest friends, and he remembers when Fordham football filled the Polo Grounds on Saturday in the fall in the thirties, while the next day, he would watch his father's team, the Giants, play to half that many on the same field. The Giants and pro football have been his life. It was Well Mara who brought Vince Lombardi to pro football.

Joe Cahill had been around football all his life. He was the sports information director at West Point during the glory days of Blanchard and Davis, and he was there with Lombardi when Army football went from the best to the worst and back again. They lived through that together, and there always was a special bond between them. Joe Cahill was as fine a man as there was in sports. He died in 1974.

Frank Gifford was a superstar in the NFL before they had coined the term. He was one of the most versatile men to have played the game, but when Vince got him, he became the spearhead of Lombardi's offense and won the league's Most Valuable Player award in 1956. Today, he is a successful television broadcaster, being one of the few authentic football stars to have made the transition from athlete to broadcaster.

WELLINGTON MARA

I was a student at Fordham, a freshman, a day hop; and Vince was a boarder and football player and sort of a hero. Wojohowicz and Franco were the big names, but everybody knew that Vince was one of the backbones of the team. I saw him play many times, but I don't remember anything particularly outstanding he did. Really, it was a team effort whenever they won a game, which was most of the games they played. They were pretty much cut from the same mold, Nat Pierce and Wojie, Franco and Vince. They were, by today's standards, very short, almost squatty and dumpy. Al Barbatsky was about six-foot one, and the ends a little bit taller than that. They played, I think, the kind of football that Vince later taught. They played bruising football. They gave you nothing and made you earn everything you got, which wasn't very much.

It was basic, I think; basic is the best word I can say for it. Naturally being a student and an undergraduate, I didn't always approve of the coaching staff, which really was great. We used to have a saying when they would make a gain that Jim Crowley was opening up his bag of tricks, which, of course, was a great injustice to a great coach I realized later.

They were basic. They blocked, and they tackled and ran and passed, occasionally; and they didn't score much, but the other team usually didn't score at all; and I think the Green Bay Packers were a direct descendent of the Seven Blocks of Granite really, except that they moved the ball a lot better than our club did.

Fordham played in the Polo Grounds in those days, and the Giants players used to go to most of the Fordham games. A typical Fordham Saturday for me was sitting in the baseball press box with Steve Owen and some of our assistant coaches and some of our players. It was always kind of nerve-racking, because you never had a safe lead, although for that team 2–0 was a big lead. I saw them beat Alabama 2–0. You always felt, "Gee, this is the team that's going to do it — we can beat anybody — bring on Notre Dame." Of course, the Pittsburgh games were great games. I don't think there were ever any greater games played.

As you know, we had three consecutive scoreless ties with Pitt. In those days, under Jock Sutherland, Pitt was really, I guess, the Ohio State or the Texas of today or the Notre Dame. They were the norm of excellence. For our team to take on this nationally known team with Goldberg and Cassiano and Stebins and Chirchunio and stand toe to toe with them and come out at least even was a great achievement we all thought.

There was a certain atmosphere, an expectancy, Monday and Tuesday at school. In-between classes you talked about last week's game; by Wednesday you started trying to sneak through the canvas to see practice, and Thursday you started to look to see if Vince's knee was all right or Frank Worty, how his ankle was and so on. Usually, we had a pep rally Thursday or Friday. Just everything seemed to revolve around what was going to happen on Saturday. I don't mean that the lessons were forgotten, but they were kind of pushed aside occasionally.

It's pretty much the same as our team today, I think. You take a deep breath on Monday and try to heal up; and Tuesday you look at the movies of Sunday's game and then forget about it and start worrying about what's to come. And as I say, along about Thursday you start to wonder whether so and so can play and from Friday's workout on, the tenseness sets in.

I think in those days, football in New York meant Fordham, NYU, and of course, we can't forget Columbia and the Rose Bowl and good old KF 79. The Giants were struggling to get on the sports pages and to become solvent. Of course, in the years that have gone by, college football has been kind of swept under the rug a little bit, and professional football, like most professional sports, has emerged.

I think there is a Lombardi legend at Fordham. You know, I sat in class with Vince at Fordham and one of our textbooks was entitled *Liberty — Its Use and Abuse,* and I believe that many of the convictions that made Vince the man and the coach and the leader that he was were formulated from that book. Anyone who was around Vince became very familiar with the phrase, "the dignity of the individual." Vince got that from Father Ignacius Cox, a Jesuit priest who taught us an ethics class, and I'm sure he got the conviction then, as I did, that the dignity of a man was enhanced by the gifts of intellect and free will. I know he also became a firm believer that this dignity was greatly ennobled when a man elected to forgo his own individual desires, and he joined with other individuals in pursuit of a common goal. Certainly the Green Bay Packers, and what they achieved, would bear out that conviction.

Vince and I sat in most of the philosophy courses together, ethics and psychology. I remember that Father Cox was the ethics professor and had a huge class — I think there were about four hundred of us in the same room. It was difficult to hold people's attention but Father Cox had a great trick. After he had made a point, he would pick names at random: "Is that clear to you, Mr. Mara?" Mr. Mara would usually say, "Yes, Father." "Is that clear to you, Mr. Peyton?" Mr. Peyton would say, "Yes, Father." "Is that clear to you, Mr. Lombardi?" Mr. Lombardi would say, "Yes, Father." Then Father Cox would say, "What's clear to you, Mr. Lombardi?" And Vince crossed us all up because he knew what was clear to him.

I think Vince was a very good student. I think he was a plugger. I think he believed in perspiration rather than inspiration. He always got good marks because I think he thought that's what he was sent to school for, and he was darn well sure he was going to get what he went after.

I think at the time you could separate "the Blocks," but I think as the years went on they tended to come together. Frank Leahy had a big influence on Vince. Vince used to like to tell a story about Spring practice his sophomore year. He had played on the freshman team, and he was going out to be evaluated to make varsity. Frank Leahy was coaching guards and tackles, and his method of evaluating was to line them up and take one at a time. Vince was the first one he took on, and Vince used to like to tell the story that Leahy had him get down in a stance and then charged Vince. And I think a forearm shiver would be a kind expression to describe what he used on Vince and Vince said — I did the only thing I know — I gave it back to him and Frank said, "You'll do, let me have the next one."

Jim Crowley was Vince's head coach, and I think of all the disciples of Knute Rockne, Jim probably came closest, because he was a great speaker — an emotional speaker. I've seen that Fordham team come down the stairs in the old Polo Grounds when it looked as though they only touched the top step and the bottom step.

I really think that most of Vince's coaching philosophy stems more directly from Earl Blaik than from anyone.

Vince wasn't particularly a psychologist. I don't think he relied particularly on getting a team up for a particular game by a locker room talk. He always was on them. He never let up, so that they were probably as ready on Wednesday as they were on Sunday.

I think at the time Vince played at Fordham that there was no particular reason to think he would become a legend to surpass Wojohowicz, who was our All-American center, and Franco, who received a great deal of notice. I do think, though, that the rank and file of the players who were his teammates always had a certain extra respect for him over and above his stature as a player.

We were together on one particular committee that I remember, the Players Relations Committee of the National Football League. It was the first time that we had collective bargaining with the players, and it was a new field for all of us. We were never involved in this before, and we had some rather heated scenes. I remember one in particular when we had gone into these meetings without any ground rules, and it just got to the point that everybody spoke up when they had something to say. One time one of the associates of the attorney for the players chimed in with a comment, and Vince answered him back — at least commented on his comment — and the attorney in question pointed his finger at Vince and said, "Hereafter you direct all your comments to me." And Vince did and they were pretty good comments too.

I remember the weeks immediately preceding the first Super Bowl. We had a pretty bitter feud with the American League, and it meant a lot to us — to the people who were from the National League — to win that first game. In fact, I sat down and wrote Vince a letter. I guess it was after I had seen Kansas City win the right to play against the Packers. I wrote him a letter and told him how much it meant to me to have the National League team win, and I told him I was very happy that the Packers and he were the ones that were going to be carrying our standards, and, of course, they really carried them.

Vince told me later that he read that to the team to impress upon them the way the other members of the National Football League were depending on them. He said it helped crystalize in his mind how much was at stake, and he used it in turn to help the players realize it.

When I got to Los Angeles, I didn't see Vince until the day before the game, and, of course, he was always about the same the day before any game. But I thought it was just intensified all the more. He really wanted to win that game.

We were making a coaching change at the end of 1953 and had hired Jim Lee Howell as our head coach. In the course of looking for a staff, I recommended Vince to Jim Lee. Jim knew Vince on a social basis. He went

Lombardi at Fordham. He only weighed about 180 pounds. (*Todd Studios, Inc.*)

home to Loanoak, Arkansas, and I arranged to have Vince fly down to, as he called it, "Loanoke," and Jim and Vince had their job interview inside a cattle corral on Jim Lee's farm down there. While Vince was on the way home, Jim called me and said, "I think he's terrific and I would like to have you hire him." When he came back, we agreed, and he became our offensive coach.

When Vince was on our staff here, he was in charge of the offense; and he was in very good control of himself, but he did have emotions and they did come into play. I remember one time in particular, we had a halfback who was having a bad practice. He ran the same play incorrectly about three times in about five minutes of practice. The third time he ran it incorrectly, he ran it for about thirty-five yards; and when he stopped, there was Vince, right behind him, somewhat out of breath. But he had chased him all the way to impress on him that he had run the play incorrectly. I remember the player's comment — he was slightly bewildered that anyone would get that upset over a mistake — and he said, "Gee, you make a mistake and the guy throws a fit on you." But he never made the same mistake again.

When I think of Vince, I really don't think of him physically so much. I think mostly of the conviction he had that youth, when properly motivated and properly led, could overcome any obstacle and could achieve any goal they were after. And I think he knew he was the type of leader that could motivate youth to do this. I believe the reason that he was such a leader was because he knew that if he had the right to exact utmost performance and devotion from someone, he also had the obligation to do nothing less than that himself. And all the years I knew him, he was always true to that principle.

I think he could have been president, and he could have been pope. In other times and other circumstances, he might have been Alexander the Great and conquered the world. Or he might have been St. Francis Xavier and converted the world, because he had the zeal of a missionary and that's the thing I always think about when I think of Vince. He had the zeal of a missionary. I think Commissioner Roselle put it very well when Vince died: it was a great loss, particularly for the youth, not only the youth who had come under him but for the youth who would have come under him and could no longer do so.

Three decades later: the "Seven Blocks of Granite" meet in reunion at a Fordham Alumni
Dinner in 1968. Surrounding Vince Lombardi are from left: Leo Paquin, end; Ed Franco,
tackle; John Druze, end; Alex Wojciechowicz (seated), center; Al Bart, tackle; and Nat Pierce,
guard. *(Courtesy, Joe Lombardi)*

JOE CAHILL

Ever since Colonel Earl Blaik took over the helm in 1943, Army football went up and up. Certainly Blaik knew Lombardi was interested in coming to West Point. After all, Army had just come off an undefeated season, and we must have had some twenty or thirty applicants to fill that job. And then, too, working for Red Blaik was the thing to do in those days. As a matter of fact, I feel quite proud about the fact that I was the one who called Vince and told him that it was his job. Colonel Blaik was in San Francisco at an NCAA meeting, and he called me and said, "Call that coach at Fordham." I got Vince on the phone and I said, "This is Joe Cahill up at West Point." He yelled, "I'll take it!"

Vince, like most coaches who came to West Point, had a lot to learn about the system. Of course, he had his own ideas about coaching, and he had to meld into a coaching staff that Colonel Blaik always took great pains in getting together. I would say that Vince possibly had some disciplinary things to consider on the coaching field in actually working with the cadets. I also think that he probably had to adjust the planning methods. For example, the coaches would get together in that office as early as eight o'clock in the morning and really not leave until well after dinner hour at night.

Though Vince wasn't a young coach compared to some of the other coaches who had joined Blaik's staff down through the years, he still had to make some adjustments in his own personal habits and approach to the game. I recall, for example, on the practice field in his first spring practice where, the perfectionist that he was, he threw his hat down immediately because one of the backs had run in the wrong direction. It became quite a scene for a moment. Colonel Blaik walked right over and had to explain to Vince that he knew how intent he was and how he wanted to succeed and how Army wanted to succeed, but that we can't display that kind of emotion on the field.

Vince's reaction was one of, "Yes, sir," and he put his hat on and I never saw it done again. I think, as we all know now, that he learned fast, and he learned his lessons well. Certainly the whole experience was rewarding for Vince, although at times frustrating. He always had in the back of his mind that this was the sure route to a head coaching job. So many others had won their opportunities this way, and Vince knew that he had the capability. He had the confidence in himself, and yet that big break just didn't seem to arrive. Now, of course, there were some extenuating circumstances. You must realize that Army had an undefeated season in 1948 and also in 1949, and only lost one game in 1950. Things were going in high gear until, of course, the football squad was decimated by the cribbing scandal in 1951 which involved a number of its football players, including Blaik's son. All of them were kicked out of school. This sidetracked some of the coaches, too. I talked to Vince and all the coaches about it, and many of the players at the time. There was a sense of great disappointment and some bitterness, naturally, because we all worked closely together. We were all part of the game, and it was a frustrating experience. I thought it was a tribute to Vince that he stayed on at that time and saw the thing through to Army's return to successful football in 1953.

He saw other guys go on to get college head coaching jobs. It often occurred to him — and we discussed it at great length — how some of the jobs would open for certain men. I know that it was a concern to Vince. He felt he had all the qualifications. He was a dynamic individual. He wanted to succeed. He felt that he could handle any job — he had that kind of confidence in himself. But the big opportunity just didn't seem to present itself. He couldn't actually figure out why. Of course, in the long run he went into pro football.

There was great elation, of course, when Vince joined the staff. He had great spirit, and all he could see was that rosy future based on what had happened to so many of his associates. Then, as time went on, I think some frustration set in. He got down near three or four years, and the big break just wasn't happening. I noticed it in our conversations many times. I used to travel around with Vince on speaking engagements, and we would get into rather deep discussion on "I wonder why?". He always felt down deep that he had as much to offer as head coach as many of the men on the staff who had gone before him.

Colonel Blaik handled all his men equally. They met as a group. They traveled as a group. Only occasionally, when they'd have a specific or special problem, would they sit with him alone. I think that this was one of the great things that Colonel Blaik was able to do. He made them competitive within their own group. They all wanted to come up with their own ideas. They had freedom of expression, and Vince, of course, contributed greatly to this because he was very forthright and outspoken when it came to football.

He was very tough when trying to sell his ideas. As a matter of fact, quite often he became irritated when he felt that he was being set down without real justification. Vince was always ready as a good recruiter. He brought in many fine football players who contributed to the Army football scene. He was thorough in everything he did.

Later, people asked me if there was a great deal of similarity between Vince and Colonel Blaik. They were two separate and distinct individuals. I do believe that Vince, through his association with Colonel Blaik, adopted some of his mannerisms. I sensed that, just watching him, after he had left West Point. However, Vince was more explosive; Colonel Blaik always seemed to be under control, no matter what the situation was. Vince was more of a friendly, out-going, party guy. He always enjoyed telling a story and more so listening to one. Colonel Blaik, on the other hand, was withdrawn. He was not a party man. He was all business twenty-four hours a day.

Vince spoke at pep rallies maybe once a year. He was an excellent speaker. You know, his background as a lawyer, and he always did an excellent job on his feet. When it came to rabble-rousing and getting them excited, he certainly could do that. It was sort of a pattern to the whole speech-making proposition. It would usually be prior to an Army–Navy game or an Army–Notre Dame game. The coaches would rotate and take turns giving the key speech. The pattern was to review the personnel on the opposing team and the problems involved. Vince would always have some excellent anecdotes to apply to the situation, and the Corps of Cadets loved it. He got a great response from them.

There was really no way to figure out in those days that one day Vince Lombardi would go on to be the greatest coach in the game. The coaching staff at West Point worked as a unit, dominated, of course, by Colonel Blaik. He ran the coaching staff. He made out the assignments, and he ran the team. There was never any question about this. For me to say that I expected Vince or any other of the Army coaches to go on to do great things would be just a misstatement.

Vince was a strong personality from the first day that I shook hands with him in the gym until the last time that I saw him. He stood up for what he believed in, on the field and off.

When Vince told me he was going to the Giants, I was very happy for him yet sad that he was leaving West Point. That big college job just never came through, and I always felt that the people at the college level never knew what a man they missed. Later, after the Giants and then into those

For The Record
By Al Del Greco

Lombardi Likes Some Movies

Oh, well, it looks as if Vince Lombardi is going to make the rounds this winter and show pictures of the Army-Navy game.

The Army backfield coach, Red Blaik's chief assistant, didn't show pictures last year. He discussed sportsmanship, studies and the boy, Flirtation Walk, and various other topics at the rubber chicken banquets. The reason he didn't show pictures was that a sailor team from Annapolis, Md., poured it into Army to the tune of 42 to 7.

It's a well known fact that Army wasn't playing football players last year after the wholesale cribbing ejections. They were playing a lot of boys who liked to play football. There is a difference.

In one short season Red Blaik and his aides really came up with something, and only need a couple of more wins for the country's elite to notice them. A Saturday win over Pittsburgh, which poured it into Notre Dame, may even have the experts picking Army as one of the country's top teams.

Naturally, Lombardi is a very happy man. The former St. Cecilia coach of Englewood had a tough time while Army was down. He had to go out and look for football players. Success lures 'em to your door step. This means that Vince at the very least should save some carfare if Army stands up under pressure. They looked mighty hot against Dartmouth, which held Penn to 30 yards rushing, but Red Blaik casually dismisses it all as an off-day for the Big Green.

The role as a signal-caller (Lombardi's task) is mighty unpleasant when the boys can't throw or run a football. Against Navy last year there were times when he was tempted to tell Blaik to call the plays. But everything looks rosy now —he has good operators on the gridiron. But can a team recover so swiftly? Pitt should supply the answer.

* * * *

Ex-Rams Mastermind Service Backs

Lombardi and Eshmont on Staffs

By LAWRENCE ROBINSON,
Staff Writer.

ANNAPOLIS, Nov. 25.—An unusual feature of the 57th meeting of Army and Navy Saturday will be a matching of wits of two old Fordham Rams—Vince Lombardi of Army and Lennie Eshmont of Navy.

Each is the backfield coach and,

Vin Lombardi   **Len Eshmont**

while top decisions will be made by Red Blaik and Eddie Erdelatz, they are bound to be consulting two of Jim Crowley's star pupils before giving final word.

To make the situation even more bizarre, backfield coach Lombardi was a Ram lineman, one of the members of the immortal Seven Blocks of Granite. Though guards are not supposed to know the finer points of play-making, Lombardi does. Blaik has tagged him one of the keenest minds in football today.

He Could Throw, Too.

Eshmont fits much more naturally into backfield tutoring. Lennie was one of the greatest halfbacks of the great Fordham prewar era—an elusive swiftie who also could punt and block with the best of his day, despite his lack of size.

He could pass, too, at Mt. Carmel, Pa., High, but an injury to his arm in his freshman year hampered his accuracy. Since graduation, Eshmont played with the Giants, three different Navy Pre-Flight teams and ended his playing days as a San Francisco

'49er, from which he came to aid Erdelatz in 1950.

Lombardi's emergence as a playmaker was no surprise to 1935 classmates on Rose Hill. Vince graduated Cum Laude, and two years later earned his law degree. But meantime he had started to coach St. Cecelia High, Englewood, where he did a magnificent job. In eight seasons, Lombardi's teams won six state championships, went unbeaten for 33 straight games in one stretch.

Three Navy Formations.

Of the two, perhaps Eshmont has more to worry about. Navy will go into Saturday's game equipped with not one but three different formations—the T, the Split T and the Notre Dame Box, a variation of the single wing.

With Bob Cameron at quarterback, Navy stays T. With Steve Schoderbek going in, the Midshipmen swing into a Split T, at which Steve excels. The reason! For two years Dave emulated Maryland's Jack Scarbath in jayvee scrimmages against the varsity and the practice has made Schoderbek letter-perfect in the optional pitchouts and running passes which are a feature of the Split T.

Both sailor signal-callers have been schooled in the single wing formations, which coach Erdelatz had installed last spring with the idea of deserting the T formation entirely. However, things still go so well with the T so much of the time, the Navy mentor is loathe to discard a going business.

Navy bumped heads here yesterday in a stiff scrum, but will take it easy today and tomorrow, with leavetaking scheduled at 9:30 a.m. Friday morning.

Army grid coach Col. Earl Blaik and his line coach, Vince Lombardi, go over game films during their association at West Point.

Newspaper clippings of Lombardi at West Point.

great years in Green Bay, a lot of these same college administrators would call and ask me if I could get them an interview with Vince and if he would be interested in taking over their school's program.

I saw Vince at a party in New York the winter after they had beaten the Giants, 37-0. We had a drink and he took me aside and told me a great story. He said, "Remember when I could not get an interview for a college coaching job?" And I said yes. So he laughed and unless you have been around Vince when he tells a story, you can't believe how excited he gets and how he grabs your arm and how much he enjoys himself. "Guess who called last week in Green Bay?" he asks. Before I can answer, he says, "The president — President Kennedy! He says, 'Hello, Coach, how are you? I say fine. He says, 'Good.' Now I'm wondering why he's calling and he says, 'Coach, I've got three generals standing in front of me, and they want me to ask you if you would come back to West Point and coach Army again.' Well, I don't know what to say. How do you turn down the president of the United States? So all I can do is kinda laugh to give myself time to think. As soon as I laugh, he cuts in and says, 'I thought that would be your answer, and I told the generals so before I called. Good luck next season and if you get here, stop by and we'll have lunch. Goodbye, Coach.' And he hangs up!"

And Vince starts laughing, and I'm laughing and everybody around us, who did not hear the story, starts laughing. He kept shaking his head and laughing that he never said 'no' but that the president of the United States took him off the hook!

I enjoyed those years with Vince at the Point and got a big thrill from his success with the Packers. But it was watching his growth as a powerful spokesman for equality and dedication and excellence that made me realize I had been close to greatness. He was a football coach, and he would not want to be thought of in any other way. But all of us who knew him, loved him and know our lives were so much richer for being his friend.

The West Point coaching staff. The man in the middle is Earl Blaik. To his right is Vince Lombardi. To his left is Murray Warmath. (New Jersey Turnpike Authority)

FRANK GIFFORD

I'll never forget that. I don't think anyone ever forgets the first time they meet or met Vince. It was in 1954 in Salem, Oregon. I had heard a lot about Vinnie Lombardi and the kind of person he was, and, of course, to me he was just another college coach who was jumping into professional ranks. He was standing outside of our dormitory at Oregon University. We were training out there, and he was standing with Jim Lee Lowell, which is quite a funny sight to begin with. Jim Lee is about six-foot six, and Vinnie wasn't short, but alongside Jim it sort of gives you a Mutt and Jeff quality. And I think the first thing I remember was that smile. When Vince smiled there was nothing quite like it.

He had, I guess, 32 teeth like everybody else, but they all seemed to be on the top and they really showed, and he shook my hand, said hello. Jim Lee introduced us. Jim is a very jolly person. There was a lot of ho-ho and a lot of laughing, and then he became very serious, and in the course of the conversation, he alluded to my having played defense the previous year and offense. We had a rather bad football team. That's putting it rather lightly. I think we won one game.

Vince said, "Well, you're my halfback this year." Of course, I didn't know how much authority he was going to have or anything else, and I went on up and checked in and I was his halfback. There was no question about it. I never saw the defensive side of the alignment again. Vince was very definite in so many ways. He was very definite about me at that particular time.

He wasn't close to anyone because we all had reservations. We had a veteran team of a lot of older fellows playing, but Vince wasn't the type of person who tried to ingratiate himself with you. He just happened to come up in the rooms in the evening, for instance. I think he felt that we were questioning his credentials, coming from college into professional football, and it never affected him on the field because he drove us as hard from the very day he got there till the day he left to go to Green Bay. In the evening he'd put in a play, and he'd stand up in the morning and draw the play out. He was very positive about it. We'd go out on the field and he'd be very positive about it. He might have been positive, but we weren't.

That evening maybe about nine thirty or ten o'clock, he'd drop around the room and maybe visit with Eddie Price or Charlie Conerly or Kyle Rote or myself, any one of a number of us. He would sit down and he would begin to laugh and he would kid around about the play a little bit. What he was really trying to find out was what we felt about a specific play, a specific formation. I guess picking our minds, if you will. All of a sudden we began to see a different person: somebody you could respect; somebody who was on your plane and yet when he was in charge, ran the show; but somebody you could have fun with, somebody you could enjoy talking with.

Those were the early days of Vince Lombardi and after that, of course, he picked up the pro game quickly. It was incredible to see what happened to him. Quite a transformation! He had a lot of help, too. I think Tom Landry contributed a great deal to Lombardi's tactical and strategical end of football.

Nobody contributed to the other end: his being somehow able to get a little more out of a man than the man thought he could give.

I thought it was a facade. We tested him in a lot of ways. We liked to needle him because he was so explosive, and I can recall one time he hated to have the players close in on his huddle while he was working. He would pick up anything, and one particular day he threw down a little piece of orange peeling and he said, "All right, all of you who are not working, get behind the orange peel and stay there," which was about four or five yards behind the huddle.

Since you would get tired in spring training, you would want to get closer to where you have to step in. You would try and cut down every possible effort you could. When he wasn't looking we would move that orange peel up and pretty soon we were right back on the huddle. He was a little explosive in some ways in that respect.

I don't think he liked to admit something he had put in was wrong or maybe a young football player had miscalculated or that he just didn't have it quite right for their ability. Well, the first thing he did when he arrived at Salem was to put in a pitchout series and an option series. Now our quarterback was Charlie Conerly, and Charlie was getting up there in years so to speak — well, I guess Charlie must have been thirty-seven or thirty-eight, maybe thirty-six when Vinnie arrived — but anyway he was too far up there to try running that option play. I don't know the kind of defensive ends Vince had been coaching against at Army, but it wasn't guys like Lenny Ford of Cleveland — two hundred eighty and six-foot six. But Charlie Conerly was great. He would run that play religiously in practice, religiously in the dummy drills but never in a scrimmage, nor ever in a game. So, after about two or three games Vinnie didn't necessarily admit his mistake in putting it in, it just kind of disappeared from our offense, sort of by osmosis. He was a big man, he didn't make many mistakes that I know of.

He could be very emotional, maybe one of the most emotional men I've ever met. I think Vinnie always kind of calculated his emotion, in other words, he dispensed it whenever he felt it was needed. It became kind of a game with us to come in after a game during those years and try and figure out what Vinnie was going to be like — whether we should have a game face on or whether we could afford a little luxury of laughter. So much depended on Vinnie's mood, and I think his mood was predicated on what he felt was necessary for the ball club. It became a game.

I don't think that Vince Lombardi went to Green Bay as the same type of coach. Those were learning years for Lombardi in terms of handling professionals, handling older men. He had been highly successful, of course, in high school and college; but this was a learning stage for him — a part of his undergraduate work — and he went on to Green Bay and certainly got his doctor's degree.

Vinnie on the sidelines was something special. I've always had the feeling that most coaches should stay home on Sunday — they get their work in and just stay away from the ball park because they couldn't really help you a lot, particularly a veteran team. I don't know how he was at Green Bay — I won't even try to speculate. Again, I think that he was different at Green Bay

On the sidelines in Yankee Stadium with the New York Giants. One of the rare pictures of Vince Lombardi and Tom Landry on the same side of the field. The player is Frank Gifford. *(New Jersey Turnpike Authority)*

than he was with the Giants. He was strictly our offense coach, but I don't think anyone on the offensive team ever looked at Vinnie as being anything but the head coach because he was that dominating. He was good on the sidelines for what coaches are good for on the sidelines. He was always working with the players. He'd see things out there that most coaches wouldn't see. He might see a tackle getting off on the ball a little slow. He might see you not getting off on the count. Those are the things he could really contribute on the sidelines. I think more of an inspirational thing than anything else. Tactically and strategically, all the information comes from above, and I don't think really there's that much for any coach to do on the sidelines, but he did a lot in terms of inspiration. If you were dogging it out there, he'd let you know pretty quick.

Frank Gifford   **65**

I don't think Vinnie ever really lost his cool with a ball player. I've heard and read of wild incidents, mostly stated and written by people who never knew the man, of all these emotional outrages and tirades he would go into. I never saw any. He geared himself, I think, according to the man. If he felt a specific ball player needed to be chewed out, well then that poor ball player was going to be chewed out continuously until he came across. I can't recall really many errors in judgment in that respect. I've seen him ride players; I've seen him ignore players; I have seen him pat them on the fanny. I really can't recall his ever making a bad error in judgment as to how to get the most out of the ball player to win the football game, and for Vinnie, that's what it was all about.

When he went to Green Bay he started collecting talent, and you could do it a lot easier then because they didn't have near as many teams. He got together a great bunch of football players, and he taught them the basics of the game as he believed: to block and to tackle and play it the way it's supposed to be played. And that's rough. You never had to worry about Vinnie tricking you. In his early days, he used to love to have one surprise play every game, but with Green Bay he didn't need that. He had such talent; he had such talented players and he got that extra little bit out of them; he was a factor in his players — the extension of Vinnie Lombardi.

Vinnie has been characterized by so many people and so many of his former players have said they loved the man. I loved him too. I look back at the years and the contributions he's made to my life, and I think he's been the single most important factor to me as an individual man. He taught me so many things. He taught me to dedicate myself. I think I would like to have my kids grow up to be something like Vince Lombardi with that kind of dedication, that kind of love of life. Make no mistakes about it, he lived every phase of it.

Vince Lombardi receiving congratulations from Pete Rozelle, Commissioner of the NFL after winning Super Bowl II. Standing to their right is Lombardi's former star, Frank Gifford, conducting the post game show for CBS.
(Vernon J. Biever)

5

The Green Bay Years

THE PLACE was typical of the small family restaurants you find in the neighborhoods of midwestern towns. There was a long bar and stools; and there were tables in the barroom and a small room off to the side, filled with dinner patrons. It was a Friday and the restaurant was crowded because of the Fish Special — one of the best bargains ever in these inflationary times. For $3.00, you got four pieces of fish, usually perch or walleye, salad, French fries, rolls and butter, cranberries, and coffee. Martinis were $.75, a draft beer $.20.

Behind the bar, Budweiser had provided a grown-up mobile of their Clydesdales. There were jars filled with hard-boiled eggs, popcorn, pretzels, sausages, and cigars. And everywhere, there were pictures of the Green Bay Packers. On the wall was a poster saying, "A Fresh Start with Bart." And there were faded pennants proclaiming the Green Bay Packers to be World Champions and saying this was "Titletown, USA."

The conversation at the bar — and throughout the restaurant — was about the Packers. In fact, we were not even in Green Bay, but in a town about 150 miles north of it where the big industry was musky fishing and talking about the Packers. The fishing for muskies had been about as successful as the Packers had been in recent years, and there was much excitement about the greatest Packer player of all taking over the team as the new head coach. Bart Starr would bring "the Pack back."

A visitor asked one of the locals about the fishing and received a shrug for an answer. So to join in the spirit of the discussion, he asked if the local thought Starr will ever bring the Packers back to where Lombardi had them. That was a mistake. Within seconds at least fifty voices told the visitor how great the Packers would be; another fifty, that they would never be as good as they were under Lombardi. And as they talked, they began remembering different games in the Lombardi years: each one was there in the "Ice Bowl" or at the Super Bowl or in Dallas. And they probably were. Finally, there was a pause and an older man, sitting at the end of the bar summed it up for everyone. "If the son-of-a-bitch hadn't gone to Washington, he'd never have caught cancer and died. And we'd still be the best," he said. And they all nodded and went back to eating.

When Vince Lombardi came to Green Bay, nobody knew a damn thing about him. When he left, he was one of the most famous men in the country and the number-one citizen of Wisconsin and Packerland. There has been so much written about him and his team that there is no need to write about it here. The reminiscences that follow give a view of the early days and what he was like to work for and to play under.

The citizens of Green Bay still have not completely gotten over the fact that Lombardi did leave and that he is dead. To the real Packer fans, he has never really been gone. What he left them is still so special that they talk about it in the present tense. There is bitterness, not much anymore, but still some. Rather, what they have is that same feeling that people get when they experience something great together. It is theirs, and it can never be changed or taken away.

Tom Miller has been with the Packers ever since Fr. Marquette paddled into the Bay and said to the Indians, "Lucky you. The white man has discovered you." Tom has seen them come and go in Green Bay, and if you were to take book on who would last longer, pro football or Tom Miller, odds are on Miller. He knew Vince Lombardi as only those who worked for the man could know him. Indeed, working for Lombardi was tougher than playing for him. At least the player could take it out on the visiting team on Sunday. Throwing a forearm at a filing cabinet might help let off steam, but it was rough on the bones. But Tom Miller has a ring with three diamonds across the top. That made up for everything.

Tony Canadeo was called the "Gray Ghost of Gonzaga," after the small school he attended in the Northwest. He played for the Packers for eleven years; they were a good team in the early forties and one of the reasons for this was Tony Canadeo. Until Jim Taylor came along, Tony was the all-time leading ground gainer for the Packers. Now, living and working in Green Bay, Tony is a member of the Executive Committee of the Packers. He, along with the other committee members, helped bring Vince Lombardi to Green Bay. The two became the closest of friends, and Tony was probably the only member who would stand up to Vince.

Today, Forrest Gregg is the head coach of the Cleveland Browns, and he is trying to bring them back to the levels of excellence they knew for so many years. If there is anybody who can do that, it will be Forrest Gregg. When he played for the Packers, writers selecting the All-Pro team each year would automatically fill his name in at the offensive tackle position. And each year, Gregg's opponents would do the same. That meant a lot more than the writers' selection. He was such a team player that when Jerry Kramer was hurt during the 1961 season, Gregg switched to guard and still won All-Pro honors. But of all his honors, probably the one that means the most to him is one that has no trophy to go with it, no silver plate or gold plaque. It is just knowing that Vince Lombardi considered him the best football player he ever coached.

Bart Starr is Bart Starr. He happens to be everything that has been written about him and more. Without question he is one of the finest human beings who has walked this poor earth. He spent more time with Vince Lombardi than any player on the Packers, and what Bart Starr is shows what that meant to him. They had a special relationship that did not have to be talked about. When Bart was on the field, Vince Lombardi did not have to worry. It was as if *he* were out there. As he always did, Lombardi got to the heart of the matter quickly, and whenever there was a discussion of who was the greatest quarterback of all time, Lombardi would say, "Who won the most championships? That's the quarterback's job." And that settled the discussion. It is Bart Starr.

Willie Davis is the president of one of the largest Schlitz distributing companies in America. He is on the board of directors of Schlitz and is a community leader in Los Angeles. He is also one of the greatest defensive ends to have ever played pro football. And, as far as Willie is concerned, the man who made him what he is was Vince Lombardi. Sometimes Lombardi would remind him of that. Willie will be in the Hall of Fame soon. That's nice. Being a Packer under Vince Lombardi, that's everything.

When Vince Lombardi and his family moved to Green Bay, the Italian population of the community was increased by four, bringing the total to twenty. Ten years later, the population was 75,987. They tell Belgian jokes in Green Bay; not Italian. And you can understand why. Two brothers, Ray and "Duds" Bilotti, had a pizza place in De Pere, Wisconsin, near Green Bay. When Lombardi and the Packers started to win, the brothers opened a fine restaurant two blocks from the Packer offices. They were businessmen and they became friendly with Vince Lombardi. Vince enjoyed them and their restaurant and would sometimes go there after a game. To the Bilottis that meant the world because their place would be jammed with people waiting to see him. They were good for him; and he was good to them. After all, is not that the way with countrymen?

TOM MILLER

At the NFL draft meeting in Pittsburgh, I met Vince Lombardi. I had heard of him because everyone in the league was talking about him as a fine future head coach. The Packers were in the market, but we had not decided who we would approach. Later, Bert Bell, then the commissioner of the NFL, recommended Vince very highly to us and so we contacted him to see if he was interested.

He was, and he came to Green Bay to meet with the group from the executive committee assigned to find a head coach. We were looking for someone who would take over this franchise, shake it up, and bring the Packers back. Vince met all the qualifications.

This was the winter of 1959. The Packers had not had a winning season in fifteen years. To say that the town was down on the team and the management would be putting it mildly. And the team was run by the executive committee of fifty or so men who represented the stockholders, who were the townspeople. And like everything else in this world that is run by a committee, the Packers were screwed up. On Monday after a game, the Coach would attend a luncheon where the committee and the guests would ask questions about the team and the previous day's game.

It was one of the great second-guessing times in sports. No coach could operate that way. Anyone could get up and make any charge he wanted or question why this player was playing and that one not. It was chaos. Finally, out of desperation and self-preservation, the executive committee agreed to hire someone who would be responsible to no one except them, and hopefully, someone who would dominate them. Vince met all those qualifications.

Vince Lombardi came to Green Bay and demanded both the head coaching job, which was his major responsibility, and the general managership. When the announcement was made that Lombardi was taking over the Packers, he was here in Green Bay and met with the board of directors and gave his plans and thoughts on how a football team and organization ought to be run. He was very impressive. After the board meeting, he met with the press, and of course, that was an impressive meeting.

That was the first time I had the opportunity to see him with the press and watch him handle a press conference. He was very dominant, very much in control of himself. He commanded a great deal of respect. And you must remember that nobody really knew anything about him other than the fact that the Maras of the Giants gave him the highest of recommendations, as did Bert Bell. The press only had the briefest of biographical material on him.

When Lombardi came here, the team was not making any money, maybe only $35,000 a year profit; it was a struggle and everything was cut down and salaries were low, both for the front office personnel and the players. The offices were in an old run-down building downtown. With the exception of a few franchises, most of pro football was like the Packers — low profits and lousy quarters.

But when Lombardi came we had the worst playing record in the game, and after the long tradition of great football in the thirties and early forties, the town was crying for a winner. So after a 1 won, 1 tied, and 10 lost record, the town and the organization decided it had to have a man who would give them a winner. And I mean the town really was putting the pressure on the organization, because as you know, this team is owned by the town.

The first thing that became apparent to us even before the players reported was the way Vince handled authority. What you felt was his dominance over all the people. His way was the only way, and he was the type of person who was very demanding. He commanded respect through fear, and people really feared him until they got to know him. Once you did get to know him, the respect remained and the fear left because you knew he had the intelligence and the ability to do what was necessary to build a winning team and a successful organization.

He was very knowledgeable about football, and he was very knowledgeable about things outside football. He ran the organization in a very businesslike way. The same way he coached. He knew how to handle players. He dominated them. He'd say to one, "You're my halfback," or "You're my quarterback," or "You're my tackle." He studied the movies that first year before summer camp, and he'd say, "That man can't play in the NFL," so he would trade him or let him go or bring another player in who he thought could do the job.

We weren't used to operating that way. When we signed a player we felt we had to keep him. There were few trades before Lombardi. Only those that benefitted both teams. But if he didn't think a player could play under his system, meaning he didn't have the fortitude, even though the player was NFL caliber, then he would get rid of him. One example was Billy Howton. Billy was one of our few stars, a top receiver, a Pro Bowl performer. But Vince did not think Howton had the dedication necessary to play for him, that Billy had too many outside interests, that his thoughts were not completely aimed at football. So he traded him to Cleveland before the season began.

Lombardi had great admiration for Paul Brown, the coach of the Cleveland Browns in those days. He knew Brown as a dedicated, successful coach and admired his methods. And Vince always liked to associate himself with successful people and have successful people around him. And so when Vince came to Green Bay, he always talked to Paul Brown about football and the players around the league, getting a line on what talent might be available through trades. I know that over the years they became great friends. And Brown developed the same admiration and respect for Vince that Vince had had for him.

But in 1959, we were hurting, both on offense and defense. Lombardi felt he had to build up the defense first because, as he used to say, "There is nothing more discouraging to a team than to watch the opposition run up and down the field at will against you." So he traded for defensive players. At that time, the Browns were at the top of the league, along with the Colts and the Giants, and they had some of the best personnel in football. Vince knew that Brown had some excellent players who were not getting a chance with the Browns because they were young and relatively inexperienced.

Two of those players were Willie Davis and Henry Jordon. Both were quick and strong, but Paul felt they were too small to play in his system. Paul had not seen too much of Willie Davis; I think that Willie was actually in the service for part of his first year with the Browns, so Paul would have had little opportunity to get to know him. In fact, they even had Willie listed as an offensive tackle for a while.

As for Henry Jordon, he never did play much for the Browns because Paul felt he had better players than Henry on his roster. I doubt that we gave up a player for either of them. Nobody wanted anybody on the Packer roster then, and so we probably gave up a couple of low draft choices.

Lombardi, like everyone else in pro football, wanted big linemen on both sides of the line. But since Vince had so much respect for Paul Brown, when Paul told him that both these men had quickness and were good football players, Vince made the trade.

Not a bad trade. A couple of low draft choices for two All-Pro players. And he also took Bill Quinlan from the Browns. Quinlan had a bad reputation, but we needed defensive help and Vince got him.

As it turned out, Lombardi made the most of it. The only regular we had on defense that was worth a damn was Dave "Hawg" Hanner. So with the "Hawg," who was great against the run, Vince put Willie Davis next to Hawg on the left side and Jordon at right defensive tackle, next to Quinlan at end. The front four was light, as defensive lines go, probably the smallest in the league. But it became a great line.

Lombardi built his front four on quickness and strength. Pro football then was dominated by the pass, and with Davis and Jordon, Vince got great pressure on the passer from the outside as well as from the inside. If a run developed, like a trap or draw on Henry, "Hawg" was there to stop it. Quinlan was very tough against the run and a fair pass rusher. But it was Davis and Jordon, because of their quickness, strength, and speed who became All-Pro performers. Willie Davis will go down as one of the three or four greatest defensive ends ever to play the game.

The real secret to Lombardi's defense was in his linebackers. They were all about six-foot three and around two hundred thirty pounds. They had speed, strength, and great range. In the middle was Ray Nitschke, later to be voted the greatest middle linebacker in the first fifty years of pro football. And on the outside, the Packers had two All-Pro players also, Dan Currie and Bill Forester. With that size and speed, they could drop off and cover on the pass; and they were strong enough to handle any runner who broke past the line or to come up and stop the runner at the line of scrimmage.

Because of the quickness of the defensive line in getting to the passer, and because of the size and speed of the linebackers, we played man-to-man pass defense most of the time. We had a great secondary — all quick, fine hitters and smart. There was Willie Wood and Hank Gremminger and Jesse Whittenton and Herb Adderley, maybe the greatest cornerback in the history of the game.

And that first year here, when the players reported to camp, I could not wait to see what would happen. I knew how demanding he was on the office people. And if he were that way with us, the players were really in for something. And it happened just that way.

He just drove the people at those practice sessions. I can see him now. He had a great knack for pointing. He'd yell and scream a lot and run after the player that had goofed up and shake that finger under that player's nose. They were all afraid of him, though later that fear became great respect and even love. But in that first camp there was nothing but fear.

Those first weeks were the hardest practices I have ever seen in football, and I've been in it all my life. He really drilled them. It was the method that he used to get the best out of a player. He always felt that a player who wasn't in condition couldn't give his all, so he drove them until they dropped and then drove them some more. So by the end of those first weeks, that team was in the best condition I'd ever seen a Packer team in, or any other.

Now he went after them on execution. He believed that you could not execute properly unless you were in condition. And he believed that good execution came from repetition and practice. And I recall his running a play over and over and over and over until the groans from the players almost drowned him out as he'd yell "run it again."

But he was a great perfectionist. Even a step, even a move, if a guy shook his shoulder the wrong way, he would say, "Do it again," over and over. He would do that all day. And the players even got so that if one would make a mistake, *they* would yell, "Do it again." But they never said it so he could hear them because they were scared to death of him. And after they would run the same play a few more times, you could hear some of them saying, "God, I hope we don't have to run it again." It was repetition, repetition, repetition, until they got it right and then he'd say, "Run it again."

That's why the Lombardi Sweep became such a successful play. Of course, he had Paul Hornung and Jimmy Taylor. He would work on that sweep until the players just could not run it any more. That's why it became so successful. After a while, everyone in the league knew it was coming but they just couldn't stop it, and that gave a great deal of confidence to the players.

But he was not always hollering and screaming. He knew how to handle players. Each player was an individual to him, and he knew just how to handle each one. Of course that took a while that first year. But he really was a master at being able to reach this man or that. Some, he'd be on all the time; some, only when they really screwed up; and some, never. He would get on the stars whenever necessary but he realized that players like McGee and Hornung and Taylor and Thurston were pros and would perform. They had the reputation of being playboys and carousers and they were. We wouldn't see them after a game until the next practice, and they might have been out all night. But when they hit that practice field, they went all out and gave a hundred percent. Vince had great respect for them. He said that if anybody could go out all night, come out here, and run full steam for an hour and forty-five minutes and still be leaders on the field, he knew they were his kind of football players. The fellow who had the ability and did not put out everything on the field was the player that Vince would get on. He was a great psychologist. He knew who to get on, when to get on him, and just how much the player could take. He knew who had the short fuse because he had one. He understood those things. He knew just how far to drive each individual. He did not know the players off the field, but he knew almost without exception how far he could push each player on the field and in the meetings.

And in those early years, even if he pushed someone too far, there was too much fear of him to ever argue back. Nobody would have ever dared argue with him. In later years, he felt that the players were finally getting to know him and to understand that he really wasn't as cold and mean as he pretended, as rough and tough as the exterior seemed. He was really a soft, kind-hearted guy. And that always showed up when the wives of the players were around. He felt that a player's wife was as important as the player, because if the wife was unhappy, he felt it would interfere with the player's performance on the field.

He was very tender and understanding if a player had a serious injury. But if he thought that somebody had a minor injury and a low pain threshold, he would drive that player and make him perform even with the small injury. He had that famous saying, "Have to play with those small hurts." The players would kid about that, but never in front of the coach. And, most of the players he had, had this high pain factor and played with the injuries and bruises.

In his early years, the players were afraid to get hurt and would play with those injuries. That helped make us the great football team we were. A lot of injuries are psychological and coach would talk to the doctors about an injured player and if the doctor said he could play even though he'd be in pain but not suffer any permanent damage, then that player was expected to play. And he did.

Lombardi probably did not have too much experience in running an organization before he came to Green Bay. But he had a natural organizational ability. After a while, we had the best run organization in all of sports. I would go with him on speaking engagements before business leaders and sit in the audience and listen to his talk, and time after time I'd hear these presidents of large corporations say that Vince could take over their company and run it better. He was so forceful. He had the knack of seeming to always make the right decision for the organization, and if the decision turned out to be wrong, by the strength of his personality, his forcefulness would make it turn out right. It was uncanny.

He had great power of some kind that I can't explain. But if he told you to do something, even though you knew it was wrong, you went ahead and did it. And most often it turned out to be right. He demanded the same inner strength from his players. He wanted them to be forceful, to commit themselves to something, and just by sheer will and hard work make it happen. Not only in football but in life.

Tom Landry of the Dallas Cowboys was quoted once as saying that the reason the Packers won all the key games was that they had "suffered" together so much. I never understood what he meant. We were the happiest group of people, both the players and the executive staff and the whole organization. It was that way because we all recognized that Lombardi's way was the winning way. Once the practice whistle blew, the players and coaches were all business. But after work or practice, this was just a great place to be. And of course, winning made it that way. I was here when we were losers, before Lombardi and after; and believe me, you're a lot happier when you're with a winner.

I like the way Red Smith put it one time when he called the Packers under Lombardi the most intelligent and articulate group of athletes he had ever covered. And Lombardi deserves the credit for that. He taught the players to think, not just to go through the motions. Not only about football, but about other things too. He never put in a play before he explained to everyone why that play was put in, why it was to be run a certain way, and what the defense would do. His passing game was the most sophisticated in football because it was based on the ability of the quarterback and receivers to read the defense and read it correctly. Of course, it helped having Bart Starr as the quarterback.

He would teach the players the weaknesses of the other team while studying the films. He'd point out this player or that one and show how he would make a mistake when a certain play or action was taken against him. Lombardi was a teacher, always, and that's why his Packers were so savvy.

Max McGee was probably the best receiver in the NFL at reading defenses and going to the open spot to catch the ball. And after playing all those years together — Starr, McGee, Dowler, and the rest — they just seemed to always come up with the right play at the right time, to be in the right spot.

Of course, it soon became apparent to the rest of the teams how the Packers' passing game worked, and other teams began to copy Lombardi's method. Now all the teams in the league try to teach their offense how to read the defensive coverages.

As the years passed and the championships began to come one after another, you could notice a change in him. He began to mellow; there was a great deal of affection for him among the players and the staff and he felt the same toward them. He would still holler and scream but the bite seemed to be softer, and the players knew that he was just trying to get the best from them.

He said on television after one of our championship games that there was a great deal of love on the Packers. He meant that they each had great respect for each other and that was true. Most of them had played together for him for a long time and there was this mutual respect and love. You could feel it. It was a tangible force.

Sometime during the 1967 season, when we were driving for our third consecutive NFL title, he began to make statements that the burden of being both coach and general manager was too much for one man. Now he wanted that third championship because no coach had ever won three NFL titles in a row. Not Paul Brown, not George Halas. Nobody. And you have to remember that he almost did it in 1963. We had won in '61 and '62, and in '63, we lost only two games. The Bears beat us both times. The Bears only won ten games that year, and we won eleven. But they only lost one time and tied three, while we lost two and tied one. So they won the Western Division on percentages.

He never forgot that. He wouldn't let anyone else forget it either. He poured so much of himself into that season that he began to believe that it really was impossible to coach and be general manager. He kept repeating it so much that even after we won that third title and the second Super Bowl, he had already made up his mind that, indeed, it was too much. So he gave up coaching and turned the team over to Phil Bengston.

At first he seemed happy, but soon there really wasn't enough to keep a person as dynamic as him busy. He knew he had made a mistake. I told him as much before he quit and afterward. And when the '68 season came on and he had to stay in the office while Phil ran the team, you could just see him suffer.

As the season progressed and the team began losing, he made it a point not to go near the players for fear of embarrassing Phil. But the general manager's job still could not keep him busy, and rumors began that he was looking for another head coaching job. I never thought he'd leave Green Bay, but we did not talk about this too much. Finally, when he asked that a meeting of the executive committee be set up, I knew he was going. By this time, the rumors had become fact. He was taking over the Redskins. He would be coach and general manager again, as well as part owner. The Redskins were in the same shape as the Packers had been in 1959 when he had come here. So ten years later he was starting from the bottom again. If he had lived, they would have won the Super Bowl a couple of times by now.

We were all upset with his leaving, and a great many of the people in town criticized Lombardi for it. But he had given us so much, and you could not expect someone as forceful and strong as he was to just sit in a paneled office.

He left for Washington sometime in February of '69, I think. He came around to say good-bye to the secretaries and the coaches and the rest of us and it was damn near impossible to keep from crying. All the women were crying. And I'm sure he was too.

We saw each other from time to time after that at league meetings, and we'd go out for a drink or two. He'd talk about the days in Green Bay, and I always felt he wished he'd never left, that he had never given up coaching the Packers. He never said as much to me but I always felt it.

He came back to Green Bay for a visit in May or June of 1970. We all

A familiar scene. Lombardi with the game ball, surrounded by the press, after a big win. (*Vernon J. Biever*)

The Green Bay Years

Lombardi's first year at Green Bay. *From left to right:* Norb Hecker, Bill Austin, Pat Peppler, Red Cochran, Phil Bengston, and Tom Fears. *(Vernon J. Biever)*

saw him at the office and it was just great. He left after a few days, and I never saw him again. He was gone in three months.

There are so many things to remember about him. I was so close to him for those nine years, but I'll never forget when he wanted to promote me to assistant general manager. I told him I did not want the job because he'd be second-guessing me and hollering at me even more then. He promised he'd not holler or embarrass me. So I took the job. In two weeks, he jumped all over me in front of the office staff. I followed him back to his office and really blew my stack. I told him he had promised to let me run things my way, that he'd not interfere, and he'd never chew me out in front of people. He looked at me and I stared right back. I was really mad. Then he started to laugh, and so did I. He apologized and said he always admired a man who stood up for what he believed in. Of course, he promised never to do it again.

And of course he did. Many times. But I guess if he could chew out Bart Starr and the rest, he could do it to his assistant. I guess you'd have to say it was an honor to be chewed out by Vince Lombardi.

Tom Miller   **77**

After the first win. They beat the Bears on opening day in Green Bay. (Vernon J. Biever)

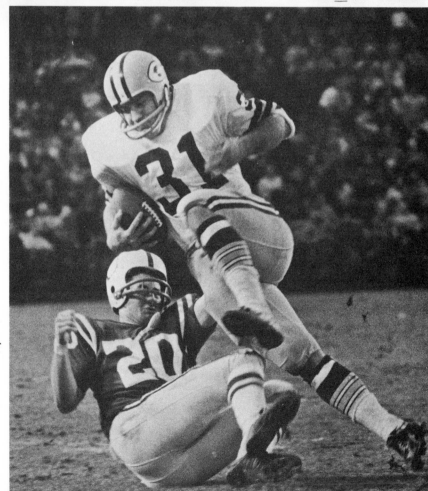

Jim Taylor doing what he did best: "stinging those defensive players." He is the first of Lombardi's players to be named to the Hall of Fame. (Vernon J. Biever)

78

Chuck Lane and Tom Miller with the Coach watching practice in the summer of '68.
(*Vernon J. Biever*)

All the way. In all their years in the NFL, the Packers never had a championship game played in Green Bay. In 1961 this was the first, and it was no contest. (*Vernon J. Biever*)

TONY CANADEO

I first heard of Lombardi reading about him when he was coaching at West Point. And being a youngster, going through the sports pages, I would read about him. I shouldn't say "youngster" because Vince wasn't that much older than me, but I used to read about the "Seven Blocks of Granite," and I knew of him then. I heard that he went into pro ball with the Giants, but I never figured he'd be the next head Packer Coach when he was at the Giants. Bert Bell had mentioned his name, but no one thought he'd be interested. We were out hunting for a coach and Dominic Olejniczak had Vince checked at the meeting. Vince showed a little interest, so he was invited up. We were very impressed the first time we met with him. Actually, it only took one meeting to decide on him.

Vince wanted a five-year contract. He felt that it would take him a few years to get the team back up where it should be. Actually, he didn't need five years to do that. The first year, if Jim Taylor hadn't burned his foot, we would have been in the championship playoffs!

I know he received a bonus after his first year. I believe that after the first year we extended his contract, you know, made it retroactive for another five years, or something like that. I know it was extended though. He did receive a bonus for the first year.

We first heard that the Giants were trying to get him to come back right after Jim Howell left in 1960. Vince said that the Giants wanted him back. But, as far as I know, the Giants didn't call the board and ask for permission to talk to him. He just wanted to know what we wanted to do. If it was "yes" we'd let him go, okay; if we said "no," it was okay too. We said "no." Very honestly "no." So he didn't have to make the decision.

The Maras are wonderful people, don't get me wrong. It might have been at a party where they suggested Vince come back. I don't think they'd do anything to try to hurt the Packers. They wouldn't tamper.

Lombardi was highly recommended by Paul Brown. Actually, we even asked Well Mara. He gave Vince a high recommendation, but he didn't think he would come. We know that the Mara's had always felt that Lombardi owed them something. I understand why. I mean, I know that they gave him his first chance at pro ball. But they also had the chance to get him as head coach before someone else asked him. I don't think that they should have felt that he should go out and get seasoning before he could take the head job. He went back to the Giants and got permission to talk to us. There wasn't anything hanky-panky about that. It was all aboveboard at the time we hired him.

I never attended a team meeting. None of the executives ever attended a team meeting. I was very impressed with him when he held his first directors' meeting. He was a domineering person, as you would say, but he had his program well-organized, like any executive would have in a big company. He told us what he intended to do and what he wanted to do and what he was going to do. And he did it. The Packers never turned him down on anything. His budget was adequate. He worked within it.

In fact, I think Vince took care of the Packer money better than he took care of his own money. He'd watch it. He was a real watchdog for the Packer Corporation. In fact, on any big expenditure, although he could do what he wanted to do, he did come and let us know what he was going to do. The board meetings with him were almost always business meetings about the organization, and very seldom did we discuss football. Basically, we never discussed football as far as what to do on the football field. The only thing he would discuss with us was Packer policy or any big contract that was out of the ordinary.

For instance, a three- or four-year contract for a player that was not at a normal price but at an exorbitant price. He would talk to us first before he got involved in anything . . . like the Anderson and Grabowski deal. He came to the Packers. He said he had to have them, but he didn't do it on his own. He said he had to have them because that was the time we were fighting the other league, and we couldn't afford to let Anderson and Grabowski go to the other league. He talked about the price he had to pay to get these guys, and it made him sick. It made us all sick.

I played under Curly Lambeau, and he always wanted to go first class. Don't get me wrong. Maybe the team couldn't afford to go first class in those days, but he always tried to do what was best for the organization. After the Lambeau era, there were a few years where it did get down-graded as far as stature was concerned. Vince brought it back to and further than it had ever been by picking the best hotels and traveling with everybody in blazers, looking alike. I think the "class" part grew up with that of the league: the rest of the league got class along with the Packers. Pro football, even in the fifties, wasn't a class sport. It was a big sport, but baseball was always thought of as number one.

Lombardi and the Packers were a happy marriage. Lombardi and the Packers together became the glamour team of professional sports. It had always been a Cinderella team, a team that came from a small town. Lombardi, first coming from West Point, a Fordham guy coming from the Giants, took over the team in an era where — maybe they were looking for an image or something — but Lombardi got to be the pro football image and brought the Packers along with him, the Cinderella team. I don't think there will ever be an era where a team and a coach are taken up by the public like the Packers and Vince Lombardi. He had such charisma in this town. He wasn't a guy that got along easily with people. He was proud, but by golly, he was successful. You know, you can say about Caesar or Roosevelt and the great leaders — maybe they weren't easy-going, popular guys — but they were successful. And regardless of what people say, they love success. The people around here love their team; and anybody that made them successful, he was all right with them. And he made them successful. I remember a comment that one of the players made in '68 before the season began. Vince now was general manager. This player, in fact, was saying in the locker room, telling a couple of people of the press, "This season would show the public, the nation, and football, who really won all those championships." Of course he was right. Then they proceeded to fall on their faces.

In a family, children, whether they know it or not, still need to be disciplined and still like to go according to the rules. There are many times when a kid wants to be told "no," which makes it easier for him to be popular and approved of, because his *parents* said "no." Now here's a guy who took a football team and gave them the goddamn discipline that they needed. It shows that people still thrive on discipline, regardless of what the present-day ball players and their union think, you still have to have discipline. You can't have every player making his own rules. Vince, to me, was a great coach because he had discipline and organization, but he also had a tender heart along with it. He did a lot of kind things that many people never hear about.

I first knew that Vince was getting, not restless, but tired of the pressures of winning. He had mentioned before the Super Bowl game in Miami, that if he won this one, he would drop out. I didn't believe him. And I proved I was right. You can't be that active and involved in football and then drop coaching, the thing that you've loved all your life, to go and sit in a press box and watch a game. That's impossible. When he first said it, I didn't believe him. He talked to me as a personal friend of his. I told him he'd never be happy doing it. He said, "You are probably right." Maybe it was his way, after reaching the top, his way of easing out, to go back East again, without just going from one team to another. I really felt that maybe he was making a big mistake, and I told him so.

Vince that one year as general manager was like a cat on a hot tin roof. He didn't know what to do with himself. Not that he didn't work hard, don't get me wrong, but when he could hear the whistle of the coaches down on the field, I don't think he was very happy up in his office. He said it was the hardest thing in the world to sit there and watch them and not be part of the decision. But he never interfered once he gave up the reins; he never interfered in the coaching part of it. He did not talk to the team at all. He wouldn't want to do that because it would be classified as interfering, I would say. He never talked to the team in a pep talk, as far as I know. He might have, without anybody knowing; but if he did, it was probably at the start of the season or at the end of the season.

I always felt that Lombardi had a unique knack of keeping a nucleus of veterans and of bringing in the right youngsters at the right time to supplement these guys. Vince believed in veterans. All good teams, if you look it up, have a certain amount of veterans on the ball club to win championships. Shula did; Dallas definitely did. Maybe that's why the Rams have fallen short because they always have too many young ones.

I remember when he drafted Dave Robinson to replace Dan Curry. I think his greatest thing was trading veterans a year or two before they were over the hill, and getting some good boy for them. Vince was not afraid to let another team get another good year out of an individual as long as he got a young guy to give him five to ten years of good service. Some of his best trades were: number one I'd say, the trade for Willie Davis and Henry Jordan and Bill Quinlan. That helped make the ball club. He got Carrol Dale from the Rams — another great trade.

How the hell he kept them motivated after all those championships was his greatest thing. Look at the fullback he got from the Rams, Ben Wilson, when Taylor had played out his option and we went to the Super

Bowl with Ben Wilson as our fullback, and Chuck Mercein came from the Giants and almost won that game against Dallas by himself. I remember Vince on the sidelines in a game against the Rams. They had him wired for sound — NFL films — and the Packers had a play to the fullback to go behind a fold block by the right guard, and he just followed the guard. And they set it up and they caught the lineback poaching. The guard wiped him out. The hole was twenty yards, and Mercein was carrying the ball and he got about nine yards before he was tackled. Lombardi was on the sideline saying, "What was that? What play was that? What play was that?" Someone told him it was a thirty-six fold. He said, "Holy Christ, if Taylor had been carrying the ball he would have gone forty yards. Well, that's all I got and he's a hell of a kid. You play with what you've got."

I heard about Vince talking to other teams when he was general manager, but I always considered it a rumor because there were one or two or three teams who tried to influence Vince to go with them. But I was in the hospital in Milwaukee with a kidney problem. Dick Bourguignon came and told me that Vince was going to ask for his release to go to a team back East, the Redskins, he thought. And I said I wouldn't give in and agree to release him. I didn't like this. I just hated to see him go, period. It was just like a guy getting a divorce, you know, if he's still in love with his wife. You don't want to see her go. We all gave our consent finally. He wanted to go, and I think he wanted to come back after he did go.

He said that to Marie when he was sick; he said that when he got well, he wanted to go back to Green Bay. He loved it here. He used to come out here to Oneida Country Club and play golf and have a ball. Not once when football started, but he'd be here on Saturday mornings after practice and play. He made it positive that he would never come back to coach in Green Bay, because once he put Phil Bengston in, he didn't want to be the guy who'd come back and make a plaything of the team. I don't think there ever came a point where it was officially thought of.

When it was rumored and then announced that he was going to Washington, I guess there were pros and cons. Some people felt he shouldn't leave, and some people felt that if the man had worked so long and wanted to leave he should be given the chance to leave. It was a fifty–fifty deal. It's hard to tell. I didn't want to see him leave, I know that. Once he made the decision that he wanted to go, I don't think it would have been very smart to keep him.

Vince took a terrific amount of criticism from the press, particularly from certain New York sportswriters about his decision to go. The criticism was based on loyalty, the team, and his commitment. And they took him to task because he had left the Packers after — you know, they brought up the Jim Taylor thing — how bitter Vince was when Taylor played out his option. They said that he established two standards: one for Lombardi and one for the rest of the world. I don't think that was fair. If, after he made his wishes known to us, if the board had voted against letting him go, I think he would have been the same kind of guy for the Packers that he'd always been. But I think we figured that he had done enough for us, and if there was one wish that we could grant, letting him leave, then he would get it that way.

Tony Canadeo

85

I don't think Vince got any financial gains out of going to Washington. I think the thing about a coach wanting part ownership of a football team is a big joke. I could say I was part owner of the Packers. I've got a share of stock. Vince could have bought a share of stock and been part owner for $25.00. So I'm a shareholder of the Packers. I've got one share.

One night we were going out to dinner in Appleton. He was going to take route 41 and go to highway 10 and go that way. I said, "Cut off at 47 and go that way." He argued that he would get there faster. Well, I went the normal speed, but I know he was doing at least ninety, just to beat us. I know it's at least two or three miles shorter the way I went. Well, you know, when we pulled up there I didn't see his car. But we waited and he went in first and he claimed all through dinner, "Yeah, I told you it was shorter." As Bill Heinz said, "If he hadn't won, it would have been a terrible dinner!"

We had some great times. Vince and I had never been deer hunting, and we went up hunting with Jack Keppler. And, you know, after playing gin the evening before and celebrating a little, getting up at four o'clock in the morning was quite hard. If anyone had said, "Go back to bed," we'd have both gone back to bed. But they took us out. We went to a place for breakfast and the smell of that bacon grease almost made us sick. But they took us out into the woods. Vince told one guy, "Now you're sure you know how to come back and get us?" We were going out to our blind, or whatever you call it. I was at one place and Vince, I would say, was about a half a block down. I fell asleep on one of those hot pads and slipped down a hill about three feet and woke up. I could hear wood crackling. Vince was in the woods crackling wood and making a fire to keep warm. I bet there wasn't a deer within twenty miles of us. I know he'd have never shot a deer because he wouldn't have cleaned it. He just wanted to go so he could say he went deer hunting. He must have had about $1000 worth of equipment. I know someone gave him a new gun, new outfit to wear, everything. We got back about noon, but that's the last time we went into the woods. In fact, that's the last time I've gone deer hunting.

When the whole club and the board of directors and everybody went out for Super Bowl I, it was quite an exciting time for the Packers. Vince was great. I went out with the team. And the directors flew out the day before the game and stayed for the game and went back after it. He liked to spend money on things like that to make it one big happy family. He kept it that way too. He kept everybody involved in things.

He was nervous before the first Super Bowl because he felt that the whole league was standing by watching, and the whole history of the Natonal Football League was resting on his shoulders. It was not only just winning or losing, but it was the prestige of the National Football League, for the first time, playing against the AFL. I think that pressure was worse than just going into a regular championship game. He was nervous and he talked about it. There was one big worry — not facing this team and not thinking his boys wouldn't play a good game — but things can go crazy in a ball game and we actually didn't start burning it up right at the start. Everybody was so nervous that they didn't get over it until the first quarter was over anyway. But I think it was harder on Vince and the Packers than it was on the Kansas City team.

They had nothing to lose. I mean, they had the game to lose, don't get me wrong, and that extra money — but the National League was supposed to be better to start off with. I don't think it proved anything really, if you want to know the truth. All it proved was that Green Bay was better. As Red Smith wrote, it also proved that Green Bay was the best team in football. That they had beat everybody in the NFL and now they had beaten the best in the AFL. Green Bay was the best team in football.

I think Green Bay, because of Lombardi, beat a lot of teams I thought were better at times. I think that he had a knack of getting the best out of a ball club, the day of a game or during the week. Regardless of what people say, his teams were in condition. But once they were in condition, he didn't overwork them during the week. He had them ready for Sunday. You've got to look at it in perspective. We're talking about a period of basically nine years in which they were the team to beat in six or seven of those years. That's a tremendous amount of pressure. Maybe some of the things I say sound corny, but he made the guys feel they were one, but there was no individual. He had some great names on that football team, but you never heard them discussed as Hornung, etc. It was always the Packers, the Packers. And the guys believed in what he was teaching.

A lot of ball players, when they get a little tired, can imagine an injury. Well, his teams were afraid to imagine injuries. I don't mean to say a guy couldn't get hurt. But when you get a little tired sometimes your imagination can put an injury on any side of your body you want. That leg all of a sudden feels a little gimpy. But his teams weren't like that — no way — and that's the difference. I think they were afraid to come to the sidelines with an injury. There were no imaginary injuries. You can watch today and a guy gets hurt and runs out and three plays later he runs in there like nothing happened. To me, the guy was tired and nothing ever happened to him. That never happened with Vince.

The best game ever played under him — perfection-wise — was the day they beat Cleveland in Cleveland. I think it was 49–17. That was a great team to beat. They had Jimmy Brown, who was a perfectionist, but Jim Taylor got four touchdowns in that game. It was a helluva game. I think that game was mechanically even better than when they beat Baltimore, because Baltimore didn't have Unitas that day. He was hurt. Hornung scored five touchdowns. But the day they beat Cleveland — O God! And then the game when they beat the Giants for the NFL championship. And that was a great Giant team — Tittle, Robustelli, Webster, Gifford, Rote — that was a great team. They demolished Huff. They blocked him everywhere 'til Sunday. The best I ever saw them play in person, I guess, would have been that Giants game.

It's hard to say who was the best player who ever played for Vince, there were so many good ones. I know he always thought Taylor was a great football player, a tough kid. Bart — I think he made a great quarterback out of Bart. I don't think there's any question about it, and Bart would be the first to admit that Lombardi made him. See what it comes to? See what I mean when you say perfection in one team? How can you pick Taylor or Jerry Kramer, or Ron Kramer, or Henry Jordon, or Willie Davis? You know, how do you say who's the best player? Herb Adderley? Ray Nitschke? Forrest Gregg?

I know who he said the best player was — the best player he ever coached. In fact, he told me one day when he looked at the films of the Packers when he first came here in 1959, spent all those hours looking at films. He told me this later. He turned to the coaching staff and said, "Gentlemen, there's only one professional player in this whole organization — number 75, Gregg." And he had all those young fellows — Kramer, Hornung, Taylor, Starr, etc. But maybe Gregg was what Vince always looked for — a perfectionist and a lineman.

Lombardi Sparked Packers' Triumph

Shower Coach With Praise After 37-0 Victory Over Giants

By BOB KURLAND
(Staff Writer)

Green Bay, Wis., Jan 2—"You can have all the fancy formations you want but it all comes down to blocking and tackling. If you have them, you're going to win." It all sounds simple the way Vince Lombardi explains the success of his championship Green Bay Packer team.

WHAT HAPPENED?

And the way the Packers massacred the Giants on Sunday, 37-0, for the National Football League crown, they certainly made it look simple.

Lombardi is still receiving congratulatory wires and phone calls for the masterful performance turned in by his team.

All doubt that the onetime St. Cecilia (Englewood, N. J.) High School coach deserves the praise, vanishes when the stars of the victory discuss the part played by Lombardi.

Quarterback Bart Starr tossed three touchdown passes in completing 10 of 17 passes and called a standout game. But when it was over, he wanted to talk about his coach.

"We had to win because we didn't want to let him down," said the signal-caller who didn't achieve his rightful place among the top pro quarterbacks until this season.

"Lombardi is a great man to work for. He wants to win and he instills it in the players. I'm really happy that I came through for him because it justified the confidence he placed in me when he traded away Lamar McHan (last season's quarterback)."

Starr couldn't seem to get the Packers rolling in a 0-0 first quarter. "We used (Jim) Taylor at the start to see how they would defense against us. After one play in which he didn't carry the ball, Jimmy told me two men tackled him. After that we used him mainly as a decoy."

Taylor revealed afterwards that his back, which was injured a couple of weeks ago, started

paining him and he asked Lombardi to take him out. By that time the Packers had a 24-0 half-time lead and it really didn't matter that the great fullback sat out most of the second half.

While the Giants were watching Taylor in the first half, Paul Hornung accounted for 12 points and went on to set a new playoff scoring mark of 19.

"The furlough helped a lot," declared Hornung, who was on leave from Fort Riley, Kan. "Although I lost weight in the Army I feel better. Maybe it helped my speed."

But it wasn't just Hornung who the Giants famed defense couldn't handle. There was also right end Ron Kramer, who proved a 230-pound unstoppable package of raw strength.

When the Packers wanted to go through the right side, Kramer, the former Michigan All-American, cleared a path big enough for the slowest man to coast through.

His blocking would have been enough but Kramer also snared a pair of touchdown passes. The first was good for 14 yards as he caught a toss over the middle and went through the Giant secondary. That made it a 21-0 game and when he beat Joe Morrison in the third quarter, the lead was upped to 34-0.

Kramer was a little happier than the rest of his mates. "I was surprised to find myself all alone behind Morrison, it's seldom I get behind any one.

"But even if I hadn't scored I

knew we'd win. In fact, we all knew we'd win ever since we took the Western title. There was no doubt in our minds."

As for his coach, Kramer said: "He's a winner and there's not a better coach in football. I thought that even before I joined the team. Look, he rules everything. You either do it his way or not at all." Kramer, who didn't play much last year, is another product of Lombardi's reclamation program.

While his players have only the highest praise for Lombardi, what does Vince think of them? "This is the greatest football team in the history of the N. F. L.," declares Lombardi.

"At midseason, when we played Cleveland, we were almost perfect. After the way we beat the Giants, I know this is the greatest."

Lombardi, who in the span of 3 seasons took a hopeless last place team and built it into a championship club which could establish a dynasty since it's a young squad, felt all last week his team would win the crown.

"I sensed we'd take them because we were ready. The boys gave me the feeling we'd do it."

Although Lombardi wouldn't single out anyone except to reiterate you only need the basic tenets of football to win, he did say: "Part of the answer to the big margin of victory is that we held the ball for 35 minutes against 21 for them."

Considering the way he thinks today it was odd to hear him say after the win: "I never thought anything like this could happen to me when I was coaching there (St. Cecilia). Probably in those days I wasn't even thinking."

As general manager of the Packers, Lombardi is going to Florida on Thursday for the league meeting. Sometime during the last week of the month he'll visit his family in Englewood, N. J., and then leave for Europe for a vacation. He'll go with a former Fordham classmate of his, Wellington Mara, the vice-president of the New York Giants.

Packers-Giants: It'll Be Close, Cold

TITLE RIVALS HEAD-TO-HEAD

By Dave Eisenberg

GIANTS OFFENSE PACKERS

No.	Name	Ht.	Wt.	Pos.	Wt.	Ht.	Name	No.
85	*SHOFNER	6-3	185	L.E.	210	6-2	McGEE	85

Each best receiver on his team, Shofner with 68 catches for 1125 yards and 11 touchdowns, McGee with 51 for 883 and 7. Shofner has edge on greater speed.

| 79 | *BROWN | 6-3 | 225 | L.T. | 245 | 6-3 | SKORONSKI | 76 |

Brown all-league tackle six straight years. Skoronski was great n first Giant game. Brown gets edge as stronger man and better over season. Rosy, however, is coming off injury to play.

| 62 | DESS | 60- | 245 | L.G. | 250 | 6-1 | *THURSTON | 63 |

Some people think Thurston is best Packer offensive lineman. More experienced than Dess. Is quicker and stronger.

| 55 | WIETECHA | 6-1 | 230 | C. | 230 | 6-2 | *RINGO | 51 |

Here probably are two finest offensive centers in pro football. Ringo probably a shade better than Thurston as top Packer offensive lineman. Ahead of Wietecha on quickness.

| 66 | STROUD | 6-1 | 255 | R.G. | 230 | 6-4 | *GREGG | 75 |

Gregg converted from tackle after Jerry Kramer was hurt. Stroud missed first Packer game. Presence helps Giants. Adds size to offensive line with 255 pounds. Teams even at this position.

| 63 | LARSON | 6-2 | 240 | R.T. | 245 | 6-2 | *MASTERS | 78 |

Masters and Gregg switched positions a month ago. Masters took hold well at right tackle. Has experience on Larson, a rookie.

| 80 | *WALTON | 5-11 | 205 | R.E. | 230 | 6-3 | KRAMER | 88 |

Walton ahead, if he has fully recovered from thigh charley horse which kept him out of Cleveland game. Very even on pass-receiving record, Kramer with 35 catches for 559 yards and four touchdowns, Walton with 36 for 544 and two TDs. Walton better blocker.

| 14 | *TITTLE | | 6-1 | 195 | Q.B. | 200 | 6-1 | | STARR | 15 |

Starr arrived as top quarterback this year, but Packers beat Giants on running and New York mistakes last time. Giants have passing edge with two great veterans, Tittle and Charley Conerly. Packers go all way with Starr.

| 28 | WELLS | 6-1 | 198 | L.H. | 210 | 6-2 | *HORNUNG | 5 |

Packers ahead all the way, with Hornung great runner, kicker and blocker, and with his substitute Tom Moore ahead of Bobby Gaiters, Giants rookie speedster.

| 44 | *ROTE | 6-1 | 200 | R.H. | 220 | 6-5 | DOWLER | 86 |

Both Rote and Dowler really ends. Both play flanker or slot back. Kyle runs greatest patterns among pass receivers. Dowler strong receiver with fine speed.

| 29 | WEBSTER | 6-3 | 220 | F.B. | 215 | 6-0 | *TAYLOR | 31 |

Taylor ripped Giants apart last time. Webster enjoyed his greatest year, but you need go no further than the figures which show Taylor second among league's ball carriers with 243 carries for 1,307 yards, an average of 5.4 per carry and total of 15 TDs. Webster ran 196 for 928, averaged 4.7 and scored twice.

| 34 | *CHANDLER | 6-2 | 205 | Punt | 220 | 6-5 | DOWLER | 86 |

Chandler better than record of 43.9 shows. Saved Browns game with booting. McGee also punts for Packers.

| 88 | SUMMERALL | 6-4 | 220 | Placements | 210 | 6-2 | HORNUNG | 5* |

DEFENSE

No.	Name	Ht.	Wt.	Pos.	Wt.	Ht.	Name	No.
75	*KATCAVAGE	6-3	240	L.E.	240	6-3	DAVIS	87

With few exceptions Giants defense superior. Katcavage had tremendous year as one of Giants Four Furies. Giants edge.

| 77 | *MODZELEWSKI | 6-0 | 250 | L.T. | 250 | 6-2 | HANNER | 79 |

Ditto for Little Mo. Modzelewski also was great all year to give Giants edge.

| 76 | GRIER | 6-5 | 290 | R.T. | 250 | 6-3 | *JORDAN | 74 |

Grier enjoyed best season. But Jordan best Packer defensive lineman. Rosy was well-grounded by Packers last time. Packer edge.

| 81 | *ROBUSTELLI | 6-1 | 230 | R.E. | 250 | 6-3 | QUINLAN | 83 |

Packers give Andy rough time too. Quinlan pursues very well. Andy is quicker, doesn't figure to be beaten twice in a row by same team. Giant edge.

| 89 | LIVINGSTON | 6-3 | 220 | L.L.B. | 235 | 6-3 | *CURRIE | 58 |

Packer linebackers come closest to matching Giants on defense. Currie has shade on Livingston as bigger man.

| 82 | SCOTT | 6-2 | 220 | R.L.B. | 240 | 6-3 | *FORESTER | 71 |

Scott has enjoyed tremendous season. Forester, with Currie, has made Green Bay one of hardest teams to run against. Giants moved best on passing last time. Packers edge.

| 70 | *HUFF | 6-1 | 230 | M.L.B. | 220 | 6-3 | NITSCHKE | 66 |

Nitschke, as service man, shared job with Bettis (no. 65, 6-2, 225). Huff, always one of best, was faster, tougher tackler this year. Giants edge.

| 49 | *BARNES | 6-3 | 198 | L.H. | 200 | 6-2 | GREMMINGER | 46 |

Barnes very fast. Defends well against passes. Tough tackler. Slipped a bit in last few games. Gremminger is solid defensive back. Giants edge.

| 20 | *PATTON | 5-10 | 185 | L.S. | 180 | 5-10 | SYMANK | 27 |

Patton great field general. Wonderful speed makes him fine pass defender. Is best in league. Symank not as fast, or as good.

| 40 | MORRISON | 6-1 | 212 | R.S. | 185 | 5-10 | *WOOD | 24 |

Wood gets edge here because Morrison converted from offense. Played first defense against Packers. Has improved steadily. Packers edge.

| 22 | *LYNCH | 6-1 | 200 | R.H. | 190 | 6-0 | WHITTENTON | 47 |

Lynch unsung hero of Giants defensive backfield. Makes enemy running around his side very tough.

(*—Denotes Superior Player.)

The game was rated close.

Graham Sees Runners Giving Packers Title

Eisenberg Sees New York Champ

Their first championship and the players carry Vince Lombardi off the field. That's Paul Hornung in front and Dave Hanner holding one leg. *(Vernon J. Biever)*

Forrest Gregg played both guard and tackle. His versatility helped the team when Jerry Kramer was injured in the championship game of '61. *(Vernon J. Biever)*

Lombardi called him the finest football player he ever coached. Forrest Gregg was so good that other offensive linemen used to study films of him to learn his techniques. *(Vernon J. Biever)*

The face of a lineman. Where they play is called the "pit." It separates them from the rest of the team. They never see the ball, seldom get the headlines, but theirs is the place where the game is won or lost. *(Vernon J. Biever)*

The Green Bay Years

FORREST GREGG

I played at Southern Methodist University in Dallas, and I was drafted number two by the Green Bay Packers in 1956. At that time there were two to three players on the Packers from SMU and some from the Southwest Conference. Bill Forester and Val Joe Walker were from SMU, and Tobin Rote was from Rice, and Doyle Nix also from SMU, and Bill Howton from Rice, and "Hawg" Hanner was from Arkansas. I knew about the Green Bay Packers, but I had no idea where Green Bay was located.

I guess I was like any other football player. I had a favorite team then, and it was the Detroit Lions. I also liked the Baltimore Colts and the Los Angeles Rams. Like a lot of other guys, especially having played all the time in the Southwest, I wanted to play for a glamour team in a nice climate and the Rams were that.

I knew absolutely nothing about the town of Green Bay and really got a surprise when I got there in the summer of 1956, a little ahead of the other players. I wasn't impressed with the town at all. It was so small that you wondered how in the world this town could support a professional football team. At that time we were playing at the old stadium, which is now a high school stadium. I had just come from playing in the Cotton Bowl for SMU in front of 70,000 people and where we had the best of equipment and the finest dressing rooms. All the facilities were first rate. Then, you get to Green Bay and take one look at that dressing room, and when they passed out the equipment that SMU would have thrown away five years earlier, it was really shocking to me.

At that time, the Packers were a fairly sound team. Lisle Blackburn was the coach, and the prior year they had been six and six and were in the race for the Conference title until they dropped their last three games, all by close scores. They had a lot of hope for the new season, and they were starting to come around from those days in the late forties when they had a lot of financial problems. In 1956, we won five and lost seven but played fairly respectable football. Bart Starr was a rookie with me, Bob Skoronski was also a rookie, and Hank Gremminger also came up with us. Tobin Rote was the quarterback, and we had a good kicker in Fred Cone, and we had a pretty tough defense, so the Packers were a sound team.

I missed the 1957 season because I was in the service, but the team had a disastrous season, winning three or four games. Blackburn was let go and they turned the team over to Scooter McLean in 1958. That year was the worst in Packer history. We won only one game, tied one, and lost ten. That was the year before Vince came.

In 1958, even though we had that terrible year, there were some good players on the team. In fact, many of the ball players who were on that 1958 team were the nucleus of the teams during the championship years. For example, Paul Hornung, Jim Taylor, Bart Starr, Ron Kramer, and Dave Hanner were there. So basically, the material was there, we had good players but we were very undisciplined. We had a lot of internal problems, not necessarily with the players, though there were some that did not get along, but there were a lot of problems with the town and what the people thought of the players. In fact, toward the end of the season in 1958, there was a circular distributed around the town telling the people to stay away from the games, since you could see the players around town and there was no need to pay to see such bad football on Sunday.

Of course, this shocked me and the rest of the team. It made us feel bad, made us feel that the entire town was down on us, that it wanted a complete new team. It never really came to a head because the board of directors squelched the petition, but we felt bad because there were so many people that supported the idea behind the circular. We lost a lot of football games and deserved criticism and we realized that, but there were a lot of things happening on and off the field. We had a lot of problems. We never found out who started the circular, but we all felt hurt that the town could turn on us like that.

At the end of the 1958 season, Scooter McLean was dismissed. During the season there were many rumors that McLean would be out, and after they had fired him, there were rumors as to who the new coach would be. In those days, after the season was over, most of us went back home. Nobody wanted to stay in Green Bay if they didn't have to. I was down in Texas at the time, and there was not much news about the Green Bay Packers in the Dallas papers. But one day I heard over the radio that Vince Lombardi had been hired as the new coach.

I didn't have the slightest idea who he was. The only thing that I knew was that he was an assistant coach with the Giants, and we had beaten the Giants in a preseason game in 1956 and 1958. So it really didn't make a big impression on me when I heard that Vince Lombardi had been hired. There was a ball player that I had played with at SMU who lived in Dallas and had been with the Giants for a short time. I saw him and he said, "Do you know anything about this Vince Lombardi who has been hired as your head coach?" I said, "No, I don't." "Well," he said, "he's a real bastard."

I didn't know what to expect, so in 1959 I came to training camp and did not unpack my bags. I didn't intend to unpack until I found out what was going on because I had almost quit after the 1958 season. I only started four games that year and became the backup offensive lineman for the two tackles and two guards. I almost quit at the end of that season, so I was not about to stick around if this new guy kept the old system.

The first day of training camp, Vince Lombardi sold me on his system. In the past with the Packers, the ball players who weren't the big stars and especially the linemen, took all the abuse from the coaches. There was this one assistant who was always jumping on my ass and rode me pretty hard. He later told me he did this because he thought I was not putting out. But the coaches never said one thing to the established players one way or another no matter how bad they had played in a game or loafed through practice, or whether they dropped a pass or whatever. They never came in for any criticism. They were the "stars," the supposed leaders of the team and the night I got into camp, I talked with Bill Austin, the offensive line coach who told me something about Lombardi. Austin had played with the Giants when Vince was the offensive coach. He told me that he was a fair man — tough, but fair — and if you hustled and worked, he'd respect you as a football player.

The first practice began about ten A.M. The offensive and defensive linemen were together with the assistant coaches; and Vince was over with the quarterbacks, the backs, and the receivers. They were running some pass patterns and the quarterbacks were throwing the ball. Vince called for all of us to come together, and as we ran over to join him and the others, one of the receivers went out for a pass. He was a heck of a football player but had a tendency to loaf in practice. He was about twenty yards down the field, and he evidently didn't run the pass pattern as precisely as Coach Lombardi wanted because the coach started yelling at him twenty yards down field and he kept yelling until the player had returned to the huddle. The year before, nothing had ever been said to that player by any coach, no matter how he loafed or goofed-off. That sold me on Lombardi.

This was the kind of coach I wanted. I want somebody who, when a ball player loafs, is going to chew him out; when he doesn't perform as he's capable of, he's going to get chewed out; and if he puts out the effort and tries as hard as he can, he'll be appreciated. And I think that is one of the big things that sold me on Vince Lombardi. I'm not saying that he didn't chew me. He chewed me plenty like he did everybody else. But one thing he never had to get on me about was loafing. I never respected a ball player that would loaf, and this was one of his big things that he stressed. He could forgive a player for not having great ability, but he could never forgive a ball player who had but did not utilize that ability.

That camp was completely different from any camp I had ever been in in my life. The previous two years that I was with the Packers, the training camp atmosphere was very relaxed. There were some scrimmages and a moderate amount of work, but the veterans had convinced the coaches that it was going to be a long season, that we could play our way into shape, and when the regular season began we would be in shape. This was the thinking of a lot of professional players and teams at that time. But Coach Lombardi completely changed our thinking on this.

We went into training camp, and you would have thought we were in college again. First thing we started on was conditioning. We thought we had left all that behind because we thought we'd "play" ourselves into shape. Not so with Lombardi. He had a very strenuous conditioning program. We scrimmaged almost every day that first year. We worked on fundamentals over and over. We started from scratch, as if we did not know a thing. He told us how he wanted things done and that's the way they were done.

From the first day you came to camp, you knew who the boss was. You knew who you had to answer to and who you had to satisfy as a football player. And as time went on, he'd chew you out in one minute but if you did something well, sometimes he'd pat you on the back. But there were not too many words of praise, especially that first year. And when you would be complimented by him, it made your day or week because it so seldom happened. Occasionally, he'd throw you a crumb and this is what kept you going. This was the way he was through all the training camps in Green Bay.

I asked Bill Austin one time after Vince had been in Green Bay about three years, when there would be some letup, especially for the veteran players. I told him I always thought that after you had become an established old veteran that you didn't have to work so hard and have to prove yourself in training camp. Bill told me that as long as Vince Lombardi was here, you'd always have to prove yourself in training camp.

And that was true. I don't care who you were — Paul Hornung, Bart Starr, Max McGee — it did not make any difference. Every year in training camp you had to prove that you could still do the job, and if there was any doubt in his mind that you could, he'd start looking for someone else to fill your position. So every year you had to prove to him you were the best man.

This made training camps under Lombardi quite competitive. In fact, I hated training camp. Willie Davis is one of the best defensive ends professional football has ever seen. And he and I are the best of friends, but in training camp, you would have thought we were mortal enemies, because we had to battle, go head-to-head. Each one of us was trying to prove that we could still do the job, and we had to prove it to ourselves and to Coach Lombardi.

We could not believe what was happening to us that first camp. We had the grass drill. Anybody who has ever heard of Vince Lombardi and his training camp has heard of the grass drill. It's just a matter of endurance. It was just murder, believe me. It never was easy and it never did get easy, no matter what kind of shape you were in. It got a little bit better as camp would continue, but he never made it any easier. And after we had finished that grass drill, we'd all spring over to the area where we did the cadence drill, and he could tell what kind of shape we were in by how heavy our breathing was. If we were not breathing too hard, he knew we were getting in shape and sometimes he let up on the grass drill by reducing the number of times we had to do it. We tried to fool him by holding our breath after getting to the cadence drill area, but that seldom worked. After all, how long can you hold your breath after a sprint? He said each year that he'd cut down on the grass drill as soon as he was convinced that we were in the kind of shape he wanted us to be, so we all looked forward to that time.

The players took his camp quite well, actually. That first night before the first day's practice, he spoke to us and told us that he was there to win and that those that survived the camp would be on a winner someday. He convinced us all that he would be there for sometime and that we had better do things his way. He said in the first meeting, "I have never been associated with a losing football team, and I did not come to Green Bay to be associated with a loser."

Coach Lombardi often said that he treated us all alike, that he painted us with the same brush. This is a military way of thinking. If one of you is bad, then all of you suffer. This is one thing he believed and one thing he practiced. However, I think he knew how to motivate each individual. To get me to do something, to perform well, he did not have to chew me out, though he did occasionally. To get me to play better, he'd just say that I was not playing up to par or that I could do better.

I wanted to please him. I had so much respect for him. So much confidence in him and I admired him so greatly that if he thought that I was letting him down, then I was unhappy and would try harder and do more just to please him. Other ball players he would motivate in different ways. He would talk to them individually, calling them aside and telling them what he wanted. Others he would chew out in front of the group. He did that to all of us at one time or another, but it worked better on certain people and so he would keep getting on them. I knew he had a good idea of each of his players; he knew just how to motivate each of us and how to get the most out of us.

I played for a lot of coaches in high school, college, and the pros. Some of these people were not really committed to winning. They thought they were, but they seemed more concerned with the playing of the game than the winning. I only play to win. I felt that if you're not going to play football to win, you might as well be doing something else.

I know that Vince Lombardi played the game to win. This was the only thing to him. He said winning is the only way, second place is nothing. You are either first or last. He was trying to accomplish what I wanted, and he had me thinking that way all my life. Vince Lombardi was the type of coach I had always been looking for. He exemplified everything that I thought a coach should be and I wanted to be part of it.

A lot of people have overplayed the fear aspect of playing for Lombardi. The fear in my mind was not him, but that for some reason I would not be a part of this team and be with this man. If you could play football and be a member of a Vince Lombardi team, within yourself you felt a great deal of happiness. It meant so much to know that I was a member of these teams and to know that I played well enough that he wanted me. It still means a great deal to me, and I know that it still means a great deal to all the guys who were part of it.

When he would chew you out in front of the others, it motivated you to not make the same mistake because you felt that you were letting down your teammates and him. Nobody wants his teammates thinking that maybe you couldn't do the job and that we needed another guy to take your place, a guy who could win.

After a loss, he wasn't tough, he was ferocious. He just could not accept a loss. He could not accept defeat. However, sometimes after a loss he might say in the dressing room that we had given the best we had and that he was not ashamed of us, that he was proud of the way we put out even though we lost. He told us to forget about the game and start thinking about the next team.

Well, this lasted from Sunday night after the game until Tuesday morning at the film sessions. And all those nice, sweet, kind words he had said Sunday afternoon somehow or other slipped his mind. He would now show you why you lost, by pointing out all your mistakes and errors to the whole team.

Normally, we would break up, with the defense going into one room to look at the game films and we, the offense, going into another room, always with Vince. However, after a loss, he'd pull all of us together and it was murder. It was one of the toughest things about playing for him. He'd point out every mistake. Nobody was spared. You might think he'd miss you on a play, but no, after the eighth time he'd run the play, out would come your name and he'd show everyone what a donkey you were.

Even after winning, if he felt we had not played up to par, he'd really get on us. One time during the early championship years, we were playing in

(Vernon J. Biever)

The Green Bay Years

Minnesota against the Vikings, and they were driving toward our goal for the score that would put them ahead and win the game because it was very late in the fourth quarter. Well, they went for the field goal, Herb Adderley blocked it and Hank Gremminger picked it up and ran in for a touchdown and we won.

I don't think I've ever seen him so upset after a game, win or lose. We had stunk up the joint and been pushed around by an expansion team, and this really made him so mad. He came in the locker room and kicked a trash can clear across the room. He kicked it so hard he hurt his toe and Dad Brasher, our equipment man, said he was going to get all plastic cans for the Packer locker rooms.

The first Super Bowl was a big challenge, not only to Vince Lombardi, but to all of us. We were playing a team that we knew absolutely nothing about except by reputation. We did not have any way to judge how good they were because we did not have a common opponent. All we had was film of two of their games. Our scouts had seen Kansas City, but that was not helpful.

But because of television and our success over the years, the Chiefs had seen a great deal of the Packers. Their disadvantage was playing us because of our reputation as the team of the sixties. I think that this was one thing that got us up for the game, making sure we lived up to our reputation.

Watching the films of Kansas City, regardlesss of the caliber of the opposition, we could see that the Chiefs had some good football players. And we knew that to win, we were going to have to come up with a good performance. And that's the way it proved out.

Although we won the game 35–10, it was still a good football game. The turning point came in the second half when Willie Wood made that interception and we scored right after that. Up to that point, it was anybody's football game.

Before both Super Bowl games, Coach Lombardi was quite nervous. He kept pointing out to us that we were not only representing the Green Bay Packers but all of the National Football League. We were the establishment, and they were the new kids on the block. Before the merger, there was a lot of ill feeling between the NFL and the AFL. And we had to prove to everybody, including the public, that we were the best league. He was quite excited before Super Bowl I. That would be the first game and maybe the most important of all the Super Bowls, because it was the first. He wanted that win, as did we all.

I'll always think of Coach Lombardi on that practice field in Green Bay, making us run the "sweep" over and over. He was so concerned that all eleven of us do it the right way; this was his secret of success as a coach. The players were involved on all of his plays but the "sweep" was his baby and we'd run it and run it and run it, until he was satisfied, and then we'd run it again. We'd all be screaming, but only to ourselves. We knew, though, that what he was doing was making us one, one unit working together to win. And we did win and it was worth all the practices and effort because, as Coach Lombardi said, winning is the only thing.

BART STARR

I think the thing I remember most about Vince Lombardi is his intensity as a competitor, his dedication to excellence, and his love for his football players. I think this is one thing that has really been overlooked about Vince Lombardi. A lot of people may not have thought this, they may not have realized it, but he was extremely loyal to the men who played for him. I think he was proud of the people who performed for him regardless of whether it was all those people who played for the Green Bay Packers or those lucky few who played for the Washington Redskins.

I met him in Green Bay in June of 1959. He called all the quarterbacks and ends in for an early session. I did not know much about the man — I had seen him on the sidelines when we had played the Giants in preseason games in previous years — but I had never met him and frankly didn't know too much about him. When we read in the papers that he had become the head coach, I just read about it, accepted it, and was looking forward to working for a new coach. When I met him that first day in June 1959, I knew we were in for a reawakening because the first time he spoke to this small group of us he was the most dynamic person I had ever heard, and I literally could not wait to get out of that office to go work out. That's just how I felt about him.

I suppose Coach Lombardi, in coming in there, wanted to make a very tough impression on us, to show us that he was not going to put up with any sort of foolishness and that things were going to be his way and only his way. And he did. He showed us the first day. In fact, there was a standing joke around after the training camp was over that if "Hawg" Hanner came back to training camp next year they were going to reserve a room for him at St. Vincent's Hospital, because he passed out a couple of times during training. It was just a vicious training camp. None of us had ever been through anything like that before. We knew nothing of what to expect, and he darned near killed half of us.

He would conduct a practice session, and he was so insistent on the type of hitting that he wanted in an effort to again develop the type of discipline that he was seeking that they just became all-out scrimmages. A dummy scrimmage was just like a collision course all day long. It was the darnest thing you've ever seen.

We tested him. I think everybody tests someone else if he's new. We had people who tested him. In fact, during his famous grass drills — where you run in place, dive on your belly, jump back up on your feet, down over on your back and back up, etc. — there were some who halfway through would just sort of peel off and not do them. They'd skip one or two and boy, the first time he caught them doing that, he just made everybody do more. So soon, the first thing you do, if you catch yourself standing next to one of your buddies who's cheating, you almost yank him up yourself because you're going to have to do extra. Plus, if he caught one he'd have him do additional ones after that, so there wasn't too much testing after a while.

I think a town, an area, a state, a lot of people get down on a team when they are losing. Coach Lombardi came in with a vibrancy that was just infectious so there was almost an immediate change. You could see it in training camp because here was a person who only asked of us that we believe in him.

He loved a good joke — a good story. He didn't like a dirty, raunchy story at all, but he loved the good story — a good joke — and he told many right before a ball game to try to loosen us up. When it was a big game and he felt we were a little tight or something, I've seen him tell a funny story right in the dressing room prior to going on the field.

One year he was going deer hunting and Zeke Bratkowski and I, in front of the team said, "Coach, we've got this coat for you to take deer hunting." He put it on, and turned around and there was a big bull's-eye target on his back. Then, of course, everybody just roared, and he got a big kick out of it.

He told us, when we were about to prepare for the first Super Bowl game against the Kansas City Chiefs, that we were under a great deal of pressure and the high reputation and tradition of the National Football League was on the line and he didn't intend to let it slip away. But he was very, very edgy all week. I think he became even more edgy as the week progressed because everybody was making the Chiefs out to be an inferior ball club — not even in the same class as we were — and we knew better because we had seen them, granted only on film, but you can recognize talent on film when you see the reactions of certain people and you see the strength and the agility of players. He was very explicit, very thorough in the things that we were doing that week, and I can recall him making a statement about curfew that if he caught anybody out for curfew it was not going to be the normal fine. He said he'd triple it, and it would be their last game with the Green Bay Packers. And he meant it! This is just how serious he took that game.

I recall his first speech to us very well. All he asked of us was for us to believe in his system. To believe that if we did things the way he wanted them done and not to ad lib and do things as we thought they ought to be done, that we would have a winning football team. He said he wasn't sure exactly how long it would take us, but he could guarantee that we would win. And so he asked us to believe in him. He was so dynamic, so vibrant, so full of enthusiasm — and speaking of enthusiasm, he would get hoarse each training camp, he would get so enthused. He lost his voice early the first year. He couldn't even speak after about four or five days; he was at a whisper. Funny, because he would yell at you and you couldn't even hear. But this is how enthusiastic he was, so it caught all of us up, and we were swept away.

I'm on Lombardi time today. That's how much I think of the man — still think of him. He just believed in being punctual and when he said a meeting was going to start at six, actually it was going to start at five of six. I can recall an incident where Willie Wood walked in one day and was actually five minutes early, but everybody was there so he started. Willie walks in at five of and got the worst chewing out you can imagine. He looked at his watch and said, "Coach, I still have five minutes," and of course everybody broke up — as he did. But this is the type of organization he ran.

Lombardi felt that Starr was not only the best quarterback that had played the game, but also the smartest. (Vernon J. Biever)

As Starr said, he never saw a camp like that first one. Those that survived went on to enjoy the rewards. (Vernon J. Biever)

Jerry Kramer, #64, keeps Alex Karras away from Starr. *(Vernon J. Biever)*

Starr is the most efficient quarterback ever to play the game. He is also the winningest player in the history of pro football. *(Vernon J. Biever)*

His first year, 1959, I didn't play too much for him. Lamar McHan played most of the year and after Mac got hurt, I played the last four or five games. I was learning during the period prior to starting myself, and I thought I had digested a lot of the things he was trying to teach me, but I didn't really feel that confident the first game or two that I was playing. Things weren't really coming into focus as I would have liked for them to.

Then the last game of the year, we were playing the San Francisco 49ers, and we were riddled with injuries. In fact, we had Lew Carpenter running fullback. They were shifting defenses on us considerably. Lombardi had been teaching us how to read defenses and everything just fell into place that day. I don't think I made a mistake calling the proper audible against their defense, and it was just a revelation for me. In fact, when the game was over I was so enthused I really couldn't wait for the next year to roll around.

You would have to have played under Coach Lombardi to have experienced his sessions Tuesday morning after a ball game. We'd come into the dressing room Tuesday morning after winning, and I think everybody really sought his praise because he was so stingy with it.

Well, we would come in on Tuesday morning after a win, and we might get the reaming out of our life. You couldn't believe the things he'd say to you. But he was right because even though you had won, he would point out your errors — your mistakes. You see this is what he was after, and we have come in there after a loss and surprisingly would have played well. We might have blocked well, we might have executed pretty well, we were just beaten by a better team, and so you really didn't know what to expect, and after a while you were quite uneasy when you were getting ready to come in on Tuesday morning.

We had beaten the Rams 6–3 in 1965, and he came in the dressing room that Tuesday morning and laid it on us like we had never had it put on us before. He said, "I don't think anybody in this room wants to play football. I can't think of a soul in here who wants to play. In fact," he said, "I don't think any of you will stand up and tell me that you do. No one in this room wants to play." Well, Forrest Gregg jumped to his feet quick and said, "But I do, Coach, I want to play more than anybody else in this darn room." And Willie Davis, just about that time had his chair tipped over, falling backward, so he had no choice but to get up too.

He had challenged us. He wanted us to stand. I was right up, right after Willie. We were practically in tears because he had challenged our very being, and again I think he had a definite purpose in doing so; because he could see we were about to be deeply involved in some sort of slump, and I think maybe this was his way of jacking us out of it.

He treated everybody most of the time with a very stern, firm approach, but he had great timing and a great ability to know that he could get more out of some people with a little more sugar than he could with salt. He had a great way of handling people, and I've always felt that your great leaders possess this quality.

I don't think he got close to many people. I don't know of any he did. There have been comments that he may have been somewhat closer to Max McGee and Paul Hornung, perhaps, than some of the other people. I think that was maybe only a surface thing. I don't think they were that close, really deeply. He may have been with Paul. He regarded Paul as one of his own children, I think, particularly after Paul was suspended. When Paul came back, he made it and made it big. Other than Paul I don't think he was ever close to anyone. He appeared to be close on the surface because he joked with them. He had a great sense of humor which has not been written of or talked about too much — a great sense of humor. And this was displayed many times to us in the privacy of these close meetings and in working around the game plan in preparing our team. He would think of something that was funny and just spit it right out. It would just break us all up, and he would do that in front of the entire squad.

The year he was retired was tough on him, and we missed him. We didn't think he would stay out of coaching because we could see how miserable he felt. He'd come into the dressing room, talk to you, and as the year progressed, he told you how much he missed it. "Gee, I made a mistake — I've got to get back in." He just came right out and told us, and we could see he felt miserable. It just showed on him, but I'll say one thing for him, he never interfered. He never interfered at all, and I don't know what assistance he was to the staff there or whether they even sought any, I don't know, but he never interfered with anything and for that I respect him.

I felt that it was just a matter of time before he came back to football because you could see that he genuinely missed it. This was his life, and he had given up his life. The big thing that he wanted to live for was football, and he wasn't going to be happy until he got back with it. It didn't catch any of us by surprise when he took that job at Washington.

The town's reaction was very mixed. I think most of the people who are what I would label nonknowledgeable football people blamed him. They just gave him hell for going. They thought it was a violent case of being a traitor. He had preached to us through the years, of loyalty, etc., and had made such an issue of Taylor leaving that these same people turned on him at the time.

But I think the people who were knowledgeable, who realized that he had given so much of himself and had really put the team back on the map, were happy that he could get back into the game. If he could not be there, at least he had left something of himself at Green Bay in the years that he was. You had to be grateful for that.

I saw him once before he died; actually twice. He came to Green Bay in the early summer of 1970 and stopped by the house. We visited for a long time and it was the only time we had really just chatted. I appreciated that so much. When he left Green Bay to go to Washington the year earlier, I wrote him a letter before he left trying to tell him how much he meant to me. Now, when he was in the house, I still couldn't tell how I felt.

The second time I saw him was that same summer but now it was in the hospital in Washington. I wished I could have seen him without seeing him.

And often as I think of him, I remember something he said to us as a team. I can't even remember whether it was before a game or just during the season. And I can't remember which season. But to me it was his most memorable line. He told us that, "The quality of any man's life is in direct proportion to his commitment to excellence." It may not have been exactly those words but I'll always remember it that way.

I have those memories but I'll always feel sorry for those football players that never had the chance to play at least one game for Coach Lombardi.

If Vince Lombardi had a favorite place on the practice field, it was on his blocking sled being pushed around the field. (*John E. Biever*)

Getting ready for the introduction are #5, Paul Hornung and #31, Jimmy Taylor, at the championship game against the Cleveland Browns. Along with Starr, this may be the best backfield of all time. (*Vernon J. Biever*)

The week earlier, Starr, #15, had his ribs bruised so badly on the first play against Baltimore that he did not play in the playoff game. Now, heavily taped and in pain, he'll lead the Packers to their third NFL title in five years and the start of three in a row. (*Vernon J. Biever*)

Pointing to a player or explaining a point, Lombardi was always using that index finger to emphasize what he was saying. *(Vernon J. Biever)*

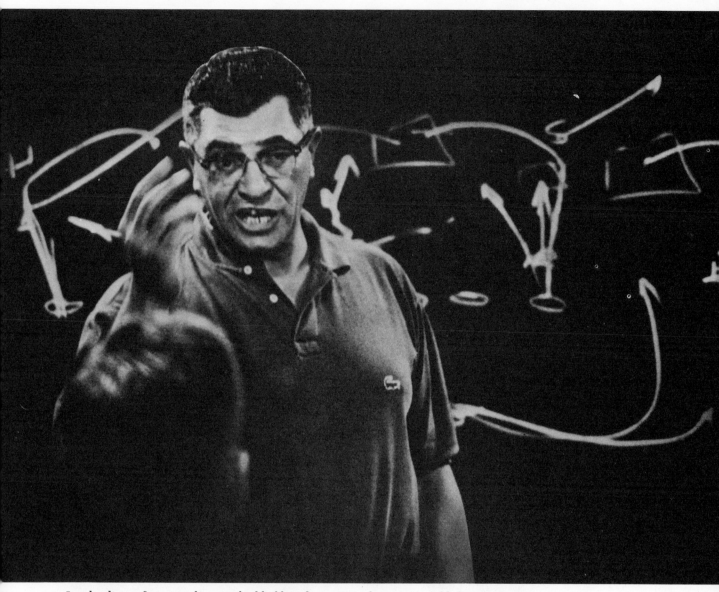

Lombardi was first a teacher. At the blackboard or out on the practice field, he was always teaching. (From *Run to Daylight* by Lombardi with Heinz and Riger. Copyright 1963 by Vince Lombardi with W.C. Heinz and Robert Riger.)

WILLIE DAVIS

I began my professional career in the National Football League with the Cleveland Browns. I came out of Grambling College in Louisiana and was a seventh- or eighth-round draft choice of the Browns in 1958. I played defensive tackle, defensive end, and was also an offensive tackle. The Browns were a fine team and had a great championship tradition.

When I found out I was traded to Green Bay, I had mixed emotions. I was disappointed as I think every athlete is when he's traded. There are a lot of things that go through your mind. But I really felt that Green Bay was going to be a test for me. If I didn't make it in Green Bay, I was going to think really seriously about giving up football.

And the very first conversation I had with Coach Lombardi in Green Bay after I had arrived was probably the most important conversation I ever had with him. He told me that the Packers had initiated the trade and that they felt that I could help the Green Bay Packers, that I was the kind of football player he was looking for.

That was all fine, but the thing that I think made me really believe in Coach Lombardi was that he turned to me and said, "Willie, what are you making right now?" I was sure that he knew what my contract was in Cleveland. I didn't answer, and he said, "Whatever you're making, we're going to give you a thousand dollars more."

Of course, financial means were not the biggest thing to me then. The biggest thing was that I felt wanted in Green Bay. So I knew that here was a man who was willing to compensate me before I played one ball game for him, and if he tells me the things that I want to hear, then this is a man I want to play for. And for eight years, it was the greatest experience I ever had.

Green Bay as a community did have some problems in the racial side of things. There had not been a great number of black ball players in Green Bay prior to Coach Lombardi's coming, and I really think that just as he made a transition in the team from a loser to a winner, he made the community aware of who could play a part in that winning. Obviously, I'm speaking of the black ball players.

What Coach Lombardi did, to the community and to the team, was to make everyone realize that if he was going to put together a winning team, he had to go for the best ball players and the most competitive ball players.

At that time there was an attitude in the town toward renting to the players. It was not only the black players, it was all of us. The attitude was somewhat hostile. Part of this attitude was somewhat the fault of the players. After all, they had been losing so much over the years that when the players got together after a game at one of the rented homes, they took their frustration out on the furniture at the parties.

But as Coach Lombardi took over the team and built pride and gave us a winning attitude, so the town came around and also developed that same pride. Within their own minds they started to search for ways that they could make the city of Green Bay more receptive to the Green Bay Packers. And obviously, this meant that they had to accept the black ball players and make them feel wanted. I can say I saw the transition take place. I saw the community go from one of tolerance of black ball players to one where there was, I felt, really no basic difference in how they approached dealing with a Green Bay Packer. In fact, I think a New York writer once called Coach Lombardi and asked him how many black Green Bay Packers he had, and he said he didn't know. They were all Green Bay Packers to him.

And I know that Coach Lombardi had that kind of feeling about the men who played for him. When he first came to Green Bay there was a black player on the team, one of the few, named Nate Borden, a defensive end. He was living in a place that you would not keep an animal in. Someone told the Coach and he gave the people renting the place hell and moved Nate out into a decent place.

My first training camp under Coach Lombardi proved to me that you had to win for this man or you were going to be in real trouble. In fact, it was physically the most demanding training camp I had ever been exposed to. When he got around to doing things like the grass drill and the push-ups and everything else that he made a part of his conditioning program, it was just too tough. We had an agility drill that started practice, and then we went from there to the grass drill and then to sprints and so on. So after the first day, there was a question in my mind as to whether I'd be able to endure. So I think right there he began to set the whole new attitude about playing the game, especially under him. In fact, throughout Coach Lombardi's coaching career there at Green Bay he always made us aware of a "price" that we paid for victory. And I know, to me, that first training camp set that "price," in terms of how we physically practiced and how we mentally got involved in terms of concentration.

One of Coach Lombardi's favorite expressions was, "There is a price you pay for victory." And I know that he constantly kept us aware of that during practice more than in the game. He felt that the game would take care of itself if he had prepared us properly in practice. And for that reason, I think that Coach Lombardi most often made practice so difficult and so demanding that really playing the game was the easiest part. The game was just really a lot of fun. That's when we really enjoyed ourselves.

I remember once we played the Rams and we had played a poor ball game, winning 6–3. On that Tuesday morning, Coach Lombardi came into the meeting room and kicked out all the assistant coaches, saying that he just wanted to talk to the players. As he started to scream and throw a tirade about how we had performed, every guy was just sitting there looking for something to say. He challenged us personally about our pride, about our willingness to pay the price for victory, and finally Forrest Gregg stood up and said, "By God, Coach, I'm willing to pay the price to win. I want to win. It tears my heart out when we don't win." And every player was waiting for someone to make a move, and I was kinda sitting there leaning back in my locker, so I wanted to get up and endorse what Gregg said, but I fell off my stool into the locker and caused all kinds of commotion. I got up and he was glaring at me. I said, "Coach, I want to win too." And he just broke up.

When I went to Green Bay in 1960, I started every exhibition game and every regular season game thereafter for the next ten years. And I can really say that at no time during that ten-year period was I ever really sure that I was going to be the defensive left-end. I think this is the way Coach Lombardi planned it. There was really no one — assistant coach, someone in the administrative office, players, groundkeepers, writers, anyone — that was ever really above Lombardi's criticism.

But he had a special way that he handled every guy. For instance, there were some he just physically and mentally went after. I mean he challenged them personally and all but said, "If you don't play the way I think you can, I'm going to personally get you." Then to others, he would just casually mention, "This is a big ball game." He had the psychological approach because he felt that he really knew every one of us. He knew what that ball player thought. He knew what was important to that player. He knew when he had a self-starter. He knew a guy he had to drive. He just knew us all.

I really do think he did know each one of us, and he did manage to get every ounce out of every player. With some he may have got it by making that player resent him enough that that player would put out so much more to prove to him that he could do it. There were players who loved him enough that they played for him simply because they believed in him and thought so much of him and because of the kind of person he was.

Because we were a team that won so many big ball games, I never knew what it was like to have played for Coach Lombardi as a loser. And I'm not really sure I could have played for him as a loser. Because I think, considering the things he demanded of us and the way he demanded them of us and how intense he was about winning, that had we been a losing team the situation would have been different. I think the players would have revolted or they would have done something. They could not have accepted the pressure that he exerted and remained a loser. I think it had a lot to do with the winning.

I really feel like he made you pay a price in such a way that you really felt that winning was the reward. It was the only thing that could justify what you had gone through in terms of practice, in terms of personal challenges, and in terms of the kinds of things he could subject you to as a person. You really felt that winning and what it brought was the only thing that would enable you to continue and be a happy part of the Green Bay Packers.

A lot of coaches are very different in practice than they are on the sideline. But Coach Lombardi was the same. You got the tempo of the game from him on the sideline. When the team was going well, he tended to try to counsel you into continuing to do things as you were doing. But if things were going bad, he was the ranting and raving personality that he was when practice was bad. He was a coach who really challenged you from the sideline many times. He'd challenge you to make the "big" play. He would scream and holler and tell you, "Get in there, Willie"; or holler to the runner about how he was running and what he was doing wrong. He was many times a real big help to us right from the sidelines in a ball game. He did not try to inject strategy from the sideline, however. He felt that that should have been done during the week.

The very first championship that the Packers won under Coach Lombardi was very important, because it made us feel we had accomplished everything we had set out to accomplish at that very first day of practice. And when we won that game against the New York Giants, each one of us said to ourselves, "It can happen and it did happen." And it brought some consolation for the disappointment we had suffered in the 1960 championship game against Philadelphia.

The next most important game we played, I think, was the 1967 Super Bowl game. It was the first. And that ball game, in particular, was a big ball game because it said that the Green Bay Packers were indeed the world champions. The AFL had been saying that we did not have any right to be calling ourselves world champions, and there was a lot of bitterness between the two leagues. We felt that by the time we took the field we were playing not only for the Green Bay Packers and all the winning that we had enjoyed, all the tradition that we had lived with, but we were playing for everything that the National Football League stood for. I think we felt that we had very little to gain in that ball game other than to maintain our championship tradition. We felt we had to win to prove to everybody beyond a shadow of a doubt that the Green Bay Packers were a team worthy of everything that had been said about us.

Coach Lombardi was not only our coach, he was also the general manager of the organization. And every year around contract signing time, he would kinda "reduce" your efforts of the past season. He would mention all the things that you didn't do well that season — and he could remember them all. I had been waiting to have the kind of year where I could walk in and feel very confident that I could ask for a raise and get it right on the spot.

This one year, after I had made All-Pro and finished second in the balloting for the Most Valuable Player, I went into his office and said, "Coach, I really had a great year. I made the All-Pro teams, went to the Pro Bowl. Coach, I was really outstanding, and I just know you're going to give me a good raise."

He just looked at me and then said, "Willie, you forgot just one thing." I said, "What's that, Coach?" He said, "Willie, I made you!" After that, I knew I'd never win a salary discussion with him. So when the next times came around, I'd just go in, have some small talk and sign whatever he gave me.

I always felt that I was a ball player who was highly underpaid! One time I thought I had him, though. I'd had another All-Pro year and I thought I'd take a different approach. So I said, "Coach, there is no way you can expect me, a $10,000 a year defensive end to stop those $40,000 a year running backs." He smiled and said, "Willie, I'm very proud of something." I said, "What's that, Coach?" He said, "Willie, I've never lost with those same faces." So he was telling me that if I wanted to go on being a winner, I'd tackle those expensive backs. And he was right.

Even though he always got the best of me in the salary discussions, as he did with everyone, I really feel that I had a very personal relationship with the Coach. I think we shared things that maybe only the two of us could discuss, partly because of the way we felt about things and partly because of things we knew were part of each other's life. One time in his office he talked to me about things that he wanted from life. He talked about how he got started, how long he waited to become a head coach, what it meant to him to see signs of success along the way, and what it meant to him to be a head coach and enjoy the success that he wanted out of life.

He told me that if I was willing to pay a price, that if I was willing to dedicate myself to the goals that I really believed in, that someday I would achieve them. And I know that he believed everything he told me, and I looked at him and understood that he was telling me that he had paid the price and that he would go on paying the price. I knew that we were not talking about money; we were talking about what it means to be a man, to overcome, to know that you did it.

I think of him often and always feel that warmth come over me remembering him and his smile. And I remember him talking to us before that Ram game. He made many speeches before many big games. But this time, it hit me something special. He told us that we should think of the Rams as someone who had come into your house and in front of your friends and your family was challenging you to prove your existence as a man. And I think that by the time we took to that field, every Green Bay Packer was not only going to win that football game, we were going to prove to ourselves our right to be called men.

To me, Vince Lombardi never left, never died.

As a pass rusher, Davis, #87, was one of the best. (*Vernon J. Biever*)

It was the Packer defense that forced the first Super Bowl into Kansas City mistakes and a Packer victory. Here Davis has forced the K. C. quarterback out of the pocket and has him running for his life. *(Vernon J. Biever)*

When Lombardi got Willie Davis from the Browns and Davis became one of the great defensive ends of all time, Lombardi considered that to be the best trade of all his career. Here is Davis walking away from Jimmy Brown of Cleveland after stopping him in the 1965 NFL title game. *(John E. Biever)*

Vince Lombardi could say more with his hands to his players than most coaches can say with words. *(Vernon J. Biever)*

The second Packer-Giants NFL title game was played in Yankee Stadium, in 1962. It was the coldest day of the year and the wind made it impossible to throw the long pass. *(Vernon J. Biever)*

Not all the games were wins. Here Vince and Phil Bengston walk off the field after his team was upset by the Minnesota Vikings in a game in which the Packers were favored. *(Vernon J. Biever)*

RAY AND "DUDS" BILOTTI

The first time we saw Vince Lombardi was when he came into our kitchen. We weren't even open yet. We were just setting up and getting organized and ready to open, and he walked in. He left the practice field and walked in and started bellowing. "Where the hell is Bilotti? Where's Bilotti?" Our cousin, who was working for us at the time and didn't know anything about football, said to us, "Who in the hell is he?" He really didn't know Lombardi at all until afterward. Then he felt like an ass when he found out it was Lombardi asking for us. Vince just left the practice field, left the guys on the field, and just walked over. He wanted to see the place as we were progressing.

Two days after we opened he came in with his wife and Bart Starr. We helped make Lombardi a success, because in the early days with the Italian population so low in Green Bay, our friends would come up and bring us Italian bread and Italian black olives and cappacola, sausage, and linguini sauce. We'd always send some over to his house. We used to kid him about that. You're winning because of us, we'd say. It wasn't on a regular basis, but any time anyone would come over from Kenosha and bring us the Italian delicacies which you couldn't get in the Green Bay area, we always made sure that he got some.

He used to ask us all the time, "I don't see any of your clam sauce." We would say, "If we ain't got it, we ain't got it." So one night he called up at seven o'clock and said he was coming out here with a party of ten or twelve. He got on the phone and says, "Got the clam sauce?" I said, "Oh, yeah." He said, "I figured you'd have it. How about I bring the stuff down and Marie goes in the kitchen? You might get an apron for her." So we're in the kitchen and Marie did the cooking. Vince made me sit down. "Now put this on the menu, ha, ha! Now ain't this great!"

You know, when he says something is great, everyone else at the table nods and agrees. He had to bring everything to our kitchen and his wife cooked. He had to have his clam sauce. Then he says to us, "Any time baby, any time." That's when we really got to know him. There were times when we'd look at him, those steel-gray eyes and that big smile, and you felt you knew him well. But you couldn't figure him all the time.

As a guest in the restaurant he was no problem at all. Terrific. No problem whatsoever. No sweat. Even on a losing night he was no problem. It wouldn't matter whether he lost or won, he was always a perfect gentleman. The waitresses and hostesses loved to wait on him.

The charisma when he'd walk in — you could almost feel it. People would have their backs to the bar, and all of a sudden, they would know that he walked in and they'd turn around. "There's Lombardi, there's Lombardi, there's Lombardi," they would say. Well you know how big our place is. A couple of minutes after he'd walk in, no matter what dining room he was in, everybody knew it. Word got around. The place went crazy, you know.

He picked our place. So by him frequenting our place the ball players didn't frequent it that much. It was a choice of either having him or the ball players, and I think we were better off having him. We gained one hundred percent because he was always bringing in people. There was always someone from New York, some friend of his from New York coming. We gained tremendously that way rather than having the ball players, who were freeloaders. You know how they are. But Lombardi was good for business.

He was always throwing parties. Win or lose, he'd come in. It was usually a party of about ten to fourteen. It would fool you. After a loss you would think that he would want to sit in a corner, but he'd say no, right out in the open. That's all right. He would phone up and say that he was coming in with a party of fourteen. Instead of trying to hide from everybody, he would sit right out in the open, even after they lost.

The customers would stare at him all the time, like any celebrity. And kids, too. I remember one kid who asked for an autograph. He was sitting with some CBS people at the time. "It would be my pleasure," he said. His voice penetrated, you know. When he got all done he shook the boy's hand and the boy started to walk away. He said, "Hey, did you forget something?" So he got a kiss from the boy and the parents thanked him.

You know, the guy was just magic. He would come into the place pretty often, but we hadn't seen him in a couple of months. So you're busy and you don't think about it right? He found out through the grapevine that the National Football League people were in town investigating gambling. So, as soon as he told us we thought they would ask questions about us. A couple of weeks after that, which was about two months since he'd been in, Lombardi came in one night at five o'clock and said, "Can I see you guys? I suppose you've noticed that I haven't been here? The National Football League people have been here checking on gambling. Do you have relatives in the scene — in the gambling business — relatives or friends?" I said, "No, sir." He said, "We checked you out and I just couldn't come here during that time." And we had another drink and he apologized for not coming. That's the way the man was.

We both talked it over, and we thought we wanted to name a room after him. This was while he was still coaching. We told him that we wanted to fix this room and name it after him. And he said, "What took you so long? It's about time someone did that!" We thought he'd say no, I'd rather not, but he laughed and said, "Oh yeah?"

Then he would come in and he would always want to take a look as it was progressing. We had it closed off. We kept saying no, not yet, not yet. And we wouldn't let him look at it.

And then we got a hold of Tony Canadeo and Marie and said that we were just about ready. Can we set this thing up for a party, a surprise party? It was just going to be a normal thing. They were just supposed to be going out to dinner with Tony Canadeo. And they came here and he saw the room. He was tremendously jolted. He really couldn't believe it that we went to all that trouble.

We didn't know how the hell we were going to unveil the pictures. You know, we had these two murals. Bill Heinz took care of that for us, and he made a speech. He opened it all up. We had a blue cloth covering the murals. It had to be blue. He roared, he laughed, he enjoyed it.

He never imposed. We always had that feeling that we were Italian, and he was Italian, and we should do just the opposite instead of trying to take advantage. We played it just the opposite. We never asked for anything. That probably played on his mind a little bit too when we said we don't need any tickets. Sure, we always needed tickets, but we always asked other people rather than him.

He was a happy man that six months between the time he retired as coach and before the team came in. You first knew he was unhappy about being general manager in the way he acted. You could just see it. He wasn't the same Vince Lombardi. It seemed like he was lost with not enough to do. A man like that has to be busy. Now he was general manager. You can be an idiot and be general manager, but with all his talents he could be general manager with one finger, right? He had nothing to do and I think that's what nearly drove him nuts.

He'd always come in to fire up the help. He'd always be teasing us and teasing the bartender, or someone. All of a sudden he wasn't doing that. He came in and sat or he'd say, "Come on over and sit." And he'd just talk in generalities, you know. He was flat. In fact, you wouldn't even enjoy it. You just felt uncomfortable, whereas before you didn't. We'd try to make him laugh and force him to talk. He was uneasy and you became uneasy.

After he came back from Super Bowl II, the following morning as a matter of fact, somebody was talking with him about retiring. Everybody felt it was in the wind. It was coming. One night I sat with him having a drink, and I kept giving him the needle. He just kept changing the subject. I was trying to get it out of him because of the rumors. And I couldn't. It was impossible. He just kept changing the subject. When it was announced, the reaction in the bar was between people being mad and some saying it was okay. I felt that the championships were over. There was a flat feeling too that they weren't going to make it.

I'll tell you our reactions to Bengston being made head coach. We heard from the ball players after the first opening day meeting. We have four or five athletes to verify it — Bengston's opening day speech. That told us the story. "If we play our cards right we can even win it again this year." And the veterans were looking at each other. "Like, what do you mean? Aren't we going to win it?" He gave them the impression that he didn't have the drive like Lombardi.

Everybody loved going to the football games. Everybody wanted not only to see the team win but to see Lombardi. When George Halas retired as the Bear's coach it wasn't the same anymore, without Halas walking down to the ten-yard line and everybody booing him. They all loved George Halas. They could hate the Bears, but they loved George Halas. When Lombardi walked down to the field with that camel's hair coat, he looked just like a distinguished Caesar, you know. He took charge.

One time Vince came in and he had a party of fourteen, and we had some friends down from Kenosha. We had mentioned in front of our friends, not the rest of the people in the restaurant, "Let's give him a nice little hand." It mushroomed. He came walking in with his group and went to his table.

Our friends got up to give him a little applause. Pretty soon the whole bar, the whole dining room, stood up and gave him a standing ovation. That was nice. We were pleased by it. Everybody did it, and he was quite pleased that he was acknowledged that way. It was just like in a theatre — a standing ovation.

This is funny. I was up in front at the bar, and he had just come out of the can laughing. I said, "What's wrong?" You could tell that he was probably mad at first, but then a second went by. "First time, first time for me," he said. I said, "What happened?" "Autographs. I was going to the john and a guy came in — I was at the urinal — and the guy asked me for my autograph!"

The greeting part was always the touchiest during the season when you had to greet him at the door. It was touchy because his wife wanted to talk but he didn't. He would say, "Hey, where's the table, where's the table?" There were times when you knew he was in a bad mood, and you'd say good evening to him and he'd grunt. That was the clue. Leave him alone. Yeah, take him to his table, but leave him alone. It was obvious, you just left him alone and gave instructions to everybody to leave him alone. You know, there was no hiding with him. You knew if he wanted to talk or he didn't want to talk. He'd let you know.

During his days here with us it was partying all the time. Always a party. That's when we did our tremendous business. You could always count on partying. Then the bars would open the first thing every morning. We'd have to open up at eight o'clock in the morning. People were still partying — the Bloody Marys. The excitement was there. Tickets were at a premium. Rooms were at a premium. Our bar business was tremendous. Saturday was no problem with $2,000 at the bar. The day of the game you'd do $2,000. After the game you'd pick up another $1,500. You'd do more business because Sunday was terrific if it was a Sunday game. Sunday morning was out of this world. We would go full blast until twenty to one. Then you'd have the rest of the afternoon to get reorganized for the onslaught that came again after the game. We found out that after he was gone things died down completely. You'd get an onslaught after the game that would last maybe an hour, because people would want to come in to use the john or something or to wait for the traffic to let up. But by six o'clock it was dead. But when he was here it would go on all night. It would just keep on going, because they knew he was coming out. He'd come out about eight or eight-thirty, and people would stay. They knew they would get another glimpse of him.

Well the third championship game was the "Ice" Bowl. There had to be an unbelievable number of drunks because they were sitting out in that cold drinking that brandy. They were on the floor by the time they entered here. They would be stone sober because of the cold, but by the minute they hit the heat of the Forum — wow! They just started to pass out all over the place.

Never once, in all the years that we knew him, did he ever come to the bar. He never drank at the bar. It was always a table or booth. At that time there were ball players at the bar and the other coaches, but I don't know what it was about not wanting to be at the bar. He did at other places, but he never came to the bar and had a drink.

I never heard of him having one in New York at the bar either. He would stand up at Manuche's when there was a whole group of people and he was visiting, but he always sat down if there was a table. And if there wasn't, he would go in the other room. He had a fetish about that, and I think he was right. If you see a guy sitting down he's having a cocktail. If you see him standing at the bar, he's getting loaded. You know, that's a fan reaction. They see one of the coaches standing at the bar, he's belting them down. If they see him sitting down with a group, they're having cocktails.

The assistant coaches and office people would come in two or three times a week. That was always the thing. You would never hear any disrespect, and then we knew the coaches real well and all the assistants. No disrespect was ever shown to him. There was one night during the draft, and they all came in at ten o'clock. Tom Miller and all the rest of them came to the end of the bar first and they were having a drink, and all of a sudden the front door opened and they grabbed their drinks and headed for a table.

The draft used to be something too. They would have these meetings up at the office, and they would order the food. Lombardi would order the food for himself and all the coaches — whoever was there for the draft. He wanted everything first class — no hamburgers and jazz like that. Steaks, I think it was T-bones. He wanted first class with the cloth and napkins. We'd bring everything up there and set everything up for his coaches in the big conference room. My cousin, the hostess, and I brought the stuff. We had to make two trips. He's picking at the hors d'oeuvres. "Pretty good. Where are the dancing girls?" I said, "Well give me an hour and I'll get 'em up here." And he started laughing. The difference in the way he took care of something, like even a dinner or a snack when his coaches were working on the draft all those hours, was that he made it first class, whereas with Devine and Bengston it was hamburgers. Honest to God, that's the way it was. Tom Miller would call and say will you send up eighteen cheeseburgers and this and that.

When we heard he was going to Washington we were sad. We didn't really want to see him go because he was really magic for us. In the early days it was naturally because he was Italian and there were very few Italians up here. When we came up north there were only about four or five families and he was about the sixth or seventh. It gave us a little in with some of the families who used to ride us. We said to him, "You're going to put the Packers on the map, right baby?" But then after that you almost forgot that he was Italian. The man was a genius, and he could have been Polish, German, anything. He could have been president of General Motors. He could have just taken anything. He didn't have to stay in sports. He made it interesting, really made the football season interesting. He made Green Bay interesting.

When he retired the people from New York stopped coming. That's the part we noticed. Ever since he left there were never any big celebrities, no big names really, who came into town anymore. It was blah again. After Lombardi, everything dropped off completely.

We didn't really notice the effect on our business, but we did notice that we weren't getting people from New York anymore. The first year wasn't bad because people were still coming down, like Bill Heinz interviewing for *Life* magazine, his first year as general manager. But then after that, after he left, even the Chicago people weren't coming up as much as they had been. It was always a big night when the Chicago people came up. But then, all of a sudden, it was no different from any other game. It used to be that there would be almost a train-load coming up from Chicago. They'd actually come up in a special train. Then that stopped. So business did drop off then.

They put the Bears game in Milwaukee instead of up here last year after all those years. I don't know what Milwaukee has over the management over here to switch that game. The people here thought it was unfair. I do too. Being in business, how can you take the Chicago Bears game away from the Green Bay people? I mean, that's really the money game, the Bears.

They must have said, "Give us the Bears game," and Dan Devine had to okay it. It had to be his decision to place it in Milwaukee. All the business places were petitioning like crazy. For fifty years the Chicago Bears played here. They always had the Bishop Charity game down there — fine. But we always had the regular season games. And then Milwaukee got it last year. The San Diego Chargers and these other clubs, you're still going to get 50,000 people at the game. But how many people come from San Diego or San Francisco? The Bears or the Vikings or Detroit, those are the games that you'd like to have up here. I'd rather have those games than see the Miami Dolphins now. Really, it's the financial end. It's better to bring fresh money out of Chicago, Minnesota, or Detroit. You need fresh money into the area.

Vince was going to Washington and the morning before, we sat down on those red couches we had then. We asked him the same thing that he said to the papers afterward — that he wanted to come back in, he wanted to really stay after he had quit, but then it wouldn't be fair to Bengston. He had the authority. He could have overstepped him, but he didn't want to do it in reality. And he felt like hell. He wanted to get back in football. He was sorry about the whole thing. He was sorry he had made the step just to quit. We sat there for about a half hour or forty-five minutes talking.

The fan reaction when they found out he was going to Washington was split. There were a lot of them mad as all hell saying, "He can't do that. It isn't right. He wasn't being fair about it." And then we had the other fifty percent saying he still had his life to lead and that's the decision he wanted to make. He did all he could in Green Bay, and he brought us to the top.

There's a lot of them that still feel that he should never have left. They still hold him to blame instead of looking back and saying, "Hey, we had him a short period of time. Marvelous! Look what he did for us." It was great having a chance to meet him. How often do you get a chance to meet that type of man? In reality he was going public. He was going out all the time. He'd play golf. People had a chance to see him. It wasn't like a celebrity who was always tied up or you never saw him. You really had a chance to shake his hand and talk to him.

The day he announced he was going to Washington at the press conference, we did a hell of a bar business. They all stayed all day and everybody was bitching. There were arguments going on back and forth. That's all it was — argument night, pro and con.

There were those who were stupid enough to say — I'd call them

Ray and "Duds" Bilotti   **123**

stupid, anyway — that he'd made a mistake. He made his mistakes. He made his mistakes even in football. My analysis is that he had this charisma that very few people have. But he wasn't a genius as far as football — knowing his football. There are a lot of coaches who know their football, probably even more than he did. But he could get something out of someone that other coaches couldn't get. He did something for us in this area.

When the town found out he was sick, even the ones who were knocking him felt sorry that they were knocking him. Headlines were always in the paper about his condition. On our end of it we held a mass for him. I don't know if anybody knew that. Yeah, we held a mass right in the Lombardi Room and we had two priests, a minister, and a rabbi come in. The team at the time was gone. They were out of town.

He was sick — very, very bad. Everybody knew it at the time and we phoned up the wives of the players and asked them if they wanted to come to this mass. We got the wives of the players who still knew him and the coaches. They all came. It wasn't in the paper so it wasn't anything that we were trying to capitalize on. We just made phone calls to certain people who were close to him and were still in town. In the Lombardi Room we had about eighty to ninety people. The priests, minister, and the rabbi all talked and said a few prayers and so forth. No publicity at all on it, in fact. We thought it was befitting that we hold something in his room.

The Lombardi legend is still as great as ever in Green Bay. The poor part is that it always will be great, and naturally, it wasn't fair to some of the coaches who followed. The thing you couldn't get across to the coaches was that there would never be another one like him, with the style he had. I believe that if anybody is going to come close to Lombardi it's going to be Starr, in a different way, a different style.

Vince Lombardi was a man who I looked up to. I think of what he has done for us. I have to take it on an individual basis. He did tremendously for the Packer organization and for the community, but then I set that aside and say, "Okay, what has he done for me?" My family was jolted when he died, because they knew what he meant to me and because I quoted his words at home. His philosophy was always quoted at home. All my young kids really cried like hell, and they really didn't know the man. You took what he was doing in football and applied it to life. So I could use what he was doing in football and apply it at home with my children.

Some of the old players like Willie Wood and Willie Davis come by. Henry Jordon, because he is in Milwaukee, we see him now and then. But we don't see too many of the others. They always talk about the "old man." To me they were pros. They might be the last of the pros, what you'd call real pros, I think. I think today we've got so many prima donnas. I'm not saying they weren't out for the buck in those days. They were. But I always thought that Vince made men of them in more ways than one; not only on the football field but also by the way they conducted themselves afterward. You could see it. That's why I say they were the last of the pros. We may not go back to that era again when it comes to professional football.

President John F. Kennedy giving Vince Lombardi an award. Notice Lombardi's left hand, patting the President on the back, as if to say "good work." (*Joe Lombardi*)

George Halas and Vince Lombardi. What a pair! The Packer-Bear rivalry has gone on ever since pro football started and Halas was part of every one of those games. (Vernon J. Biever)

For some reason, Lombardi has been credited with inventing the "grass drill." He did not. He just used it more effectively than anybody else. It's easy. Run in place at full speed, raising those knees as high as you can: then throw yourself on your stomach, roll over, jump up and start running in place again. (Vernon J. Biever)

Everyone had to run through the rope ladder after doing the "grass drill." This helped their agility. (Vernon J. Biever)

When there was something going on that he did not like, Vince Lombardi let you know about it. *(Vernon J. Biever)*

In Super Bowl I, the defense closed off the run. Here middle linebacker Ray Nitschke is about to put the wood to the running back. *(Vernon J. Biever)*

Here, during the third quarter of Super Bowl I, Willie Davis, Henry Jordon and Ron Kostelnic tackle Len Dawson of the Chiefs for a big loss.

Jimmy Taylor's last game as a Green Bay Packer. This run set up the last Packer touchdown in Super Bowl I, as they won 35-10. *(Vernon J. Biever)*

Vince Lombardi really wanted to win that Super Bowl game. *(Vernon J. Biever)*

One could tell exactly how the Packers were doing just by watching Lombardi on the sideline.
(Vernon J. Biever)

6
Run to Daylight!

IN THE FALL of 1963, *Run to Daylight!* was published. It is still in print and selling. And the only reason that it was ever finished is Bill Heinz. When we first started to put it together, Lombardi had just won his first NFL title. It was winter of 1962, and Lombardi agreed to participate as coauthor of a book about a coach and pro football. We did not have a title.

The first editorial meeting took place upstairs at Toots Shor's; that was always a good place to get a lot of details worked out. Along with Lombardi were Robert Riger, the artist and photographer who would illustrate the book; Red Smith, whose by-line would be carried on the title page as editor of the series, and Tim Cohane, sports editor of *Look* magazine and an old friend of Lombardi's from his Fordham days. Vince wanted Tim to write the book.

After the book's concept and how the book would be put together were discussed, Tim Cohane said, "I'd love to be a part of this. It is going to be a great book. But I'm not your man. You need a great writer for this. The guy you should get is Bill Heinz." Smith and Riger agreed that Heinz would be the ideal choice. Lombardi did not know Bill Heinz, but if Cohane recommended him, that was fine. There was only one problem: according to Smith, Heinz was working on a novel and could not do the book.

But Red called Bill and found out that Heinz was finishing his novel that spring and could work on the book, if he liked the idea and liked Lombardi. So we had another meeting with the same cast, except that Heinz replaced Cohane. It was a fine meeting and everyone seemed happy; the project would start that summer in Green Bay. But there was still one real problem: someone had to go out and get the material to write the book from Vince Lombardi. That someone was Bill Heinz, who already knew that Lombardi would be a very difficult coauthor.

The book idea was exciting and new to Lombardi and he was very enthusiastic about it. When Bill got to Green Bay, Vince and Marie insisted he live with them. After all, should not coauthors be together? After four days, the romance wore off, the drudgery and hard work of writing a book took over, and Vince Lombardi, coauthor, became Vince Lombardi, golfer.

Those were the days before the Packers reported to camp, and Bill knew that once the team arrived, Vince would have even less time for him. But somehow, following Vince around the golf course, at dinner, and at the office, the thing started to take shape. And when the team came in, though Bill had even less time with Lombardi, he could study him as a coach. It was fascinating to him, and the players were great.

It was Marie Lombardi who saved the day. She knew the players so well that she was able to give Bill insight into the men who made up the Packers. The decision to write the book around a key game during the season was Bill's. It turned out to be the Lions game, a classic of football games and football literature.

Marie Lombardi is responsible for the title, *Run to Daylight!* We were in Manuche's for dinner one night, Vince and Marie, Bill, Red, and me. Vince asked Bill what he was going to call the book. Bill said, "I'm using the working title of *Six Days and Sunday.*" Red Smith said, "If you do, the book will end up on the Biblical shelves in the bookstores." Many other titles were tried and all sounded just as bad. Finally, Marie said, "Vin, why don't you call it what you're always yelling at your backs to do, run to daylight?" When she said that, the book became *Run to Daylight!* And broadcasters everywhere soon had a new phrase to add to their lexicon, "He's running to daylight, fans."

The critics were most kind, and phrases like "best book ever written on football" and "handbook for fans . . . work of art" and "remarkable" and "great writing achievement" appeared across the pages of the newspapers and magazines that reviewed the book.

In the Lions game, the focal point in the writing of *Run to Daylight!*, the Packers won when Herb Adderley intercepted a pass by the Lions' quarterback, late in the fourth quarter and ran it back to give the Packers a good field position for Paul Hornung's field goal. Later, in the Lions' locker room, Alex Karras, the Lions' great defensive tackle, was so mad at losing, he threw his helmet at the quarterback. For seven weeks, the Lions waited until they got the Packers again and then on Thanksgiving morning, in Detroit, before the traditional national television audience, they killed the Packers; they literally destroyed the vaunted Green Bay offensive line, sacking Starr eight times. It was the only game the Packers lost that year and one of the worst defeats a Lombardi Green Bay team ever knew. Although the Packers went on to beat the Giants for their second NFL title, the Lions told everyone they were the best team. They couldn't wait to prove it in 1963.

As fate would have it, when *Daylight* was published, the Packers were in Milwaukee for their most important game of the early 1963 season. Their opponents were those same Lions and it was going to be a blood-feud. On Saturday before the game, Vince Lombardi and Bill Heinz made a personal appearance at two of the largest stores in Milwaukee to autograph their book. The crowds were large and Lombardi was thoroughly enjoying himself, playing the author bit to the hilt. At the Boston store, there was a big, orderly crowd waiting in line with their books for the coauthors to sign. Heinz and Lombardi were seated behind a long table in the book department, and as the purchasers passed before them, offering their books, signs and loudspeakers directed additional potential buyers to Lombardi. Among those led to the scene were two elderly women, wearing black dresses with white lace collars, later described by Heinz as looking like two escapees from a road company of *Arsenic and Old Lace*.

"Which one is the band leader?" one of the women finally asked another spectator, a young man who, obviously awed by finding himself in the presence of the great coach, had been intently watching Lombardi for the past ten minutes.

"The what?" the young man said.

"Lombardo," the second woman said. "The band leader."

Heinz, listening to all this byplay, looked up and said, "Oh, you mean Guy Lombardo? He's right here," pointing to Lombardi.

"Good," the first woman said, "but what are you doing autographing books, too?"

"Me?" Heinz said. "I play clarinet in the band."

"Oh no, you don't," the second woman said. "We recognize him, but we never saw you before."

"C'mon, c'mon," Lombardi said to Heinz. "We've got books piling up here. Stop talking to the people, and keep signing."

"Yes, Coach," Heinz said.

The next day the Packers beat the Lions, 31–10.

BILL HEINZ

Vincent, you know, didn't have too much respect for the press. He admired them as writers, considered them to be professional writers. But if you take a group of one hundred football writers, let's say, you would be lucky if you could come up with one who was capable of putting in an offense, putting in a defense, or scouting the opposition. So Vincent had very little regard for the foolish questions that he had to be subjected to. I remember once when I was out at Green Bay a young writer came in from out of town — a free-lance writer, a serious young man, nice and rather shy. He was around about three or four days. I happened to come out of the Coach's room, and he said to me, "Is the Coach in there?" I said, "Yeah, do you want to talk to him?" He said, "Could I?" So I went in and Vincent's sitting there getting out of his field gear and he looks up and says, "Oh, it's you!" I said, "Yeah, that young writer is out there and he'd like to talk to you." He said, "What does he want?" I said, "He's a reporter, Vince, and he wants to ask you a question or two." "All right, all right, send him in," Vince said. So the writer went in and about ten minutes later he came out and said, "Gee, thanks very much."

Vincent and I got in the car and went back to St. Norbert's to have lunch. On the way I said, "You know that young writer? He's a very good writer." "How do you know?" Vince said. I said, "Because I've read his stuff. And I want to tell you something else. He's a very shy young man and he has a job to do, and the way you're treating him you could be giving him an inferiority complex." He grunted and on we went.

We came back for afternoon practice and were walking off the field. Let's say the writer's name is Pete. Pete is fifty feet ahead of us and Vincent says, "Hey, Pete!" The kid turns around. Vince says, "Any questions you got?" We went back then to St. Norbert's where they have a tradition called the "five o'clock club." All professional football teams have it. It's where the coaches and their friends gather for a drink or two before they meet the team at mess.

So Vincent's sitting over in the corner reading the *Green Bay Press Gazette.* Somebody's out in the kitchenette getting the ice ready. The French doors open, but very tentatively, and in comes young Pete. Vincent looks up and says, "Hey, Pete. Come here, come here. Get him a drink." Pete says, "I can get it." Vincent says, "No, get him a drink. Get him a drink." So they brought him a beer or something. And Vincent says, "Any questions you want to ask?" This went on for three or four days, and finally, another noon time came and Vincent and I were driving back to St. Norbert's and he says, "You and your Pete!" I said, "What's the matter?" He said, "Inferiority complex! I'm getting an inferiority complex worrying about him!"

Vince was always a big-city guy, and I think that once he had built the team at Green Bay, once he had established in his mind that he could take the material that he had and by developing and training and coaching build that dynasty, the challenge was gone. I think that one of the big invitations that Washington, D.C., represented was, again, taking a club that was down at the bottom of the league and building it up. The second thing was that it was a big city, and he was a big-city guy. The third thing was that he could have a piece of the ball club, which he could never have at Green Bay. Those are the reasons why I think he left. He came out of Sheepshead Bay, New York; he was always around New York. New York was "it" for him. You can't take the city out of the boy. Vincent would come to New York and would walk out of the Waldorf or some other hotel, and people on the street would say, "Hi, Vinny, hi Vinny!" I was in New York a few times with the late Mayor O'Dwyer when he came back from Mexico, and the truck drivers would stop and holler, "Hey, Bill!" Vincent had the same thing — truck drivers, taxi drivers, people on the street — he would puff up.

Vincent, in life, tried to eliminate all the nonessentials and to concentrate on the important things he was doing. After the first three or four days of working with me as a coauthor, the romance of being an author was wearing off. One of the things Vincent considered to be nonessential was the anecdote that a writer needs. One night I said something about an anecdote, and he said, "Anecdotes, anecdotes. You always want anecdotes! Why?" I said, "Vincent, for the same reason that when you put in a play with the Packers you don't just tell them to play. You walk to the blackboard and you diagram it. The anecdote is the illustration of the point we're trying to make." He said, "All right, all right, I understand. What anecdotes do you want?"

Many forces impel all of us no matter what we are doing in life. I always felt that one of the strong motivating forces behind Vincent, that made him work so hard to be something big, was the fact that he was born an Italian–American at a time when they were called "wops" and "guineas." As recently as fifteen years ago, I know for a fact that Vincent did not get college coaching jobs that he wanted because he was an Italian–American. It follows very naturally that after he got to Green Bay you never heard words like "guinea," "wop," "spic," "nigger," or "kike."

I think one of the reasons that Vincent quit coaching at Green Bay was that he had built that team from nothing, from the bottom of the league, and he'd climbed that mountain. That was done, and he was a builder. When the Washington job came up it was the same kind of thing again. It might have been a higher mountain, I don't know. But it was another mountain for him to climb.

Vincent was probably the most totally competitive — around the clock, through the calendar — man I have ever met. It didn't matter whether the game was golf, whether he was pitching pennies, or whether the game was Super Bowl. I remember one night when we were in Green Bay, Tony Canadeo (who had been a fine back with the Packers many years ago) and his wife, Marie and Vincent, Bard Lindeman, and I were going to go to dinner down at Appleton. Tony Canadeo and Vincent got into an argument about the shortest route to get to Appleton. Tony is a little competitive, too, you see. So we get into the car — Marie, Vincent, Bard, and I — and go ninety-five miles an hour to beat Tony Canadeo to a restaurant in Appleton. I'm glad we beat them, because if we didn't it was going to be a dreadful dinner!

As a coach, of course, Lombardi was meticulous about details. He would work hours or days on small things. But when it came to details in his past life that were not pertinent to playing football, he had little regard for them and no memory. As a matter of fact, after we had worked on the book for about three or four days, he said to me, "How are we doing on this book? Are we doing all right?" How could you tell him that we weren't? And I said, "We're doing fine, Coach, but you don't have any audio-video recall." He said, "What's that?" I said, "That's just something I made up, but it means that you don't remember what things sounded like, who said what, or what things looked like in your youth, your adolescence, or two days ago." He said, "That's right, you're right."

So, I don't know, weeks later I had a few things that I wanted to get out of him if he could recall them, and I cornered him and said, "Vincent, when you were playing football for St. Francis Prep, you had a great day against Boys' High." He said, "I already told you that." I said, "I know you did, but I have something I want to ask you. As you were getting out of your uniform, pulling the jersey over your head, you had the feeling for the first time in your life that football was the great game — that football was the thing you wanted to do in life." He said, "You've got that." I said, "I know I've got it, Vincent, but will you listen to my question? The question is, what color was the jersey you were pulling over your head?" He said, "Do you need that?" I said, "If I'm going to describe the scene, I need it." He said, "I don't know that." Well, by a phone call I found out that it was dark blue and red.

Another time, I was sitting there with Vincent along with Dick Voris, who had formerly been a coach at the University of Virginia and who was on

Vincent's staff at Green Bay. I said, "Vincent, while you were at St. Cecilia's you won twenty-six games in a row. You won six state titles." He said, "What about it? You know that." I said, "I have it. I want to ask you to reconstruct the scene visually. What were the colors of St. Cecilia's?" He said, "You've already told me I don't know anything about that audio-video thing. How do I know that?" And Dick Voris said, "I know what colors you wore." Vincent said, "How would you know that?" Dick said, "I came up and scouted you once." Vincent said, "What colors were they?" Dick said, "The time I scouted you, you wore white jerseys with dark blue." Vincent said, "He's right."

Vincent was an imposing man even when he did not intend to be imposing. He was an absolutely marvelous host. When you went to a restaurant with him it was fun and laughs. But, typically, let's say he was taking you to a favorite Italian restaurant of his, and after everyone had looked at the menu, he'd say, "The linguini with clam sauce is great here." And everyone would order the linguini with the clam sauce. He'd probably have the Veal Parmegiana.

When we were working on *Run* and we would talk and he would make a point that I didn't necessarily agree with, I would usually let it slide. If it was not important to me, I'd give him ground there. It was difficult to keep him on one train of thought to develop a scene I needed for the book, and I tried to avoid things that would take his mind off what we were talking about and where I had him headed. If I started disagreeing with something he said and it was unimportant, then I'd never get him back on the track.

Vince Lombardi was probably the most vital human being I have ever met in my life. I have a special pantheon of heroes of my own whom I have collected in more than thirty years in this business. I call them my Armageddon squad because they're not going to win that last battle, but they are going to make a great show before they go. Vincent is not only on that squad — he's the leader!

Action from the Lion-Packer game in 1962, the "game" in *Run to Daylight! (From* **Run to Daylight!** *by Lombardi with Heinz and Riger. Copyright ©️ 1963 by Vincent Lombardi with W. C. Heinz and Robert Riger)*

Author Vince Lombardi reading from his masterpiece. It is a great book, beautifully written, thanks to Bill Heinz, and filled with fine illustrations, thanks to Bob Riger. (*Bob Shaw*)

Some of Lombardi's intensity on the sideline. *(Vernon J. Biever)*

It's over and Lombardi offers condolences to the Detroit coach, George Wilson. To the left is co-author Bill Heinz. *(Vernon J. Biever)*

7
The Media
and Vince Lombardi

NOBODY GOT BETTER press than Vince Lombardi. Forget the reasons, it is a fact that he had the best of it. And yet, he never got along with the press. Maybe the reason why was his exposure. It often is all too easy for a coach or a player to become too familiar with the reporters and broadcasters; they have a job to do and so does the coach.

Lombardi had a captive press in Green Bay and Milwaukee and he knew it, but I never heard or saw him demand that something be written or deleted. The same with the broadcasters. But he really had little time for the press. He was too busy to worry about what someone would write about him or the team. Later on, however, he became much more aware of what was being written.

He did not like questions right after a ball game from the press. He made that quite clear to everyone. And he did not like the television people who were always sticking a camera or a mike in his face or those of his players. I guess you have to agree with him on that. The sideline is no place for a mike or a camera. He was all business and expected them to be. After all, he did not go into their trucks and tell them which picture to use.

He really never trusted the writers, and with a few exceptions, notably Bill Heinz, he was never close to them. He felt the same way about the broadcasters working around the team. If they were local, he treated them like his captive press. If they were from out of town, he avoided them. He knew they had a job to do but he did not concern himself with that or them, unless they were from New York.

One of the biggest projects undertaken by the Lombardis was to make sure that Chuck Lane, the Packer P.R. man, got married and settled down. They were very close to him and wanted to be sure he would find the right girl and be happy. But Chuck Lane has done very well, and he is still single.

Chuck was there from 1966 through Lombardi's going to Washington, through the years with Bengston and the debacle of the Dan Devine days. He quit Devine on a matter of principle. Chuck Lane is now back with the Green Bay Packers and working with Bart Starr. It looks like a long haul, but if there is anyone who can bring the Packers back, it will be Starr. And Chuck Lane will be very helpful to him in doing it.

Ray Scott began broadcasting sports in 1937 in Johnstown, Pennsylvania. He worked for a small radio station, and he did everything there — announced; sold, wrote, and tried to collect for spots; and usually cleaned up after work. He talked the station into doing a daily sports show, which he broadcast, and the next year he talked the station into covering high school football and basketball, which he covered.

Ray Scott was the voice of the Green Bay Packers during the Lombardi era, and to many, he was the best play-by-play man in all of broadcasting. He was judicious with words, trusting the intelligence and knowledge of his viewers to be able to see and understand what they were viewing. He was objective, never giving in to the rooting for the home team that is so much a part of broadcasting today. If the Packers' opponents made a good play, he said so; and if the Packers fouled up, he also said so.

Ray Scott did not editorialize on the air. Opinions were left to the summary of the game; never interjected to disconcert the viewer. And when the game was over, you knew you had been treated to a professional broadcast.

In 1953, Scott and others talked Westinghouse into sponsoring pro football on a national basis, and Scott became the play-by-play announcer for the Saturday night games. The major networks would not touch pro football then, so the package wound up on the Dumont Network. Generally speaking, they had the worst stations in every market. They went head-to-head with Jackie Gleason on CBS, *The Show of Shows* with Sid Ceasar, and they beat the competition in every market. For the first time, national sponsors became aware of pro football's potential.

Dumont dropped out of broadcasting and in 1956, CBS picked up the NFL. Because a friend of Scott's was doing the Steelers games, CBS asked him if he'd do the Green Bay Packers games.

Green Bay was not a successful team and had a very small network as far as viewers were concerned. Their major market was Minneapolis–St. Paul. CBS promised that if Scott did a good job, he'd get moved to a bigger network later on. In 1959, after three terrible years, Lombardi came to Green Bay and Ray Scott suddenly, like everyone else, was rescued. He then had one of the choicest jobs in football. With the exception of 1964, Ray Scott was the voice of the Packers for twelve years.

As he says, he was a lucky man. Those years with the Packers and Lombardi were the great years of pro football and television.

Jerry Izenberg happens to be probably the best writer doing a daily sports column in America. He is also a successful director/writer of television specials. Izenberg spent a great deal of time with Vince Lombardi and got to know him about as well as any writer did. They had a great deal of respect for each other, and because of that, they would fight every once in a while. It took a brave writer to take Vince Lombardi on in a one-on-one shouting match. But after it was over, they still were friends. Izenberg won a number of awards as a writer and columnist, and he was also nominated for an Emmy for writing the television documentary, "A Man Named Lombardi."

CHUCK LANE

The story has it that Lombardi himself hired me. The truth is that Lombardi took Jim Fink's recommendation, and I'm sure, some words from Max Winter, the president of the Minnesota Vikings. He built his own impression, and then allowed Tom Miller to handle the interview.

I interviewed with Tom Miller after having come to Green Bay. I walked into the Green Bay office cold turkey. And all of a sudden I'm looking for work. I'm looking for work in the NFL, they're looking for somebody. They're looking for somebody young, they're looking for somebody single to handle the P.R. job in Green Bay. I happened to qualify by those standards. They hired me, or agreed to hire me, and I spent about a day or two in the Green Bay office. I'd never met Vince Lombardi. Pretty soon this was a little embarrassing to me, and I'm sure, embarrassing to him. There was this very formal atmosphere around the office.

It was April 1, 1966, when I reported there, and Vince came back from the spring meetings in Hawaii a week later. I walked into his office and introduced myself. I said, "As long as I'm working for you I should meet you." I stuck out my hand and he bellowed and laughed in his typical deep chuckle.

I'd always been a Packers fan. Growing up in Minneapolis you are subjected to Ray Scott and the Green Bay Packers. That was the NFL broadcast you received on television.

Vince Lombardi had a way of enveloping people around him, enveloping them in a certain dynamism, or whatever you want to call it. He was a very dynamic person. Whoever came into the room — even if Richard Burton had come into the room, or Joe Namath or Prince Philip — whoever it was, at whatever level, I think Vince Lombardi would have dominated them. Because he had that certain charm; he had that certain ability and strength of character. He didn't have to say it. He didn't have to shout. He didn't have to point that twenty-seven-inch index finger of his. All he had to do was to be there. His charm, his personality radiated. He didn't have to tell you he was Vince Lombardi. You *knew* he was Vince Lombardi. You accepted it, and that was enough. Henry Jordon came out with a famed quote, "He treated us all alike. Like dogs." This is probably the most inaccurate quote about Coach Lombardi. He treated everybody extremely individually. He'd try to treat everybody alike. He would shout, rant, and rave at everybody. Yes, he shouted at a lot of people. But for certain people he realized that shouting was not a way of motivating them. He had a great ability to read people and understand where their nerve endings were. He'd shout at some and cajole others, and they would respond.

I was on the practice field one day and Bob Brockman from the *San Francisco Examiner* was there. Bob had billed himself as a close friend of Coach Lombardi. For all I knew, he was. We went out to the practice field on Thursday prior to playing the 49ers, and Bob was in town to cover the game. He came out there to see his "close friend," Vince Lombardi. We start walking across the practice field and I can hear this shouting in the distance, but this was nothing new. Boyd Dowler was running the sideline pattern going down the field. As he passed me, he said, "Get the hell out of here. I think the old man's after your ass."

I couldn't believe it. So I kept right on walking toward the center of the field where the press were to stand at practice. And Lombardi comes running across the practice field, screaming and shouting. I can't believe this. Nonetheless, he expels us from the practice field. Being thrown off the practice field is no big thing. Other people have been. So we go up to the office building. The scene changes; I'm walking down the office hallway, and I run across him and he's just livid. You know, the veins are sticking out on his neck and he's yelling and screaming and carrying on about how I brought a spy to practice. Well, you know, in the middle of the season a guy gets tired and you lose a little bit of your cushion, I suppose, between sanity and insanity, and I've got this man standing in front of me hollering and screaming and shouting about my infidelity which, Lord knows, didn't exist.

So I just teed off in return. I don't know why. It wasn't a planned thing. I told him, "Goddamnit, if that's the way you want to treat your friends it's all right with me, but don't involve me in it." I told him that as far as I knew Bob Brockman was a personal friend of his, and I was bringing him out to practice and we were getting there right at the end of practice so that he would have a chance to see you and the guy wouldn't come around and bother you in the dressing room. I said that I'd done the best I could to bring the two of them together at the most convenient hour, and if that wasn't good enough then, Goddamnit, it was his own problem. He could just run him off at his own leisure. I would be Goddamned if I was going to be berated in front of people like that. Lombardi softened up, backed off.

He tested the mettle of people. I think he knew who he could push and who he couldn't push. And this was the way he tested you. It got to the point, through the years, where he became, I suppose, more at ease with your character and your personality. I never once heard him holler at Bart Starr. But I heard him rant and rave at Fuzzy Thurston a great deal. He knew Fuzz could take it. He knew that Bart was a highly sensitive and emotional person, who would not respond this way. I think he played people. He hollered and screamed and shouted at Tom Miller. For better or for worse, he found out through years of experience that I could be motivated better with praise. A pat on the back would motivate me ten times more than a shout. But the man had the sensitivity to understand this.

He had a very captive press in Green Bay which I don't think he ever particularly appreciated. Maybe he did inwardly, but he never admitted to it, and he never allowed anyone into the privacy of his own thoughts. When he was on the road, he seemed to let his hair down more with out of town writers.

We were playing the first Super Bowl in L.A., and people absolutely deluged him with the comparison bit between the AFL and NFL, at that point between Kansas City and Green Bay. He would not say anything about it, and somewhere in the course of the press conference, which was held the night before the game, Art Daley felt, I suppose, a need to stand up and ask a question because he was from Green Bay, a city that was represented in the Super Bowl. I don't even recall the question now — something like comparing the Kansas City Chiefs to the Dallas Cowboys, something like that. Coach Lombardi absolutely took him to task and just flayed him right down to the bone. Yet, somebody from outside this area, an NFL city or anywhere else, could have asked him the same question and he would, I'm sure, have just ground his teeth and the veins would have stuck out another half-inch on his neck. But he would never have come down like he did on Art Daley. All of us were terribly embarrassed for Daley, because the man is extraordinarily well-meaning, a very pleasant man — a journalist who's been in the business for years and years. He'd been very good to the Packers, and yet Lombardi let him have it.

I'm sure Lombardi apologized later because that was his nature. But the apology was always private. You never found out about those things. John Proski, the guy who takes care of the playing field — John must be close to sixty or sixty-five years old — was once shouted at by Lombardi in front of the squad about the condition of the playing field, which was probably not well-founded. But he came back to John privately, after he had just embarrassed him in front of the entire football team and apologized. And John said, "I'll be Goddamned if I'll accept your apology. You chew me out publicly, and I'll be Goddamned if I'll have your private apology."

I don't know that Lombardi ever apologized publicly. I doubt it. But I think after that Lombardi had a great deal more compassion and feeling for John Proski because Proski stood up to him. He was always testing your character — always testing your strength, your mettle, or whatever — and I think he had a great deal more respect for people who would stand up and be counted.

For one thing, nobody ever handled him. I don't care what anybody has to say — people like Jim Kinsel, Don Weiss, people in the NFL office, who were probably the best group of public relations people ever in existence, either politically or in the sports field or anywhere — nobody has ever handled Vince Lombardi. The best you could hope for was a tie. I had the ability to realize that it was his signature on the lower corner of my paycheck, so he was the first person I had to please, and I think that he had a certain respect for my ability to judge a situation. I won't say that he ever came to me for advice, but I would make suggestions constantly. That's really the role of an employee, whether it's in a professional football league or wherever it is. You know, you have a certain experience in your field, and it's your responsibility to give your employer a certain feedback in your area. I hoped to have given him feedback with what I thought he should say, with what I thought the press expected, and how I thought the thing should be set up. But with his strength of personality, he would do it in his own particular manner, which worked out very well. For him to be anything but himself was a loss, because his own strength, his own personality was far above anything else. The man could survive on his own strength, his own character, his own personality totally and singularly. There was no reason to settle for anything else.

I think he was sensitive enough to know how others felt about him. I think he knew that I had a great deal of respect for him. I did. There were times I wanted to get him around the neck and just throttle him, and five minutes later I wanted to put him over my shoulder and carry him around the room. But that was the typical Italian personality and temperament, or whatever you want to call it. He knew that I liked him.

I only had three years with him, two when he was head coach. Both of these were Super Bowls; the third year he was general manager. I think the most enjoyable times I had with him were those that were never chronicled — like moments socially when I happened to be thrown together with him. I don't mean to imply that he sought me out socially. It was just when we happened to be together socially. I revered those moments. When he left Green Bay he asked me to drive him to the airport. We drove out to Oneida Country Club to pick up his golf clubs, and then we drove to the airport, and in that time we exchanged thoughts about where the National Football League was heading, about the management of the Green Bay Packers. Before that we had always spoken in terms of Jerry Kramer's twisted ankle, the condition of Bart Starr's arm, and whether or not the scoreboards were operating properly. But on this ride we got into larger subjects. We talked about philosophical things. It was probably one of the most enjoyable conversations I've ever had with a human being, this ride in a Corvette, with a full bag of golf clubs, on the way to the airport. Here we are in total confusion — you know, when you put two men in a Corvette with a set of golf clubs it gets a little congested. And yet, we were driving to the airport discussing all these things. I imagine it's a fifteen-minute drive; I wish I could relive those fifteen minutes. Fantastic! The man was extraordinarily well-versed in understanding people, in understanding situations, and the long view versus the short view. I would venture, that if he had lived, we would never have had the player strikes we've had. We would never have had the unrest we have had. We would, perhaps, have never had the death knell sound for pro football. I don't think we're there yet. I don't think pro football has died. I don't think the death warrant has been signed, but we do have problems, and I don't think we'd have these problems today if he had lived.

I think he quit because he had painted himself into a corner, and he had put himself into the general manager's role because he was afraid for himself physically. He had some physical problems at that time. He was blacking out. Believe it or not, he was the world's worst hypochondriac. The players alluded to that. In fact, they said that their injuries never bothered him. That's the truth, but yet he'd have a hangnail and he'd scream like it was the Third World War.

He had great fear for his own sanity, I think, for his own physical well-being. He realized what being the head coach and general manager and of repeating the world championships meant. He knew what it was doing to him. I think he would have loved to let his guard down. He would have loved to have been a human being. He was an extraordinary human person. He did not allow himself to be one as head coach and general manager of the Green Bay Packers. It drove him to physical endurance that perhaps he was not up to.

Very few knew about his physical problems. He would closet himself and go off to his coach's locker room. I know that Vince, Jr., knew about it. I know that Sid Hartman, the sports editor of the *Minneapolis Tribune*, knew, but there were very few others. I think that this was what drove him out of coaching. I don't know whether it was the physical situation or knowing quite frankly that he had driven the squad for three straights. I just think that he realized that he had driven this team as far as they could go. There was no way they could win four in a row. And for that reason I think he got himself out of football. I think he knew that he had driven this club as far as he could. The reason why he couldn't come back to Green Bay as head coach is that he had installed his number-one lieutenant. Lombardi was forever preaching service to the club — the team was greater than any individual — yet he realized that the thing was spent. He knew it was over, I think.

And he knew also that he had put in Phil Bengston as head coach, whatever the motive was at that time. He realized, during the course of Phil's first year, what the weaknesses were and he was dying to get back and take over the thing. But I don't think that he felt that he could come back. He'd painted himself into a corner. He couldn't come back. I think that killed him. He was like a caged tiger that year he was away. That's why he had to go somewhere else.

The city of Green Bay, Wisconsin, is celebrated for its paper milling and its Green Bay Packers. Its paper milling doesn't get the publicity. The Green Bay Packers do. The whole social mood of the city is centered around the success or failure of the Packers. That's one of the things that made losing in Green Bay so unbearable. That's the same reason that made winning and success and pride — pride in the organization, pride in the leadership, pride in the performance of the players so important in Green Bay. Winning in Green Bay can be one of the most beautiful things in the world. You work for twelve months a year to win games in fourteen consecutive weeks. When you do it's beautiful, when you don't the world knows about it.

I think that he could get blood out of a stone. I don't think it made any difference to him who he hired. He could get the work and get the performance out of his people. And he did, indeed, get the work out of his people, whatever their strengths or weaknesses were. I think that's illustrated by the fact that when he was gone, or when people left him — nobody who ever had worked under Lombardi, coached under Lombardi, or to this day had played under Lombardi, has really done it, has really made it in a big way. And I think that this is what Starr's greatest challenge is. No great "Hall of Fame" type quarterback has ever made it as a head coach. This is Starr's challenge.

We all shared the same relationship with the head man. He was up there, and we were all down below. All of us shared an area that was subordinate to Lombardi. I think we had a great fellowship, we had a great feeling. We all knew we'd face the fire, we'd face the test, and it gave us a great fraternity. I think the players had a feeling for the people in the front office and we had a great feeling for them. But here again, I was separate from them. I was twenty-three years old when I got the job. The ball players during the Super Bowl years, I would say, were closer to the twenty-eight to thirty age group. They had been through an awful lot with Lombardi, and I was just coming into it. There were people on that club whom I would consider to be great friends of mine. They accepted me right away.

There was tremendous respect, fear to a degree, but primarily respect for him. I think respect is something you earn. You don't decree it, you don't demand it, and certainly you don't buy it. You earn it. Vince Lombardi earned respect from his football players. And they respected him a great deal. A lot of them came out in public and said that they didn't approve of the way he did things, they didn't approve of the way he ordered people, they didn't approve of the way he drove people. But they respected the way he got things done. As years have gone by and as these men have matured, I think they appreciate this more and more. I feel the same way.

Lombardi's martinet reputation comes from a group of people who saw him only briefly. People are always seeking to pigeonhole other people. The same with a personality I meet, the girl I date, the people I encounter on the practice field. I want to pigeonhole that person. It's a tendency that we all have, I think, in our interpersonal relationships. If people met Vince Lombardi and heard him shout, rather than going into the depth of his personality (which was considerable), they would find it more convenient to say that this guy's a wild-eyed shouter. He's a martinet. He's a cruel son-of-a-bitch. Write him off. Other teams called him "the Jap" because of his grin. I think we tend to classify people by their physical appearances, be it black, white, Italian, or whatever. We tend to pigeonhole, we tend to put a tag line on them. I think this is where his martinet image came from. There were very few people who bothered to get into him. And there were people who did, like Jim Murray of the L.A. *Times*. Jim understood Vince and was one of the first people who came to his defense after the *Esquire* piece by Leonard Schecter, who flayed him just terribly. It hurt Vince Lombardi to the quick, really bothered the hell out of him.

And yet that attack, I think, was the one major force that turned public sentiment to Lombardi. Unfortunately, I said this to Dan Devine. And I think that Devine felt that because the *Esquire* piece turned public sentiment toward Lombardi, he would try to plant a piece in *Time* magazine, which he did. And this would turn public sentiment pro-Devine. It didn't. Instead it just alienated him with the community. I have a strong feeling that this is what Devine felt, but it backfired tremendously and eventually cost him his job. Well, if Devine didn't understand then, he must have understood when all of the reputable writers and broadcasters came immediately to the defense of Lombardi and said that this was completely unfair. Red Smith did a column. Jim Murray did a column, Cosell did a piece on his radio show — everybody in the world.

The reason that they came to Lombardi's defense is that responsible journalists in this country understood the depth of Lombardi's commitment. They realized the reasons why he was doing it, and I think they understood him. He was a very difficult man to understand, but he was a sensitive man. I think that when a person is emotional and sensitive his feelings are on the surface. Maybe that makes them a little bit easier to feel and understand. I think you get more playback from a person like this.

Schecter came in like any other writer. He was to do a piece on the

Green Bay Packers and did not declare himself as intending to do a hatchet job, which he indeed did. We welcomed him as we would any other writer. Just as we have you [the author] in camp today. You come in and declare you want to do a book on Lombardi and Starr. We give you the same treatment that we would a man who had a bad reputation. It's our job to try to sway ill-feeling people to a positive vein just as it's our job with people who come in and have positive predeclared motives to further those feelings.

After we beat Dallas for the NFL title, I remember the bus ride to the hotel. It was an emotional time, a very emotional moment. We had a get-together down at the Hilton Hotel in Dallas. I think it was the Hilton, but anyway it was a hotel we hadn't stayed at before or since. Fuzzy Thurston — Fuzzy was really the welding force that got this club together — was singing, "He's Got the Whole World in His Hands," and it was directed to Vince Lombardi. The radiation, the warmth, the personality flowing out of this one man — he could be extraordinarily nasty, but conversely he could be extraordinarily warm. I feel sorry for the people who saw his extraordinarily nasty side, because he could be ten times warmer than he could be nasty.

When I think of Lombardi, I picture him as tense and driving, not only demanding of others but of himself, extraordinarily well-prepared. And I think that follows the excellence angle. I found him to be an extremely emotional person. I suppose this goes back to his Italian background. Football is a very emotional game. It's the nature of the sport and the nature of the people who make the sport. It's the nature of the American people, and that's why it's been a great marriage — football and emotions and Vince Lombardi. He knew how to play by emotions. That's why the Packers were as successful as they were in the big games.

My fondest memory of him is his laughter. I think his laughter was an emotional outburst. I am a person who appreciates people's emotions. I love a person at his leisure. I love a person when he lets himself go. I think that's when a person really declares himself, when he lets himself go. His laughter, his ability to relax, the character that he exhibits at this moment.

I think another example of a person's character is at a moment of great stress. As I look back, I would say if there was a time I was proudest of him it was during Super Bowl I when he was being hounded by the press. He would not allow himself the luxury of comment. The Kansas City Chiefs were like an expansion football team in the National Football League. They had not been in existence that long. They had been playing with inferior talent, and they did not meet up to the measure of the Green Bay Packers. And he would not allow himself the luxury of saying that they didn't.

I had to be at practice because he was such an explosive character. In fact, I was there for every single practice they had. If I was not there and if there was a writer or a broadcaster or a cameraman who transgressed and got out onto the field and what not, well it was my fanny. It was the guy's fanny initially, but eventually mine would get flayed and broiled, and God knows what all shortly after that. So I had to be there.

The practices were highly organized, very autocratic, you know, "I am the coach and you will do as I damn will you to do it." The film sessions were totally different. And I had the privilege of getting into these things and finding out that he had a great interplay of ideas and philosophies with his players. There was a great input by the players, by McGee, Hornung, Starr, Gregg, etc. These people would suggest things while watching the films, things that could be done and things that couldn't be done. I was just utterly amazed at the interplay of ideas, the free flow of philosophy that existed during their film sessions. I didn't think this existed. And to have watched his practices you would not think that anybody would have dared to speak up in the course of their film reviews. But, in truth, there was a great interplay.

He did scream and holler when a guy made a mistake. He did indeed. But I think it was such a professional organization that people realized themselves when they were erring. The screaming and hollering has been overplayed. Granted, there was a great deal of this that went on, but there was also a great deal of interplay.

Red Smith called the Green Bay Packers the most intelligent and articulate group of athletes he's ever covered in his fifty years of covering sports, and he covered Notre Dame, the New York Yankees, St. Louis Cardinals — you name it, some of the great teams. I think every organization is a reflection of its leadership. Vince Lombardi was highly intelligent and highly organized, highly disciplined, and very articulate. I think the Packers were a reflection of his leadership. NBC and CBS both mentioned this to me in the first Super Bowl. Both networks were covering the ball game. Both said that they had felt the Green Bay Packers were monsters, but they thought that Lombardi was highly articulate and that the team was a reflection of that.

But the team had great individuals, in terms not only of athletes but also in terms of personalities. That's why they were chosen by Lombardi. Making it in this football club as an athlete was not enough. They had a lot of great athletes, but you had to have that great character to make this ball club. I think he was right. You win in this game with character, depth of character.

Willie Davis told Jerry Izenberg that he had a great fear. His great fear was that he wouldn't be part of the organization. He said that this motivated him more than anything. With all the hollering and screaming and shouting, he wanted to be part of the Green Bay Packers. We lost that when Lombardi left. The man was great force himself. When he was no longer "coach," the Green Bay Packers started to lose. They didn't have that great character behind them They didn't have that great drive — be it fear, motivation, whatever it was.

I think his greatest moment was championship number three. It's what he had striven for in 1961, 1962, and 1963. He lost it in 1963. In 1964 he fought for it and didn't get it. He complained about second place being a place for losers. In 1965 he won it. In 1966 he won it. In 1967 all cannons were loaded for three straight. This was his greatest moment, and this is what put him out of the game.

When things were going well on the field, Lombardi would be a real cheerleader. *(Vernon J. Biever)*

Bart Starr was as professional off the field as he was on and he, along with the other Packers, had a great relationship with the Press. *(Vernon J. Biever)*

Contrary to popular myth, after a game, Vince Lombardi could smile and talk to newsmen and broadcasters without snarling. Of course, before this interview, they have just beaten the Dallas Cowboys in the "Ice Bowl" and have won their third NFL title in a row. (*Vernon J. Biever*)

The resignation. The press conference was held at the Oneida Country Club where he was a member. Because of the emotion of the moment, Vince wrote out his speech and then did not answer questions. *(Vernon J. Biever)*

Vince Lombardi congratulates his successor, Phil Bengston. *(Vernon J. Biever)*

RAY SCOTT

It is almost impossible to begin to talk about Vince Lombardi and the Packers because you really never know where to begin. They were a terrible team in the three years I covered them before Lombardi came, but these were the players that would form the nucleus of his teams. And if I were to say I saw greatness on that field before Lombardi, I would be inaccurate. I saw frustration and lack of discipline and poor organization.

The late Scooter McLean was the Packer coach, and they won one game, beating the Eagles. They almost lost that one also because of an on-side kick that the Eagles recovered, but time ran out. And they tied one with the Detroit Lions. The rest of the games were losses, including a 56–0 loss to the Baltimore Colts.

I attended the draft meeting following that season, and that's the first time I became aware of Vince Lombardi. I met him briefly, but I don't remember if he had accepted the Green Bay job yet or not. I don't think he had because I would have spent more time with him. Of course, I had heard about him and a whole lot of people thought he would be a great head coach when he got his chance. It was a question of where he was going to wind up.

When it was announced that Lombardi would take over the Packers, I called Tony Canadeo, who was on the executive committee, to get some inside information on the man and the deal they gave Lombardi. They were all very high on him, Tony said, and had given him virtual free reign to run the club. They had given him this power because they felt they had to. The franchise was shaky and the Packers were not getting good television money. In fact, the first year I was doing the Packer games, in 1956, I think the Packers got just $35,000 for their television rights from CBS.

My first actual chance to talk to Vince came sometime during the preseason game period before the 1959 season. And what he said to me, in effect, was that he had heard that I was an excellent broadcaster and that he was glad to have me as part of the family. He made it obvious from the very beginning that whoever did the television and radio was part of the Packer family. This meant a number of things to him. It meant that you were totally loyal, that you would be invited to dinner parties and cocktail parties that were very exclusive, your wife would be included as part of the family, and it was really an honor.

He was just great around women, and women automatically liked him. And when stories would get into the press that Lombardi was a dictator, or obnoxious, or mean, my wife and others would fight anyone who wrote or said that. He was always courteous, considerate, and pleasant to women, and that's the way they knew him and loved him. He was a total gentleman.

During that first year, it was obvious to me that he was no ordinary coach. He had an almost fanatical desire to have the team turn around immediately. And yet, I know he was a realist, because I honestly believe that he was not expecting them to be as good as they were that first year. If you'll remember, they almost tied for the division title.

The people in Green Bay were won over immediately. The past had been so bad, and now it was obvious that they had somebody who was going to bring the Packers back so they just loved him. He was treated in almost total awe.

That first year, there was no doubt in my mind that the Packers were going to be winners. No doubt whatsoever. So all of a sudden, the defeatism that you as the broadcaster pick up covering a losing team is gone.

The most memorable games I covered during those years would have to be the back-to-back championship games against the Dallas Cowboys. One was in the Cotton Bowl on a good field in 1966. This game determined who would represent the NFL in the first Super Bowl. In that game Dallas had the ball in the closing seconds and could not score. But I can't think of that game separately because the next year, the game was played on a horrible field in sub-zero weather in Green Bay and as fate would have it, the Packers had the ball in the closing moments, and they did score.

Those two games, back-to-back were the most dramatic. But the game, the aftermath of which I'll never forget, involving Vince was the Colt game in 1966. The Packers had defeated the Colts in the Western Conference playoff in sudden death in Green Bay the year earlier. There was a disputed Don Chandler field goal that tied the game and the Packers won in overtime. People in Baltimore were incensed, and I guess they still are to this day, claiming that the field goal was not good.

The town was very outspoken about it, and so were the Colt players. As good scheduling would have it, the first game of the next season was played in Milwaukee between the Colts and the Packers, with the Colts still crying about the Chandler field goal. But because Vince was the way he was, you never heard a word out of the Packers. I knew that he wanted to say they should settle this on the football field.

I don't think I've ever seen a Packer team more ready than the team that night. The Colts scored a field goal, and that was it for them. The defense dominated Unitas and the offense controlled the game. The Packers won 17–3, I think, but they really dominated the game. There was no doubt which was the better team.

And I remember going up to Vince's suite in the Phister Hotel that night about two hours after the game. I can still see him sitting in a chair, holding on to the game ball the players had given him. He was so keyed-up that his hands were still shaking. I know that had to be one of his most satisfying victories.

You never heard much out of Vince before a game was played. To me that was a key to his great success. You never heard him say that the Packers might lose because of injuries or anything. After a loss, he never complained about the officiating. I asked him one time about why he never talked about injuries as other coaches did — and do. We were in his game room at his home in Green Bay and he said, "If you were with the Packers and were a sub and if you read in the paper on Thursday that I or another coach had suggested that we were going to lose because the 'regular' was unable to play because of injuries, how would you feel? If I suggested we were going to lose because you were going to play, you would not feel very confident in your-self." His answer was so obvious that I was ashamed for having asked. But I can remember so many coaches crying the blues because they had injuries and setting up their alibi in case they did lose.

Heck, I can remember so many times when there would be two or three or sometimes four regulars out of the Packer lineup for key games, and you never heard a word from the man. And I think that is another insight as to why he was such a great coach: he never let anyone on his team ever think that he did not belong with the Green Bay Packers.

Vince after a loss was one of the most intriguing men I've ever seen in sports. When Billy Martin was a coach with the Twins, he had never met Lombardi even though he played with the Yankees when Vince was with the Giants. In those days, I made it a practice to take a good friend to a Packer game in Green Bay at least one time during the season. So this time we went with the Martins and this time the Vikings were the opponents. We had a regular routine during those years. After the game and after I had finished the commentary or the after-game interview, we would all meet at Tony Canadeo's house. Then after an hour there, we'd go to the Lombardi's. And after an hour or so there we would go to dinner.

This time, the Vikings won the game. It is a bitter loss to the Packers. It was only the second game the Packers lost that year. We went to Canadeo's and then after an hour, I say to Billy that it's time to go. He asks where and I tell him, Lombardi's. Billy says that I'm nuts if I think he's going over there after what happened that afternoon. I tell him we always go over there. Well, it's apparent that Billy is afraid to go over there since he's never met Vince. So anyway, we go over. And after we drop off our coats in the living room, we head downstairs to the recreation room. Now I always let Vince know who we were bringing as a guest, so he knew Billy was coming. We barely get to the stairs before Vince is there shaking Billy's hand and saying how much he always wanted to meet Billy. Billy can't believe what's happening. Lombardi's just lost a tough game and he's acting like meeting Billy Martin is the biggest thing in his life. Well, Vince took Billy over to a corner in that game room, and they talked by themselves for forty-five minutes.

I asked Billy later what they talked about, and Billy said that they talked about Casey Stengel. Vince wanted to know about Stengle and how he handled the players and what Stengle was really like. Billy has told me over and over since then that that was the most inspirational, greatest time he ever spent. In five minutes, he had forgotten the whole game, let alone who won.

When they played Dallas in that first championship game, the Packers took the ball the length of the field on the first series and scored. Then they recovered the kickoff and scored, but missed an extra point. They got the ball again and they were on their way to another touchdown, and it looked like they are going to blow the Cowboys out of Texas. Elijah Pitts fumbled, and the Cowboys recovered. The first guy to pat him on the fanny and tell him to forget it was Vince Lombardi. To him, a fumble was not a mental mistake. On the other hand, they could be winning by 40 to 0 and complete a pass and some Packer lineman would be called for holding and he'd blow sky high. And you did not want to be that guy. He'd take the longest route back to the bench. So as a result, I don't think it was luck that they did not make mental mistakes in big games.

The Sunday after Vince's funeral, I had a 49ers game to do. Dick Nolan was then the coach and was a great disciple of Lombardi's. And we got talking about him and his teams. I said, "Dick, when was the last time you can remember a Packer team making a mental mistake in a big game?" And Dick laughed and said he could not remember any mental mistakes by them. He agreed that this was another of the reasons the man was such a great coach. A man could feel he had played his best game physically, but make a mental mistake, and Vince was all over him. But drop a pass in the clutch, or fumble, that was part of the game and Lombardi would never get on a player for that.

Before Super Bowl I, we were in Dallas the night before the Packers and Cowboys game and I was having dinner with Bill McPhail and Pat Summerall of CBS. In the past, when there was a championship game, the announcers for the two teams split the duties on the game. So I asked McPhail who was going to do the Super Bowl for CBS. I knew that the NBC team representing the AFL would be Curt Gowdy and Paul Christman. McPhail said that if Dallas won, Jack Buck would definitely not do the Super Bowl and if the Packers won, there was only a ten percent chance I would do the game.

I was flabbergasted. I had been told by others in CBS that if the Packers won, I'd do the game. The same for Jack Buck. I blew my stack, and at the production meeting the following day, I took Jack Dolph outside and told him if someone other than me did that game, assuming the Packers beat Dallas, that I had no intention of honoring the remaining two years on my CBS contract. Jack said I was childish and unprofessional, and I told him that if I were in a room with all the CBS sports executives, there would be only one pro in the room, and the name was Scott.

Sometime later, after the Packers had won and were in Los Angeles, I got a call from Jack Dolph. He had some news for me, some good and some bad. At this time, NBC was trumpeting the fact that they had, in their opinion, the best announcing team in television in Gowdy and Christman. So it became, as far as the networks were concerned, a battle for ratings between CBS and NBC. So Jack Dolph told me that I was going to do just half the game.

Since CBS was afraid they would lose the rating game in New York, they wanted Jack Whitaker to do the other half with me. I told Dolph that that was acceptable to me. But to me it was sheer nonsense that whoever was broadcasting the game would determine what station or network was watched. I told McPhail that CBS would win the rating battle. Not because of me or Whitaker or CBS, but just because there were more NFL fans than AFL and CBS had more stations. After all, CBS had more viewers during the regular season of pro football. Habit was going to win it for CBS.

There was great pressure — great, great pressure. CBS brass made it difficult all the time. Jack and I had to prepare for the biggest pro football game ever and at the same time make those executives stay out of the professional business of putting on a telecast of the game.

There was great pressure on the teams. It was fantastic. But as usual, the Packers veterans were very confident. I saw Max McGee in the lobby of the Sheraton West Hotel maybe two days before the game. In the Dallas game, Boyd Dowler had caught a slant-in pass from Starr and was three steps into the end zone when Mike Gechtner hit him a cheap shot at the ankles and Dowler flipped into the air, landed on his shoulder and separated it. McGee, who was near the end of his career, played the rest of the game.

Anyway, McGee told me in the lobby that if he got into the game, they would never get him out. I asked why and he told me he had been looking at film of the Kansas City secondary, and he felt that there was no way they would stop him. And true enough. Dowler got hurt right away again, and Max came in and had the kind of game that men dream about. He caught seven passes, scored two touchdowns, and was just great. In fact, there is a great picture of Max smiling down at a Kansas City defender after he had scored, and that grin said it all.

There was no doubt in my mind that those Packers were never going to lose that game. There was just no way that Lombardi would let them. After it was all over, some of them said, jokingly, that they were afraid more of him than Kansas City. Afraid to face him in that locker room if they lost. I think he had them convinced that they would all go to some football purgatory if they lost it.

Lombardi made Super Bowl I a crusade — and one that he was going to win. During the season, he kept everyone hungry, including the broadcasters. He never let up on the quest for that championship. But looking at him after he had won the Super Bowl, you had to know how happy he was. His smile was fantastic.

In February after the game, I was the toastmaster at a banquet in Pittsburgh that Hank Stram, the Kansas City coach, attended. We were seated next to each other on the dais and Hank said to me he still felt that they were the better team. And I said, "Hank, let me tell you something. If you had played for a hundred more quarters, you were not going to win. That game, Hank, you were not going to win." Now maybe I felt like that because I was so immersed in the Lombardi thinking, but to me there was no way he was going to allow that Packers team to lose that game.

I heard later that there was a lot of panic among the NFL owners at halftime when the score was only 14–10 in favor of the Packers. But there was none in the broadcasting booth. Fortunately, in the booth, we don't have the production people, the management brass. You have the professionals there to do a job.

I think that there were two years that Vince did not think he had the horses to win the NFL title. One was in 1965 and the other in 1967. But he did win in 1965 after that overtime game with Baltimore and they beat the Browns for the NFL title. There was no Super Bowl that year. The reason I say I don't think he thought he had the horses was that they had had a bad year in 1964, coming in second to Baltimore, which then lost to Cleveland, and he felt that the team was one year older and needed some new blood. But they won some games they might have lost and somehow hung together to win.

In 1967, I know he felt that the dream of three in a row might sustain the team to make it, but he felt that there were better teams, younger and stronger. The 1966 team has always been considered as one of the greatest in all the history of pro football, and maybe it was, but Vince himself, as far as I know, did not rank it with the 1961 and 1962 teams.

As I recall, the Packers had clinched their division title early and went out to play the Rams, who were very tough and fighting Baltimore for their division title. Both had better records than the Packers, and the Packers had nothing to win that day in Los Angeles. Well, as you remember, it was a great game with both teams coming from behind. The Packers led late in the game and all they had to do was punt the ball downfield and hold on for a minute or two. When the Rams blocked the punt and scored to win the game, that meant that they would play the Packers in Milwaukee for the Western Conference crown. And all of the Ram players and fans and officials were cocksure that they would beat the Packers. As I recall, even the bookmakers made the Rams a touchdown favorite.

But as far as I knew from talking to Vince, he could hardly keep from grinning after the Rams won and made so many statements about beating the Packers. He now had the psychological weapon he needed to get his team ready for the playoff game. And I know he never let up on them from the time that game was over. I think he said to himself, "We've got them now."

Packers players told me later that on the field in Milwaukee prior to the game, the Rams team of that day was the cockiest team they had ever been around. And this is exactly what I'm sure Vince expected — that the Rams would be cocky while he had the Packers ready to just bite nails, they were so ready to win that game.

When the Rams jumped off to an early touchdown and then recovered a fumble deep in Packers territory and looked like they would get another quick touchdown, you could feel the concern all over the stadium. But the Packers held and then blocked the Rams field goal attempt and that was the end of it. The ball game was over for Los Angeles. The Rams were never in it after that, and for the next three quarters, the Packers gave the Rams a lesson in the game of football that those players and coaches will never forget. I can't say if that was the best coaching job for one game that Lombardi ever did. All I know was that there were a lot of so-called experts, including Packer writers and fans, that had conceded the game to the Rams. Not Vince or his team, but he never said anything before the game or afterward, except in the locker room where he said to all the press, "We were magnificent."

There had been speculation all season as to whether Vince was going to step down or not. Everyone knew how much it meant to him to win that third NFL title in a row, and the thinking was that if they did, he'd give up coaching.

Late in that 1967 season, after the Packers had played the Vikings in Minnesota, I was in the locker room and Vince was talking to the writers, including my brother Hal, who was and is the director of sports for the CBS station here. Vince, in response to a question, told everyone that he felt that the two jobs, head coach and general manager, were too much for one man to handle. He said one could not do justice to both jobs. Someone asked him if he were going to drop one of the titles and he would not answer.

So, the night after the Packers–Cowboys game, or the day after the NFL title, my brother went on the air and unfortunately used the statement, "I have learned that Vince Lombardi is going to resign as coach of the Green

Bay Packers." I didn't know about the broadcast and I was playing gin rummy at the country club I belong to when I got a phone call. It was Tom Miller, Vince's assistant.

And Tom said, "Ray, the Coach is very disappointed in you." I said, "Tom, what the hell are you talking about?" And he said, "Disappointed about what your brother said last night." And I said, "Tom, I don't know what you're talking about. What did my brother say last night?"

Looking back now, I remember sensing that Vince must have been right at Tom's elbow, because Tom would pause between answers. And Tom would say, "You know what he said," and I would say, "Tom, no, I don't know." In fact, I said, "Tom, come to the point. I'm in the middle of a gin game and I've got a good hand. What the hell's on your mind?" And he said that the coach feels you have violated a confidence. I kept telling Tom I did not know what he was talking about. And he told me about my brother saying that Vince was resigning as coach of the Packers.

Well, for the six years that I was the broadcaster for the Twins in baseball, if my brother went on the air and said anything about the Twins other than the score, I was automatically accused of feeding him information. And in this case with the Packers, it was assumed by Vince that I had told my brother.

First of all, I did not know anything about Vince planning to give up the head coaching job, and all Hal had done was put two and two together, having been present when Vince talked about the heavy burden of being coach and general manager. Vince had won his three in a row, the Packers were a sure pop to win the Super Bowl over Oakland, and so Hal figured what better time to resign. And I'm sure had Hal not used the phrase, "I have learned," which was automatically filled in by Vince and others to mean "I have learned from my brother," that there probably would not have been this uproar with Vince.

So, after Hal's broadcast, Vince was deluged by the press from all over the country, asking if the story was true. And with each denial came more speculation and stories. Vince came out and said that Hal had done a disservice to the team and to the town. I'm sure he was worried that this publicity and speculation would take away from the team in its preparations for the Raiders.

I wrote Vince a letter. In it I said that I resented any implication that I had been disloyal to the Packers. I said that since the time I first became the Packers telecaster, I had been privy to many secrets, that I had had many, many opportunities had I chosen to "violate your confidence," and this I had never done. Then I said, "I look forward to telling you in person at the Super Bowl."

As it turned out, the Packers stayed out at the Galt Ocean Mile in Ft. Lauderdale and CBS insisted we stay down in Miami, so I did not get the chance to see him face to face before the game. However, before the kickoff, we saw each other on the floor of the Orange Bowl and chatted about the game before I left to do the telecast. The Packers won, but I still felt very strongly about the incident. He did not say anything.

We had no occasion to be together after the Super Bowl until the

Thousand Yard Club had its annual banquet. I was scheduled to be the M.C. and he had announced his retirement as coach of the Packers and was now just the general manager. George Allan was to be the featured speaker, and there was a cocktail party prior to the dinner. I would say that Vince and I were within a foot of each other for an hour or so, and he never spoke to me. I guess I was too damn stubborn to start it, so we just sat there and ate and drank and made small talk to those around us. I figured that if that's the way he wants it, that's all right with me. The president of the Thousand Yard Club was sitting between Vince and me at the head table, and in the course of eating dinner, Vince all of a sudden looked over this man, looked me right in the eye, and said, "Coach, you're still the best." And then he looked away.

While in his own mind, I'm sure Vince felt I was the "Packer broadcaster," he never ever suggested to me that I should do anything a certain way. He was never critical of anything I ever said, never asked me to be a rooter. However, I know he was very difficult with a writer who would write things he did not like. He looked on the writers covering the Packers as part of the team — they should never write anything negative. Maybe I was lucky because of the way I do a football game. I always let the picture tell the story. I did not need to tell the viewer that somebody did so and so. Maybe I just did not say enough to be criticized.

I appreciated being taken into the inner circle because I had a chance to see the real Vince Lombardi, who was a paradox in many ways. He could be warm and friendly like few men I've ever known. But I know that he had such a tremendous control over himself that he could just literally turn things on and off. He could be demanding, he could be autocratic, and at times downright nasty.

One time, the season ended on the West Coast. It had to be one of the early years because most of the time they were going into the championship playoffs and those always were in the East. The Packers always threw a big party after the last game, and all of the players, their wives, if there, members of the organization at all levels, and close friends were invited. And like everything the Packers did under Lombardi, the party was the best.

Anyhow, at this party, I was standing with a drink in my hand talking to Tony Canadeo near the buffet. The team had won its last game against the Rams and everyone was in a good mood. One of the writers who had covered the Packers from Milwaukee, Chuck Johnson, was in line with his plate to get his food at the buffet. He had just finished a book on the Packers that fall and had been close to the team in the bad times as well as at the start of the Lombardi era.

Vince came up to Chuck and ordered him out. Just told him to leave the party and get out! Well, Tony and I could not believe it, and Johnson was embarrassed and so were a lot of others. But Vince just told him to leave. And Johnson left and did not say a word. Tony and I asked Vince what that was all about, thinking Johnson had written something critical about the team or Vince. But Vince said that he was doing Johnson a favor. Lombardi's logic was that he had done Johnson a favor, because if something happened later at the party that would put a player or a coach or a guest in a bad light, Chuck would have had to wrestle with his conscience as to whether his loyalty would be to the paper (to report the incident) or to the Packers (not to report it). So Vince said, in effect, he had done Johnson a favor; he took Johnson out of any position where he had an opportunity to witness anything. And I'm sure that in his own mind, in his own way of thinking, this was entirely right and proper for him to do.

I think in his own way, Vince tried to browbeat the Green Bay press. That included Milwaukee writers. He did not want anything negative if at all possible to be written about the Packers by those who were with them the most. And here again, strictly by coincidence, I was fortunate in that I did not live in Green Bay. I came in to do the games but I was seldom around during practice, except for a little during preseason when I'd come over to see how the new team shaped up, and of course, before all the championship and playoff games. And in all those years I never flew on a Packer charter. Never flew with them and never asked.

On the other hand, with the outside press, he had his favorites. Red Smith, Tim Cohane, Copper Rollow in Chicago, Jim Murray in Los Angeles, and some of the other New York writers were people that he felt close to and relaxed around. Not in the press conference after a game; then they were all treated the same. But after the game you'd see Smith or Izenberg or Murray at his home, if it were a game covered by the national press. I don't ever remember a Green Bay writer or broadcaster invited to one of those parties. When the Packers were on the road and he had his "five o'clock club" in his suite, the team writers would be invited along with the assistant coaches and the executives of the Packers and any other friends. But I never saw that in Green Bay.

He talked to these outside writers more "off the cuff" than the locals because he totally trusted them. He had known them longer. And they in turn honored that confidence and never violated it. They had their stories and did not need some sensational piece from Lombardi to help them write their columns. So it was a comfortable and at the same time professional relationship he had with them.

But it also caused him a great deal of hurt one time. I was with him in Los Angeles when the infamous *Esquire* piece that was written by Leonard Schecter hit the street. He was crushed, totally crushed. He looked at me and said, "Coach, I'm not like that. You know I'm not like that. You know I don't talk like that."

As I recall the details of that story, the writer came to camp under false pretenses. He came as if he were writing something else, and this is something that Vince could never understand. He could not understand how a writer could come into the Packer camp, be entertained by them, fed by them, housed by them, and then write a story that was completely false and not about what the writer said he was going to write. And I don't blame him one iota.

He was very aware of what his public image was. Very aware. And what Schecter had done, and *Esquire* also, hurt him. Almost as soon as the article was out, however, many writers came to Vince's defense, and the public sensed that Schecter had "jobbed" Lombardi. There was a great deal of sympathy for him, and I think, maybe, a softening in the way the public looked at him.

One time earlier in his career in Green Bay and before he had made an impact on the public, he was to receive an award at the "Dapper Dan" dinner in Pittsburgh. This is a great sports dinner every year, and I was asked to present the award. I quoted a phrase out of a column that Arthur Daley had written about Knute Rockne and applied it to Vince Lombardi. I said, in introducing Vince, "To say that Vince Lombardi is just a football coach is like saying that the Metropolitan Museum of Art is a building on Fifth Avenue. It does not even hint at the treasures inside." And I meant it. When I got home after the banquet, I received a letter Vince had written in longhand. It was a very warm thank you note for the introduction. He was a very appreciative person, and he thought of those little things. I wished I'd saved it.

I did the Packer games in 1968. And when Vince went to Washington, I did some of his preseason games and a few regular season games. When we had been together years earlier on the West Coast in Los Angeles, I took Vince and Marie out to hear some jazz. He became a great fan. We were down in New Orleans for the Super Bowl game between Kansas City and the Vikings and I was walking down Bourbon Street with some friends, and I hear this voice from across the street yelling, "Hey, Coach." There is only one voice like that, and there were Marie and Vince and another couple. So we all got together and spent the rest of the night listening to jazz. That was the last time I saw him alive.

I was in Washington when he was in the hospital and was at Duke Ziebert's restaurant when Marie came in with some friends. I sat down with them at the table. I told Marie that I wanted to go and see Vince. She said, "Ray, I don't want you to see him. I want you to remember him the way he was, because the Vince Lombardi that you knew is dead. They are just keeping him alive."

Looking back now, even though I felt I should go, it was probably for the best because I have many pictures of him in my mind and all of them are healthy, strong, and virile.

To my way of thinking, Vince Lombardi and Branch Rickey are the two most unforgettable men I've ever met in sports. They made an impact on their sport that will be felt for a long time to come. Even now, people are always comparing Don Shula and his great Miami Dolphins teams to the Packers. The same with the Pittsburgh Steelers and Chuck Noll. No matter what team or which coach becomes the new genius of pro football, they will always be compared to Lombardi and his Packers.

Lombardi made an impact on football as no other coach has or probably ever will. Timing was so important, as it is in so many things. He had the Packers dominating pro football, as no team had before or since, at a time when pro football was the thing to watch in person and on television. It is a sport so perfectly suited to television. And it looked like Vince Lombardi, pro football, and television were made for each other. I don't think anyone who has ever seen Vince Lombardi on the sidelines can ever forget the man. Volatile, demonstrative, filled with all the emotions. When he was unhappy, you knew he was unhappy; and when he was happy, you could see it and feel it and understand it.

When you played the Green Bay Packers, you played Vince Lombardi. He made the Packers an extension of his personality. You did not think of the Packers without automatically thinking of Vince Lombardi.

And for me, I was the luckiest man in the world. I was the Packers broadcaster, and I was with Vince and those players through it all. It was the greatest break I ever had. And it all started with an apology.

Red Smith

No Arms When Tittle Can't Throw

NEW YORK—Polar gales clawed topsoil off the barren playground and whipped it in tan whirlwinds about the great concrete chasm of Yankee Stadium.

The winds snatched up tattered newspapers, more newspapers than people can find in all New York these days, and flung the shreds aloft where they danced and swirled in a Shubert blizzard straight out of "East Lynne."

It was a scene of wild desolation, and down on the sideline in left field stood Allie Sherman with his troops around him, a little man among monsters. A blue knitted hood framed his face, a face as bleak as the setting. This was Washington at Valley Forge, complete with all the trappings except snow to set off the bloody footprints.

Across the field from the coach of the football Giants, the scoreboard told its cold factual tale:

PACKERS 16, GIANTS 7

One minute, 50 seconds remained in the struggle for the championship of the National League, but no hope at all remained for New York. Sherman's men had no arms to combat and no armor to fend off the finest team in the professional game, the defending champions from little Green Bay, Wis., established once more as despots of the mercenary world.

Bushville, U.S.A.

"When was the last time," a fellow had asked on the eve of the game, "when a single sports event coming up created excitement comparable to this in New York?"

"The second Louis-Conn fight," one man said.

"Maybe a little more recent than that," another said. "Maybe the last Army-Notre Dame game here in 1946. There've been lots of sellouts since, of course, at World Series games and the Giants' regular games, but they happen so often there's nothing special about them in a town like this."

A town like this? This was Bushville, U.S.A. "Beat Green Bay! Beat Green Bay!" the crowds in Madison Square Garden chanted Friday and Saturday nights. "Beat Green Bay!" the Stadium mob was bawling an hour before yesterday's kickoff, and even during pre-game exercises every alien member of the Packers was thunderously booed, every demigod on the Giants cheered to the cold skies.

"The radio says," a guy reported, "that traffic is bumper-to-bumper all the way down to Philadelphia, to catch this on television. Imagine going down to Philadelphia on a Sunday? What's happening to the human race? What is this, anyhow?"

Three-Way Test

What it really was, it was a test of football, of fortitude, of stupidity. As to fortitude and stupidity, there were 64,892 immortal souls in the Bronx playpen, and even if you count expectant mothers as two there are not that many men, women and children in the city of Green Bay, Wis. They paid either $8 or $10 each to go out in 20-degree temperatures that dropped steadily as the day wore on, and they sat it out as the bitter winds rose above 30 miles an hour, stiffening their ghastly grins.

As to football, it was as simple as a lesson can get. The cold and the wind made the forward pass a weapon of dubious value, and the pass as thrown by Y. A. Tittle is the Giants' major weapon.

It is an article of faith with Vince Lombardi, the Packers' coach, that football is a game of blocking and tackling. When weather conditions make a match anybody's game, rely on it—it will be Lombardi's game.

That's how it was because that's how it had to be. In the first half the Giants couldn't handle Green Bay's defensive line, the New York blockers didn't knock the tacklers down and the Giants couldn't move. The Green Bay running attack set up a field goal by Jerry Kramer and the Green Bay defense forced a fumble that opened the way for the Packers' touchdown.

The Giants had one big chance in the first half, and the Green Bay defense wiped it out as a big, wet thumb swabs chalk off a slate. Ray Nitschke, the Packers' great linebacker, deflected a pass by Tittle which might have meant a touchdown, and the wobbly little pop-up fell into the paws of Green Bay's Dan Currie, who ran the ball out of the danger zone.

Name of the Game

So it was 10-0 for Green Bay at the half, and the Giants hadn't been in the ball game. They got into it in the second half thanks to a tremendous effort by their defensive unit, which scored New York's only points by blocking a punt and falling on the ball in the end zone.

That made it 10-7 and lent an element of suspense, to a struggle which had been fiercely unspectacular. But it also underlined a significant fact—that in 10 quarters, counting back through the second half of their mid-season meeting in Milwaukee last year, the Giants' offensive unit has not scored a point against Green Bay.

Suspense endured a long time. Jerry Kramer's second field goal made it 13-7 in the third period, but that put the Giants only six points back, where they still could win with a touchdown and conversion. There was 1:50 to play when Kramer racked up his third goal and the ball game.

The Giants are great at bean bag, the throwing game. When the name of the game is football, take the Packers.

Sam Huff of the Giants, #70, fighting with Jimmy Taylor of the Packers after the play is over in the 1962 title game. There probably has never been a more fierce, vicious hitting game than this one. *(Vernon J. Biever)*

The Media and Vince Lombardi

Vince Lombardi was presented the game balls from the first and last victories of the 1966 season. He's shown squeezing the ball after victory over the Colts and holding the Super Bowl trophy. (*Vernon J. Biever*)

The interception by Tom Brown, #40, of the Packers in the Dallas end zone that ended the Cowboys' chances to tie the Packers in the 1966 NFL title game. (*Vernon J. Biever*)

JERRY IZENBERG

I had heard of Vince Lombardi when he was at West Point coaching Army, but the first time I ever put the face with the voice was when he was an assistant coach with the Giants and I was covering them for the *New York Herald Tribune*.

He was a horrible, dreadful man in the dressing room, as far as reporters went. You see, you have to understand the Giants' situation at that time. The Giants' situation was different. They did not have a head coach; they had a head smile. Jim Lee Howell, who replaced Steve Owen, was the head coach by title. Owen had gotten out of touch with the modern game, and typical of the Maras, they were very concerned about what the press and the public would think, so they replaced Owen with Howell, who was a popular, old Giant and a very affable old man. It was obvious that he was not going to be able to do the job.

Tom Landry became the defensive coach and Vince became the offensive coach. I was very, very young then, and I thought that if you wanted to find out about the team, you talked to the coach. And you'd say to Howell, "Why did you kick the field goal?" and he'd say, "Ho ho, you'll have to ask Vince that. Ho ho." The same with Landry. Anyway, you'd go to Vince and he was very, very suspicious by nature. If you could ask a question in technical football jargon, then he would answer you in that language. But if you asked something like, "Why did you decide to pass on third down?" you'd get some horrible look and an answer that you could not print.

I remember talking to him in front of his locker as he was trying to get ready to go on the field. This was not an unusual time to visit, and you would ask a question and he'd grunt. He was not as belligerent as he would become later, but he almost answered every question with a yes or no. But if I had asked him to diagram a play and explain it to me so I could explain it to my readers, he would be very pleased and take the time to give me more detail than I wanted. He mistrusted any question that he felt was not a "pure" football question.

Remembering now my attempts to get more from Vince than just pure football, I have to remember that he was also trying to learn about the same players I wanted to write about. He had left the ordered world of West Point and was coming into the world of professional football. So maybe, looking back, he could not give me that insight I wanted because he was learning, too. And unlike most assistant coaches, Vince was really running that offensive team. He was totally immersed in the game. I think if we had sent in the tackle from the other team with a list of questions to ask Vince, we'd have gotten a better interview.

I went into the service for a few years and when I got back, the Giants had won their first NFL title in years and Vince was the man responsible, along with Tom Landry and his defense. Now he knew his players and there was more of a feeling of respect and confidence in Vince from them. They knew, like the defensive players knew, that they had only Lombardi to answer to, and it was almost like there were two different teams playing for the

Giants. To the defensive players, Lombardi was just a guy they were happy to watch scream at the offensive players. They had more contact with the trainer than they did with Lombardi.

In 1961, I saw Lombardi and his Packers a few times. The *Herald Tribune* had Bill Wallace covering the Giants full-time. The Giants were still big news in New York then. Red Smith covered pro ball whenever he wanted, but as the featured columnist, he went wherever he wanted. So my job was to go to the other big game that Sunday and sometimes it would be a Packers game. After all, they were becoming the "super team," and we had to cover them. So I'd usually come into town on Friday or Saturday, depending on where the game was, and I'd catch that "five o'clock club". It was not really a good place to socialize then. Vince kinda divided the room up with the writers on one side and he, the coaches, and the Packers officials on the other. I'm sure it was not planned, but it just felt like that. He'd say hello and make sure you had a drink, and then he'd retreat to the other side of the room.

You felt like you were being ordered to have a drink and it seemed that even Olejniczak, the president of the club, was being tolerated somewhere between the writers and "family." And Vince did not seem to be comfortable around any special guests from Green Bay. He had not really come, at that time, to love the people of Green Bay, and so when some of the "stockholders" were invited to the party, he was very uncomfortable. Also, he was still working on the upcoming game, and these social moments interfered with work. Actually then, these get-togethers were not all that pleasant and most of the time when I went it was because I was looking for Tom Miller to make sure I had my press passes and ticket. If I waited for them to be delivered to my room, I'd have missed a lot of games.

After the game, and after writing the lead story for a morning paper, I very seldom had time to go down to the locker room and visit with Vince or the players. The deadline was too close. But in 1962, when I was writing the column for the *Newark Star Ledger*, it was a whole different thing; and Vince became very important to me.

I'd have to say, as Muhammad Ali became important to Howard Cosell, if you can understand that, my relationship with Vince and his team became very important to me. I liked Vince very much. But I had very ambivalent feelings about him. There were times when I detested him. But I liked him very much, also. As I began to know him, I began to find out more about him, and I found that he was as deficient in many areas as I was. But he covered them up much better.

In 1962, the nature of our relationship changed. Then I would go into Green Bay three days before a big game or whatever and wherever. And we would spend a lot of time together.

Now Vince had the world divided into two areas. Forget all the legends. With Vince, there was "us" and "them." You were either an "us" or a "them." There was no middle ground on this thing and when I came in on a Wednesday, I was an "us." First of all, I was coming from the New York area and I was one of the faces who had been around the Giants locker room, so that made me an "us." And this is one of the things that pissed off the

Milwaukee writers. That Vince would confide in us and speak to us, and he would treat them like dogs.

So it was great. He'd tell me to come out to the house or we'd have to have dinner or meet after practice in the office or whatever. Except, "Don't come to my practices!" He really believed in keeping all writers and visitors away from the practice. And yet, there would be three or four hundred people, standing or sitting along the street side of the practice field watching the Packers work out! That's what made him seem so maniacal. There is no way there are any secrets in football. But there we were in November or December, still having secret practices, with the fans sitting fifty yards away!

One day, before a Bears game, the Packers came out to that parking lot and walked over to the practice field. And as I'm watching, along comes Jimmy Taylor wearing Willie Davis's number and Davis has on Taylor's and Starr has on Adderley's and Adderley is wearing Hornung's and so on. And so after practice, I went up to him and said, "That was beautiful. Who do you think is not going to identify Willie Davis or Paul Hornung, just because they changed numbers. Have you looked at them lately? There is a difference between Davis and Taylor, Hornung and Adderley!" And he just brushed me aside. He had done what he wanted and the "secrecy" had been maintained.

Before the game, he would be open and frank and talk about the players, the other team, what he thought; he would really be open. But then he would cut it off. He had a mental clock. He would allot you whatever he thought was necessary and when he started looking at his fingernails or out the window, you knew it was all over for the day. And if you did not get up and leave, he would get up and say good-bye and walk out. Boom, that was it.

But he was very friendly. Then they played the game. After the game, he would be impossible! He was surly and he was hypertensive. That may be a contradiction, but he was the only man that could be both at the same time. It was now the "us" and "them" time. And now the edge that you had going in as an "us" and not being a local writer was gone. Now I'm a "them," and we had some horrible confrontations after games. I always felt he was worse when he won than when he lost. When he lost, there was always kind of a deflation in him so he could not work full-time at being a son-of-a-bitch. There is no question, in my mind, that Vince Lombardi on Monday after the game was a different animal than on Sunday, and I use the term "animal" advisedly because that's what he was after the game.

A great example was the Packer–Colts game in Milwaukee in 1965. I don't remember if it was the opening game or the second game of the season, but the Packers knew they were going to have to beat the Colts if they wanted to win the Western Conference title. Hornung missed the game because he was hurt. In the first quarter, Taylor, who started the game hurt, was hurt again and left, and he didn't play anymore that day. Then, before the half was out, they lost Starr. Now they played the second half, as I recall, with Zeke Bratkowski at quarterback, Tom Moore and Elijah Pitts as the running backs, and there were no others on the bench. They won, 20–17! They had just beaten the other best team in football; Zeke was great and Max McGee scored the winning touchdown on a pass from Zeke late in the game. It was a hell of a game.

Afterward, in that dressing room in County Stadium, we all crowded around Lombardi and he was absolutely impossible! We all had planes to catch, as did the Packers, and deadlines to meet and he was so miserable to all of us that nothing was happening. Nobody wanted to ask him a tough question! So I said, to get something going, "Did you ever think you could win a game without Starr, Hornung, and Taylor in the lineup?" He said, "Certainly!" I said, "You mean you never had any doubts?" He said, "I told you, certainly!" He was getting red in the face. So I said, "Look, I'm not trying to badger you. Let me ask you this a different way. Did you ever think you'd have to coach a game without them?" So he says, "That's a very stupid question, Mister!"

I really got hot. "Well," I said, "I don't think you coached such a brilliant game, Mister." So he said, "How dare you say that. You don't know a goddamn thing about football!" And I said, "Agreed. And how dare you tell me my question was stupid. You don't know a goddamn thing about journalism. You stick to football and I'll stick to journalism. If you don't want to answer, don't answer." He looked at me and said, "What do you want to know?"

So we went through this thing and he explained the adjustments as sparingly as possible. You could see him thinking that he did not want to tell us everything because some day he might have to play another team or the Colts without Hornung, Taylor, and Starr, and he did not want them to know how he did it. Like there were no game films for the others to study. But he did explain, and I got a good column out of it.

That was on Sunday and I was really steaming and so was he when it broke up. On Monday, there was a call at my office and then it was transfered to my home. I picked up the phone. "Hello. Jerry, I'm sorry if I was out of line yesterday. It was not a smart question, but I think I overstepped my bounds. Okay? Good-bye." Click. He never even identified himself. That was Vincent.

Those were my early dealings with him. Nothing changed a hell of a lot. I think he tried to change very hard, and I think he finally understood the press as part of his job. Although I think he hated that part of his job. On a one-to-one basis, he could be very informative and cooperative.

I've often thought about Vincent and his relationship with the press. You know the press is a very important part of a coach's job. It can be very cruel, very unfair. It can hurt him. The press can be conned by the coach and help him where he doesn't deserve to be helped. It's a many-edged sword. But in terms of Vince and his personality and his absolute paranoia with what he felt was right and what he was going to do, had he started in New York, Chicago, Los Angeles, or Philadelphia, he would not have made it. Not because the press would have driven him out, but because they would have made his life miserable; and secondly, he used the press in Milwaukee and Green Bay as his own public relations firm. He bitched about them and was horrible to them, but goddamn it, he used them for what he wanted in the paper and for what he did not want in the paper. And I want to make it clear that I feel that the writers are not at fault. The fault lies with the publishers of these papers. I can't say with certainty that Vince ever did it, but from being around those writers, you knew that with a phone call, their asses could be fried. And that made a big difference in how they wrote about the Green Bay Packers. But as far as his relationships with the non–Green Bay Packer press, I think he made an effort to understand the writers and I think — in fact, I know I did — the writers tried to think before they asked the question.

He had another misconception and that was that New York had the greatest press in the world. I don't necessarily agree with that. But he did, and he respected a lot of New York writers because of their professionalism. As he got to know other writers from other cities, as he got to know them personally, he began to respect them and that helped him later with the press.

I think he became more understanding of the press and began to go out of his way to be more accessible. But his going out of his way was just standard procedure for another guy. So you really can't measure him against others in the same position. I don't think he ever thought about helping a new or young writer. He feared the young writers, the new guys sent out to cover the team or to do a story on him. He feared them in the same way a veteran player fears the rookie on the squad. You know, the kind of "Is this guy going to make his reputation off me?" type of thinking.

One of the reasons the Packers and Lombardi will be remembered so greatly, this thing called the Lombardi era, is because of the players who were on the team. And I don't mean because of their football talent only. But the press had labeled this team and this time. And after them came the phoney magazine literati and the pseudo-book writers who always come along after the press has discovered something and it becomes fact.

Well, Lombardi had a remarkable group of players. And when he got there, though they were not much as players, they had had those bad years and had acquired the taste of speaking out on whatever they wanted. After all, when you lose year after year, you soon develop a thick skin and a quick tongue. There was no discipline, and guys did whatever the hell they wanted. I remember one writer saying that in those days, the players would take themselves out of the game and put themselves back in whenever they wanted. So the guys he inherited and kept were not reluctant to talk. And since he could not get new players, he had to make those that he had work. Look at them. There was Bill Quinlan, who had a bad reputation but was available so Vince took a chance on him. Henry Jordon, who the Browns didn't want and the same with Willie Davis. Then there was Paul Hornung, who should have been cut by the Packers earlier. Vince, by legend, says he looked at film and made Hornung his halfback. Bull. He had no other backs and if he had, he'd probably have gotten rid of Hornung just on reputation alone. And then Ron Kramer, who one day became the best tight end in football but when Vince got there, he was a bum. And Starr. Nobody in the league thought he'd make it. There was a whole team of misfits, free-swingers, malcontents, failures, and locker-room lawyers.

But he had to go to these guys because he needed a football team, and nobody was going to give him other players. So he told them that he was tough as nails and would trade anyone at the drop of a hat. He threatened them in every way, but as long as they put out on the field, he didn't care what they said in the locker room or to the writers. He worked them so hard it became difficult to interview, since many of the players passed out on the sidelines.

They knew that Vincent was in a hurry to win. Hell, the guy was forty-six years old, and he had never coached in the NFL as the top man. And they knew that he would look away from what they did or said if they could perform, as long as they did not embarrass him or the Packers. So that was the tone of the team as he took it over.

As new people came to the team, as the years and the winning started to come together, they became a part of this locker room. Football players live in the locker room. If you talk to them and if they are honest, the thing they miss most is being with the players in the bus, at the training table, in the locker room or wherever the team is. Nobody misses getting the crap beat out of him. But after they have gone, what they miss is the guys. And so that tone in the locker room is very important to a team. After Vince left and the veterans retired, the coach they had put a clamp on their freedom. I don't know if that is the main reason they never have been a winner since, but it is not the same organization and probably never will be again.

The enormous fear that these guys had for Vince was not a physical fear. Willie Davis said it best to me one night in the Northland hotel before the game with Dallas in 1967. I asked him about this fear and how I could not understand it. I asked him how he could be afraid of a man with a pot belly who ran around and screamed. Willie said, "Look at me. I'm 250 pounds, six-foot four, in great shape, and I could break this man in half. I am not afraid of him. I am afraid of what he can do to us." And then he went on to explain. "His biggest threat is that you are not a Packer."

Now, as I'm listening I'm shaking my head because this sounds like something out of P.S. 107 at halftime where you're told you're not good enough to play for the Black Dragons and represent the blue and gold, or something. But this is something that the man really did. "You're not a Packer, you're garbage. I'll get people who want to be Packers." And Willie said, "In the beginning, you don't pay any attention and you laugh and wonder who in the hell he thinks he's kidding. And then you begin to see guys go and then you begin to think about what it means not to be a Packer. Well, the first thing it means, and this is before the Super Bowls, it means about an extra seven or eight grand a year.

"And you know that he's going to have the Packers in the championship every year so, right away you know it's going to mean you'll lose out on a lot of money if you're not a Packer. Then along comes the Super Bowl and all of a sudden, it means more money than any team has ever won and if you're not a Packer, you are not going to get any of that. So, you understand why it means a lot to be a Packer."

If you hear it explained the way Willie did, you can understand why it means a hell of a lot to be a Packer. A guy can pick up twenty-five or thirty grand extra being a Packer. And they did believe in him and themselves, and that fear really drove them to listen to him.

Another example of their belief in Vincent was Fuzzy Thurston. Before Super Bowl I in Los Angeles, I saw Fuzzy sitting on the balcony looking at the pool that he was not allowed to swim in. Vincent had this thing about swimming and stretching muscles and ruled the pool off-limits. Fuzzy had only seen movies of the Kansas City Chiefs and he had to take on their best player, Buck Bucannan. He seemed very relaxed and when I asked him about the game, he matter of factly said that they would win.

Fuzzy was a typical Green Bay Packer veteran. At that point, all the veterans were getting bald, had a little pot belly; in effect, they were starting to look like me except Vincent would not let them grow a beard. But they still had that great ability; they had been to the mountain so many times that they knew how to handle things.

When Fuzzy said they would win, I asked how he knew. He said, "We have never played them or anybody they have played. We don't know much about them. They may be as good as we are, as players. But we will win because we have the greatest coach there ever was on our side. And I'm not taking anything away from their guy. But not even God himself, coaching Kansas City, is going to beat our man."

The Packers trained for Super Bowl I in Santa Barbara. Lombardi wanted to stay in Green Bay until the week before the game and then stay at Rickey's in Palo Alto where the Packers always stayed, but Rozelle overruled him. This was the first one, and it was going to be the damn best press coverage that the sports world ever saw and both teams would be available. So the Packers came to Santa Barbara.

One day, Jack Murphy of the San Diego paper and I drove up to the Packers camp. The drive was really beautiful. The surf was rolling in and the water was Nile green and the beach was clean. None of that Asbury Park pollution. The hotel was a pretty little place and the pool, which was empty, gave the place a courtyard effect. There was a sailboat on the horizon and it was just perfect.

The first guy I saw was Vincent. He was standing on the porch by himself looking nervous. It was an hour before practice, and he wanted to make sure the bus was on time and he was yelling for Chuck Lane. He was always yelling for Chuck Lane. He blamed Chuck for everything that happened from inclement weather to a leaky toilet. But he said hello and he was really cordial.

I was somewhat surprised that Vincent was so pleasant. There had been a lot of pressure put on him to win this game. Not that he needed any, because he put his own pressure on. But Wellington Mara was writing letters about being the league standard bearer and everyone else in the league and NFL fans all over had been trying to get to him and tell him what they expected. So he wanted to get away from everybody and take his team to his own location. But here he was and here we were and there were a hell of a lot more of us on the way, each day.

Anyway, we said hello, and he kept asking anyone who walked by where Chuck Lane was. Nobody could find Lane. Lane was a bachelor in California, and he knew what he was doing. After saying hello and asking if I'd seen Lane, the next thing he said was, "You can't go to practice." The season was now thirty-eight months old, so I figured I'd live without going to practice. So to change the subject, I said, "Vince, this is a beautiful place." And he said, "Yeah." I said, "No. Really. The guys must like it." He said, "Yeah." So I said again, very cleverly, "This is really beautiful." And he said, "That's the trouble. It's too goddamn beautiful to train for a football game!"

He said it was okay to talk to the players but to make it quick. So off he went looking for Chuck Lane, and I talked to Fuzzy Thurston.

The day before in Long Beach, I was at the Chiefs' camp and talked to Buck Bucannan, the man Fuzzy would be up against. I wanted to do a traditional piece about two guys who were going to go head to head, especially since these two had never played against each other and didn't know anything except what they could get off the films.

Bucannan was a massive man — got to be one of the strongest men ever to have played the game. And if you go back over those films as a fan, you must say it was the most enjoyable matchup in the game. They were just great for each other. They brought out the best in each other. And if there were another dozen or so Bucannans on the Chiefs, the game might have been closer.

I remember after the game, a veteran of the Chiefs came out of the locker, one of the guys that was with them when they were the Dallas Texans. He said, "I just feel like I got into a fight in a back alley. I've been stomped. And I'm glad I was able to get out of the alley, alive." That was pretty much the attitude of most of the Kansas City players. Except Bucannan. He was screaming in the locker room still in his uniform about a half hour after the game was over.

He wanted to play them again the next day. And he meant it. He kept saying, "I'm sorry, this team is not 35–10 better than us. I know it. I want to play them right now." He was livid and he was not blaming anyone else. But he felt justified. He had played an even game with the guy he was up against and that guy, Fuzzy Thurston, was as good a guard as there was in the game.

That game, I felt the Kansas City players worried about the Packers; and mostly, they worried about Lombardi. I really think so. No player admits that, but the Lombardi mystique was what they were playing. Remember that they had never, never played a game against him. There were few men in their league that had ever played against him. They had seen the team on television or caught a film clip or read a story and I know that several of them had read *Run to Daylight!* and were very impressed with him but none of them had played against him. And in the coffee shop before the game, about three days before, I sat with E. J. Holeb.

Now E. J. Holeb was as good a football player as they had in that league. He'd been a number-one draft choice of the NFL also. He was as good as there was in either league. And he said, "Look at me. My palms are sweating." And they were! And I asked him, why? "Well, I think of the money and that's part of it," he said, "and I think of the prestige, and that's part of it. But playing these guys is most of it."

But I think he had it in reverse order. And I don't mean it was fear by any stretch of the imagination. I can't believe that E. J. Holeb would be afraid of Godzilla. But it was the questioning of the unknown. Do we, the Chiefs, really know anything about Lombardi and these guys? And they wondered if anybody could be as good as these guys were supposed to be.

Jerry Izenberg   171

Before the game, there were terrific demands on both coaches by the press. They had them out there two weeks before the game and by the time I got there, at the start of the last week, there really was not much different that could be asked. Vincent was very charming and everyone commented about how accommodating he was, and what a change there was in him. Well, one thing Vincent was not about to do was give the Chiefs anything that could be used to get them up. Also, he was well thought of by the press because he kept to himself except when he had to be in L.A.

I remember while I was in New York, before going out there, I saw a picture coming over the wire and I could not believe it. Here was Vincent, with two girls in bathing suits, holding a football, smiling and happy. I never found out how that happened, and Chuck Lane swears that Vincent gave approval. It must have been for an old friend.

I guess that shows how relaxed Vince was. Maybe he was agreeable because he wanted to keep the pressure off the players. The very fact that he made that comment after the game that the Chiefs were not as good as the Cowboys or Colts, that they were middle-level NFL or something like that indicated how relaxed he was. Then everybody jumped on him for saying it.

Of course, the game did not prove anything. The Chiefs lost 35–10. How many other teams did the Packers beat that year by that score? Vincent's clubs were not high-scoring teams, and there is no doubt in my mind that they had to work for that thirty-five points. But given the same intensity of that game and put the Bears on the field, they might have scored eighty points if he had turned them loose.

I think he was very patient at Super Bowl I; at Super Bowl II, he was even more so. His biggest problems were behind him then — the Colts, Rams, and Cowboys. Oakland was nothing.

They played so many great games. I was out in Green Bay for the first Giants game, and I saw him the night before in a restaurant with Marie and friends and he seemed very relaxed. I can't tell you anything about the after-game celebration in the locker room because I was assigned to cover the Giants.

In 1962, they came to Yankee Stadium to play the Giants again in that terrible wind and cold and they won, but there was nothing special in Lombardi's press meeting after the game. One of the writers tried to draw him into discussing the viciousness of the game and he suddenly got very surly and was not cooperative at all after that. There had been some controversy. Jimmy Taylor and Sam Huff tried to kill each other and the Giants' defense was gang-tackling Taylor all the time. In a fit of rage, Taylor, after he had been tackled on the frozen ground, bit an exposed calf and he heard this scream, looked up and saw Modjeleski and said, "Sorry, Mo, I thought you were Sam." But that's the kind of game it was. And Vince did not have much to say.

I was out there in 1965 when they played the Colts in the playoff and it should have been an easy game for them since Tom Matte was playing quarterback for the Colts. But after the first play, Starr was on the sidelines and the two teams beat hell out of each other, and the Packers finally won on a Chandler field goal. The Packers were a very battered team and the Cleveland Browns were coming in to play them for the title. Since I was already there, I spent Christmas week in Green Bay!

There were only four of us in the hotel in town and I went every day to the Packers offices. It really was a pleasant time. I wanted to be home; there really wasn't much to talk about but surprisingly, I enjoyed it. The press conferences were delightful. I remember someone saying to Vince, "Well, now, how do you decide to go for the field goal?" And he says, "I say to myself, I think I'll kick a field goal." So now, since I asked the first dumb question, I'll be creative and go back and reconstruct this moment of crisis on the sideline against Baltimore. So I say, "I mean, like what are the mechanics? What's going on on the bench?" He says, "I turn around and I yell, 'field-goal team.' "

He was quite affable. But a couple of years later, I was back for their third in a row against Dallas and I remember his being quite depressed. He was upset with the press, in particular the piece that Leonard Schecter had written about him in *Esquire*. We talked about this, and it's the only time I ever remember his trying to make a case for himself. Always, he assumed that the case was there and you were too dumb to see it, and so he would just ignore you until you understood him. And if you never did, he did not care.

The piece was very strong; it dealt with Vince's language on the practice field and the "grass drills." The biggest thing that had upset him was that his mother had called him in tears. I'm sure that she had not read it but someone had told her about it, especially the part about his language. This was an old Italian family and she was quite concerned about the image of her son.

He asked me that day to wait after the press conference was over and we sat and we talked. He said, "I don't know what to do. I mean, if you don't talk to people you're damned. If you do, you're damned. Here I am. I open up our place to a guy and look at what he does to me." He was very hurt by it. And he had a point. What could he do about a guy like Schecter, how could he protect himself?

I told him that he had brought this on himself. I frankly said that he antagonized everybody in the world, for no reason whatsoever and that you've got to learn to treat each writer as an individual. You can hate a guy or you can bar a guy, I told him, but you can't turn on everybody over this incident. And I told him that this was a case where a guy does a hatchet job on you, an unfair piece of reporting, and yet he's going to get a sympathetic ear from a lot of guys you have been unfair to.

We sat there for about forty minutes talking about it, and I have never seen him so emotionally distraught. He did not yell or scream. He talked very quietly about the injustice of it. He felt very, very deeply about it. I don't think he ever got over it. But I do think that after that, he did approach people just a little bit differently. He handled the *Esquire* incident very well: he marked it down as a hatchet job, did not issue any statements, and publicly ignored the whole thing.

But it really upset him. And he kept referring to his mother and saying that it was times like this that made him want to quit.

I had no knowledge of Vince's illness until he checked into the hospital in the summer of 1970. But he did undergo a major personality change after he beat Dallas and then won the second Super Bowl in a row. Of course, he now was a football coach without a football team to coach. And as much as he loved golf, he couldn't play that every day. He'd watch another guy coaching his team and he'd see the team going badly and he died a million deaths up in that glass booth, trying to stay out of Bengston's way. But his simply being there made Bengston's life difficult and Vince knew it.

If there were any signs that Vincent was ill before he went to Washington, I don't know of them. And if Vince thought there might be a problem, he had probably convinced himself that it was not valid or given himself some explanation for whatever he thought might be wrong. Or maybe some doctor had given him an explanation that satisfied him. Remember, Lombardi was a man who would not look at his health as a problem. He was just too strong willed and too sure of himself to admit there really might be something wrong. And there was no doctor in the world who was about to tell Vince Lombardi to have a complete checkup.

He did go into that first Washington training camp as the old Lombardi. Very much so. He got down and blocked against Walter Rock, the big tackle. He ran around hitting people with his baseball cap, challenging people. He was almost maniacal in his approach to it, but he was enjoying himself in an insane way. It was vintage Lombardi and any Packer who could have seen that camp would have been right at home.

I noticed the change after the first season with the Redskins. It was like he had returned for a second life. I must say that he seemed very, very happy. He was mellower, he was no less intense than he had been. But when I was covering a couple of their games, I noticed that he seemed to put the game behind him sooner than he did in Green Bay. You could talk to the guy more. Now his wars with the press seemed almost a game to him, and he was enjoying himself with them because before these meetings had almost seemed like vendettas.

I think he saw himself doing something that nobody had ever done before. He was coming back, taking over another terrible team, and he was going to win more Super Bowl games. No doubt about it. He thought he'd coach for a thousand years.

In retrospect, after that first season in Washington, I think he knew he was not well. He had changed in so many ways. And I don't mean physically. I would see him at the league meetings in New York, and he was so much more interested in what was going on in the country than he was in talking about football. He had very strong feelings about America, strong feelings about injustice, and strong feelings that the American system would always work everything out.

This was the time when kids were burning flags and there was a great deal of questioning about our system and its values — not only by the kids, but by many people. Vietnam was still going on. It was during these times that we talked and no one will ever convince me that Vincent did not see himself moving into the political arena and bringing back the American values as he saw them.

He had taken to wearing an American flag in his lapel, which I had never seen before, and he had begun to make speeches about America and football. When you talked about the war in Vietnam, it was "my country, right or wrong," and you felt that he felt that he was not doing enough for America.

Of course, this is perfect hindsight, but it really looked like this was a man putting his house in order. He had gone into many business ventures and he was thinking of what would be left for his wife and children, when and if anything happened. Now this may not seem strange to normal people, to have wills and insurance and things like that, but as long as I had known Vincent, football was everything and he never looked past that.

I always thought of Vincent as a little bit left of center, socially and politically. He really was concerned with social injustice. He fought very actively for racial integration within the league, and there was complete integration on his teams. In the town of Green Bay, it was the same. He stood up when he did not have to stand up.

I noticed this at the league meetings. They have this thing where one afternoon the coaches sit in little rooms and the writers come around and visit and it's all very informal. Anyway, I saw this change there, with Vincent. I remember discussing the Vietnam War with him. I remember discussing America and kids with him. I remember his deploring the lack of discipline within the country, and I remember that every time a guy would drop by and talk football, as soon as he left, Vincent would go right back to the subject of America.

And also at this time, there was the player's union, which he considered a threat to the game. And it seemed that he felt that he personally had to force a showdown over this. Somehow, all these things seemed to blend in his mind — America, discipline, order, the union. Looking back it seems now that what he was saying was, "Okay, I've got enough strength left, let me get this thing settled, this thing with the players." Because he really did love football. He felt a debt to football, and he felt it was for the good of the game that they get this thing settled. He was willing to fight any battle, fight any lawyer, take on anybody for the good of football, or what he saw as best for the game.

But another side of him never changed. If you were to ask me to describe quickly what I see in my mind when you say Lombardi, the first image would be of him screaming. There he is standing on the sideline in that silly sun visor they wear on sunny days in Texas or Los Angeles early in the year. And he's screaming and hollering and his neck is red and the veins are jumping out and you wonder what in hell could have caused that reaction. That's one way I remember him.

Another way I remember him would be in a place like Manuche's. He would be standing and the bar would be very crowded, and somewhere in the room would be his brother Joe. There was a certain stability about this. He liked having his brother around. He liked screaming at Joe, but it was that "one of us and one of them" thing again. Eddie Breslin would be there. He did not like to sit, especially with the predinner crowd. He wanted to be able to see everyone in the place. He would probably be talking about Fordham or talking about some place they had gone to on the road for a game, and he saw this singer and she was great. The singer might be someone like Sophie Tucker. And the thing I always remember about times like this is that his laughter would fill the room and everybody would smile no matter where you were in the room.

These places were always where he felt comfortable. You could take him to the finest of restaurants, and he loved good food, and he'd laugh and smile and sign the menu for the fans who came around and he'd have a nice time. But he'd have a *great* time in a place where he knew every one of the people. That meant much more to him than the times he'd go out in Green Bay and have everybody bow to him. He liked the deference and the people, but this was different. Here, he was first among equals. There, in Green Bay, he was emperor. But here, he really liked being with his equals, because he could make those equals also understand that he was first among them. And he pushed all the time he could into those moments because they were so few and so relaxed.

The third thing that comes to mind when you say Lombardi to me is the day of the funeral. Labor Day in New York. I remember parking the car and walking up Fifth Avenue, and you could shoot a cannon off in Manhattan and not hit anybody. Then I got to the church, St. Patrick's, and the police barriers were already up. It was about three hours before the funeral and there were already people standing there, behind those police barriers.

Now there were not any ten thousand people there. That's part of the legend because gross exaggeration helps build legends. I would guess there might have been fifteen hundred people, maybe two thousand. But most of them had been standing there since early morning. I walked up to a man standing behind the wooden horse across Fifth Avenue from the front of St. Patrick's, and I asked him why he was there. He was alone and he had come from Ohio and all he said was, "I simply wanted to be here."

He was not crying or sobbing. A lot of people were. He had driven all night from his home in Ohio, and I can't remember the name of the town but it was middle-sized and somewhere in the center of the state. He looked tired, but I'll never forget his explaining it so beautifully, "I simply wanted to be here."

And I remember the stubbornness of the man. I had written a book called *The Rivals*. I autographed a copy and sent it to him. A couple of days later he calls me at home and without saying hello or who he is, starts in on the book. "Jerry, I just read *The Rivals*. Greatest book I ever read. I grew up on those Giants and Dodgers baseball games and I hope everybody in the country gets a copy." Now I'm not modest but I know the book is not the greatest so I say, "Thanks, Vince, but it's not the greatest book ever written." He's all over me saying that he thinks it's the greatest and he's going to tell everyone to buy it. Somehow, I'm protesting that it is not the greatest, and he's getting madder and madder and telling me to be quiet, that he says it's the best and that's that. So I say, "How would you know? All you ever read is a missal and the Packer playbook!" And he says, "This is a great book. I don't care what you say. I say it's a great book and it is." And he hangs up.

Mention Lombardi and I remember Baltimore and the scene after the game in 1967. You have to understand the nature of the rivalry between these two teams. They were playing some of the greatest games against each other in all of football. In fact, they were the greatest games. There was nothing like them and for pure violence, they were classics. There was the game in the fog in Baltimore, with Hornung scoring the five touchdowns, and the playoff game in Green Bay. They were forever playing each other for the conference championship because fate and an appalling ignorance of geography by the NFL owners had put them in the same division.

So now they came into Baltimore and they lost the ball game in the most incredible way. The Packers were winning 10–0 in the fourth quarter, and the Colts scored with about a minute and a half left in the game. And the Colts missed the extra point! So it does not take any genius to figure out what the Colts have to do. The score is 10–6 Packers and if you did not say on-side kick, join the Packers players. Because that's what happened. With everybody in the world knowing what was going to happen, the Baltimore kicker tried an on-side kick. Now these are the Green Bay Packers, the greatest team in football with the greatest coach the world has ever seen. And the kick went about *thirty yards* downfield among all those Packers, and they miss it and a Colt falls on it. Next play, Unitas hits his receiver and it's seven more for the home team, and I suddenly do not want to go to that press conference and talk to Lombardi. It was the kind of game that Green Bay never loses, and when I saw him downstairs, he was livid.

You could say his language would peel the paint off the walls, but there is no paint on the walls of Memorial Stadium in Baltimore. You're lucky to have walls. But he is screaming so much the stone is starting to chip. And here comes this guy into the room with the rest of the press, and he has this copy of a book written by Bart Starr. And he starts yelling, "Coach, Coach." And he's asking questions about the game and Lombardi is looking at the guy and you know he is not too happy to answer anybody's questions. But this guy keeps asking about the on-side kick and Lombardi is answering through his teeth, which are smoking from the way he's grinding them. Finally, Lombardi says, "Wait a minute. Wait a minute. Who do you work for? What paper are you with?" And Vince is really upset. And the guy says, "Oh, I don't work for any paper. I just wonder if you'll autograph my Bart Starr book for me."

Lombardi starts screaming, "Lane! Chuck Lane! Lane, get this guy out of here! Lane! Lane! Where in hell is Chuck Lane!" Well, I'm laughing so hard I have to leave or else. And Lane is upstairs in the press box where the publicity man is supposed to be. But he blamed Lane for that guy getting past the guard and never forgave him. But then he also blamed Lane for not covering the on-side kick.

One of the greatest Lombardi stories I ever heard — and now that we have talked about the Colts, I have to tell it to you — is the Alex Hawkins story. Alex Hawkins was a back drafted by the Packers out of South Carolina. You must understand that Alex Hawkins is a free spirit. He also has a good reputation as a football player and Vince makes him second- or third-round choice. Alex Hawkins is going to do what Alex Hawkins wants to do, and if you ask him, he'll concede that.

Now Lombardi has a rule, no wives in training camp. Hawkins not only shows up with a wife, he shows up with a pregnant wife. A very, very pregnant wife. When Lombardi hears that Hawkins is there with his wife, he blows at Hawkins about "You were told," etc. Now, when he sees the wife and sees that she is about to whelp at any second, he does not know what to do. Finally, Lombardi decides to bring Mrs. Hawkins to his home and gives her to Marie to take care of. So Mrs. Hawkins is living with Mrs. Lombardi and Mr. Hawkins is training under Mr. Lombardi.

And Alex is catching hell. First of all, he's doing everything wrong, which all rookies do in Vince's camps. Secondly, when Vince chews him out, Alex answers back! Now it has gotten to the point where Hawkins has developed a rash and he's scratching the rash, and every time Vince yells at him the rash blooms, and when it blooms he scratches it, and every time he scratches it the rash bleeds. Now they are wearing T-shirts this day and the blood is soaking through his practice jersey. The rash is up around the shoulder.

This goes on day after day. The team is in De Pere, Wisconsin, and Alex only gets to talk to his wife on the phone. She's telling him how wonderful the Lombardis are and he hates Lombardi's guts and he is sick from the rash. Hawkins is making more and more mistakes and Lombardi has made up his mind that he is going to trade him. He thinks Hawkins can play for somebody, but not for him because of his attitude. There are some other guys as good, so Vince will try to put him with another club. But he is not going to trade him until after the baby comes!

Practice is getting worse and worse. Hawkins knows that it is all over because Lombardi is not even bothering to scream at him anymore. He just ignores Alex. One day during practice, Vince calls Alex over and tells him that his wife has gone into labor and is at the hospital with Marie. He gives Alex the rest of the day off and when the baby is born, Alex is traded to the Colts.

Mention Lombardi to me and I remember the time Bob Skoronski was at an ice-cream parlor in Green Bay with his children. This is in the early summer before camp had opened and they had just won another championship. Bob likes ice-cream and after getting cones for his children, he orders one for himself. The family walks out to the parking lot, and as Bob is walking toward his car, he sees Vince pull in and he knows the coach has spotted him. So he turns and waves to Vince with one hand and in the other is the ice-cream cone, which he promptly hides behind his back. Now here is this huge man, maybe thirty-two or thirty-three, cocaptain of the World Champion Green Bay Packers, hiding an ice-cream cone from his coach! And it is not even in season!

Why is Lombardi still such an influence today? Well, for one thing, he set standards that have not been excelled. In any business, there are measuring sticks and in his business, he and his team are still the standard against which all teams and coaches will be measured. Two Super Bowls in a row, five NFL titles in seven years (three of them in a row), six Western Conference titles; all of these are records that may never be matched.

Secondly, he had a great edge coaching in Green Bay. Tiny, little loveable Green Bay. That's very important because here comes the little town against the big town, and everybody is really rooting against the big town. And making this small town the football capital of America adds to the myth.

And I think the route that Lombardi took to success made an important contribution to the legend. You know, by-passed for coaching jobs at the college level, not getting his chance until he was forty-six years old.

People like winners and his teams were that and they were colorful. He was colorful in many ways. He gave the impression of being a general and that appealed to many people. It is the American dream come true. Here is the grandson of Italian immigrants of humble beginnings, the playing of a sport like football, the struggle in the backwoods before hitting the big time, all of that contributes to the legend and keeps it alive.

If you ask me why Lombardi is still so viable today, I'd have to tell you that I'm a bad choice to answer that. For me, he's important because he taught me about dedication to goals and things like that. I could compare parts of my own life to his. Actually, I've been too close to him to be objec-

A winner, Willie Davis, #87, of th Packers, smiles as he goes off the fiel after the Packers won Super Bowl The unhappy player, #86, is Buc Bucannan of the Kansas City Chief (*John E. Biever*)

tive. To understand why he is viable, you should go out on the street and stop twenty people and ask them about Vince Lombardi. And I'm sure you would be amazed by their answers. Maybe someone like me could interpret the answers, but I've just been too close to the whole situation and to the man.

I think that — and maybe this is his appeal to a lot of people — he represents in his field of endeavor, as near perfection as you can get. And since this field is pro football and since pro football has become so dominant and so much a part of America, he is even more of a factor than the president of General Motors. Even though the president of General Motors can have a huge impact on my life and everyone's through the economy.

But Vincent was dealing in an area where people could watch him and understand what was happening, and he was the best in his business. And for that, he had enormous impact.

Also, I think he would have been extremely successful in politics. I would have loved him for a mayor. I would have been fascinated by him as a governor. And I think I'd have been scared s—less of him as a president.

There will always be this image of Lombardi yelling. It cannot be called inaccurate. *(Vernon J. Biever)*

180

THE SPORT OF THE '60s

TIME

THE WEEKLY NEWSMAGAZINE

GREEN BAY COACH
VINCE LOMBARDI

The Packers were voted the team of the decade (the 1960's) and this drawing of Vince Lombardi appeared on the cover of *Time* magazine in December of 1962, just before the championship game with the Giants. (*Copyright Time Inc.*)

8

Three in a Row

VINCE LOMBARDI was always aware of his place in the history of football. He wanted to leave a legacy of victories that would be unmatched in the game. And he did. No coach has ever won so many games over the same period of time as Lombardi. But that was not the most important thing to him. He wanted to win more championships than anyone else. He knew that many teams and coaches would win many games, maybe even more than he and his Packers. But he was damn well sure that he was going to win the most championships and his ultimate goal was the winning of three NFL titles in a row. No team and no coach had ever done that before.

The team he had to achieve that third title was not the powerhouse of 1961–62. Nor was it the jewel of a machine that won the first Super Bowl. The names may have been the same in most positions, but age and years were beginning to take their toll. And he knew it. He knew that if he did not make it in 1967, he'd have to rebuild the whole structure and start all over. So he just made sure they couldn't fail to win that third championship in a row.

He drove them to that championship. He played without Hornung and Jimmy Taylor. And in the early part of the season, not only did he lose to the Colts on an on-side kick, he also lost his starting backfield. Still, nothing was going to stop them. And by sheer will power, he took them all the way. Indeed, this may have taken everything out of him. It was his best coaching season.

When Chuck Mercein played high school football at New Trier in suburban Chicago, he made All State, along with Dick Butkus. He went to Yale and became a star in the Ivy League. Unlike Butkus, who became a star at Illinois and later with the Chicago Bears, Mercein never became a "star" in the National Football League. But hundreds of great players in the history of the NFL never got what Chuck Mercein has, a championship ring with three diamonds across the top. In fact, only thirty-nine other players have that ring. Mercein was not a superstar in pro football; but he became one on the frozen turf of Lambeau Field on the 31st of December in 1967. His star shone briefly but brightly and the three diamonds testify as to how brightly it shone that day at 13 degrees below zero.

CHUCK MERCEIN

In 1964, I was the second-round draft pick of the New York Giants. Tucker Fredrickson was their first choice; in fact, he was the first choice of the whole NFL draft that year. I was the twenty-ninth player picked. Also, I was drafted by the Buffalo team in the AFL, but at that time they held a secret draft before the season had ended. They were trying to get to college players before the NFL draft.

The Bills people came to New Haven and offered me a lot of money. It was very tempting because I was broke, living in a third-floor walk-up apartment, and my wife was working while I went to school. I told them there was no way I was going to sign because I wanted to keep my amateur status so I could compete for Yale in track that coming spring. I was a shotputter, and I was ranked in the top ten in the country.

I decided on the Giants and signed a very good contract. I got a three-year, no-cut contract and the total package was a lot of money at that time. That was also the year Joe Namath signed with the Jets and the big money was starting to be paid to the rookies. Nobody was sure who was worth what, but I got a big bonus and felt I was paid quite well.

Allie Sherman was the coach of the Giants at that time. I don't have too many friendly thoughts about Sherman. At the time when I joined the Giants, Allie had traded some great old Giants veterans, like Sam Huff and Rosey Grier, and he was trying to remake the Giants. Things were not going too well when I joined the team.

We had one good year while I was there. We were 7–7, and I led the team in rushing, even though I was hurt quite a bit. But Allie was getting more and more frustrated and frantic, and he was starting to do a lot of strange things and was acting in an emotional way. It was not a happy period for me and for the people of New York.

Wellington Mara was a very fine man. He was fair to me. Later he was helpful in getting me to the Packers, but the only thing at that time was that he gave Allie total control. He was not in the forefront of management, as far as I could tell.

The Giants were a first-class organization in terms of travel arrangements and equipment and things of that nature. It's just at this time that I was there, they were floundering, frustrated with their won–lost record, trying to find a replacement for Y. A. Tittle and to rebuild the team. It was a team in flux, and we would have Gary Wood at quarterback one time, and then Earl Morrell and Fran Tarkenton came in, but I was only there for a few weeks while Fran was with the Giants. There was a lot of uncertainty about who was staying and who was going, and this contributed to the mistrust of Allie and the organization.

Being a rookie and then a second-year man, I was completely enthusiastic about playing. I was very discouraged about not playing more than I did when I always performed well. I'd get in a game and get eighty-five yards, one hundred yards, and then I would not play for a while. They did have Tucker and he had a good rookie year, but he got hurt the next year and I got my chance.

And I was in the top ten in the league in rushing before I got hurt. My injury was a strange happening. We were playing the St. Louis Cardinals in Yankee Stadium, and we were down on the infield part of the playing field. During the football season, they lay sod over the infield dirt. Gary Wood threw a swing pass to me, but he underthrew me by a good five yards. I tried to scramble back to recover the ball, because I was not sure whether it was an incomplete pass or a lateral. The play was long dead because it was a lousy pass.

But as I was going after the ball, the turf under my feet gave way, and I was on all fours trying to get the ball. Larry Stallings, the Cardinal linebacker, had a cast on his arm and he teed off on me as I was on the ground and hit me in the kidneys. They swelled up right away, and I had blood in my urine for quite awhile. The right side of my back looked like a football was sticking out, and it was very painful. Of course, I did not play much the rest of the season.

I never really got back with the Giants after that. I came to summer camp the next year, 1967, but never did play a lot during the exhibition season. I had made the team, the forty-man roster was set and I was one of the forty. But during the last exhibition, our middle linebacker was hurt and Allie Sherman got Vince Costello from the Browns to replace him. Since I had a no-cut contract and a good salary, Sherman figured nobody would pick me up, and he had to make room for Costello so he told me I'd be put on the taxi squad.

So I just languished for a few weeks. And to keep in playing shape, I volunteered to go and play with the Westchester Bulls awhile. I was really glad I did that because it kept me in "game" shape. I was upset, naturally, and my pride was hurt that I was in a lower league. But it was good that I did that because when Lombardi called a few weeks later, I was ready.

I had been a kicker in college and Sherman brought me back up with the Giants one more time. We were playing the Steelers and I had this groin injury which limited my abilities as a kicker. I told that to Allie, but he wanted me to do the extra points and field goals anyway. I had not kicked in months and I could not lift my leg above my knee. Sherman told me on the plane going to Pittsburgh that if I missed a field goal or extra point, I'd be gone again. How's that for building confidence? This is the kind of rationale he ran the team with. And as it turned out, I made a short field goal and an extra point. But on the extra point, we had an infraction and we were pushed back fifteen yards; then I was kicking from the 24-yard line and I blew it! And I knew right then, as I came back to the bench that that was it. The next Monday he told me he was putting me on waivers again, and I told him I never wanted to play for him again. I told him I was not a kicker but a runner, but he did not care. Nobody was doing anything running for them anyway, and I felt I could do better but he did not care.

When I left, even though it was the third year of my "no-cut," and I always hoped I'd play for the Giants again, I knew it was all over for me in New York. I knew also that I'd not go back down and play for the Bulls.

I had played in the College All-Star game for Otto Graham against the Cleveland Browns and had had a good game, catching a touchdown pass from John Huarte and kicking a field goal and coming in second in the voting for

Most Valuable Player. And I only knew one other pro coach personally, besides Sherman, and that was Graham. He was coach of the Washington Redskins at the time so I called him.

He said he was very interested in talking to me and would I come down so he could have a look at me and see if I was all right physically. I got down there and worked out for a few days and he said, "Great." He said he wanted to sign me, but that he was not quite ready for me for the upcoming Sunday. So it was done except that he did not sign me to play.

I came back to New York and I told my wife that we were going to Washington and I was going to play for the Skins. I was pretty happy about it. She packed the car and we were ready to drive down to Washington.

I did not know this, but that Sunday that I did not play for the Redskins, the Packers were playing in Baltimore against the Colts. In that game, always a brutal battle, the Packers lost both starting running backs, Jim Grabowski and Elijah Pitts. And lost them for the season. Often when Lombardi and the Packers were on the East Coast for the game, Vince would give Well Mara a call or vice-versa, just to say hello. This time, after the Colts game, Lombardi called Mara and told him about losing his starting backfield! He was upset, to say the least, and he had only one healthy running back left, Donny Anderson.

What transpired is hearsay but it seems that Mara told Vince that I was on waivers. He did not know that I had been working out with the Redskins. The way I hear it is that Well gave Vince a good recommendation about me. I had had a good game against the Packers one exhibition season so Lombardi knew who I was.

Coach Lombardi called me at home that night and I was shocked. You know, it isn't every night that Vince Lombardi calls you and all I could do was say "Hello." He told me the situation about Pitts and Grabowski and said, "We are going to go to the Super Bowl again and we have a great team, and I think you can help us right now and I want you to come out here right now. Get on the first plane you can get to Green Bay and we'll sign you when you arrive." No nonsense! Bing, bing, bing — right on the line. And I said, "Well, I've been down to Washington and they want me to sign." There was a slight pause and I immediately made up my mind, without consulting anyone I said, "I'll be on the next plane." I got off the phone and said to my wife, "Unpack the car. We're not going to Washington. I'm going to Green Bay."

I wanted to be there so much I caught the last plane out of New York to Green Bay by way of Milwaukee. Pat Peppler, the director of player personnel, met me and took me to a motel because it was very late. Next day I came to the offices and met the Coach. He was very businesslike. He was very nice and complimentary. He said he was happy to have me and reiterated that he thought I could help them right away. He asked about my contract, said fine, they would match it with the playoff money as a bonus.

Forrest Gregg was the first player I met. He came up and shook my hand and said, "I'm really pleased to see you. You can really help us." It was great. Bart Starr was great; they all were. There was immediate acceptance by everyone. This was the most wonderful experience in my life. Here was a team of veteran, many-time champions, guys that had been together for a long time, and they were just great. I felt wanted and comfortable with them.

I took the playbook home and I studied it like crazy. The system was very much like the Giants system, because Lombardi had put in the Giants offense when he was there and they had not changed it that much since he left. And that was eight years earlier. So there wasn't that difficulty in getting the plays down.

I had three days of practice with the team, and then we went to Milwaukee to play the Browns. They had a good team and the game was to be a good test for the Packers. Well, we won 56–7, and I played about half the game and did well. What an experience. Just a few weeks earlier I was with the Giants, who were losing something like fifteen in a row, and suddenly, I'm playing with a team that wins 56–7! These guys were great.

After that, I played more and more. Ben Wilson had come to the Packers from the Rams that summer; he was the other fullback. Ben had some injury problems so we split the position. I played on the special teams also. In fact, Coach wanted me to return kickoffs if anything happened to Herb Adderley, who teamed with Travis Williams as our kickoff return men. I was amused and I asked, "Why me?" And he said, "I think you can do it. I've seen you catch them before and you have the speed, because when you played us, you returned them against us." I was very surprised because I thought nobody ever remembered that I returned kickoffs in the NFL. But he did.

Before a couple of big games, he'd come up to me and say, "Remember, we have all the confidence in the world in you. You can do the job and get it done. Just do the best you can do, not any more." Just the opposite from the "If you don't do it, you're gone" kind of attitude I'd left in New York. It was a great feeling.

This man was the most fair man I have ever met in terms of handling people. He could be caustic and rough when he felt it was needed. He could be terribly hard on you. He was very big on discipline and did not allow for mental mistakes. He expected 110 percent out of you and if you did not give it, you caught hell. But you gave it. And you played hurt. I played more hurt there than I would have playing somewhere else. It was just expected of me and all of us. In that Cleveland game, I came up with a hip-pointer. I never even told him. I never even went into the training room about it, and with an injury like that, you sneeze and you think the pain will never stop. I played the next week. I had a shoulder separation and never missed a game. It was minor in that the pain wasn't that bad, but I could not raise my arm more than three or four inches. He got that out of his players. There were not too many guys in that training room or that whirlpool.

The players themselves exuded tremendous confidence. You never went into a game with them not believing that they would not win. There was never any doubt. That game against the Rams in Milwaukee and that last drive against Dallas — there was never any doubt. I never looked around and thought that we were not going to win. There just was never any doubt on the field, in the huddle, or on the sideline. And because they felt like that, I felt the same way.

I struck up good friendships with the players. Marv Fleming and I became good friends. Jim Grabowski was very helpful and not the least bit jealous that I was playing and he was injured. The assistant coaches were very proficient and helpful, but Vince was just such an overwhelming factor that they did not have much influence on the club. That's why Phil Bengston had such a rough time after he took over. They worked for the man just like we did; he did not have a favorite assistant nor did I ever know him to socialize with them.

The first time I met the whole team was the Tuesday morning after I arrived in Green Bay. And that was the weekly film reviewing day. I had no idea of what was to come. I had not played yet nor had I practiced with them; I was the new kid on the block. I had met some in the locker room the day before, and Gregg and Starr had said hello, but this was the first time I was with the whole group. Coach introduced me to the team and said how happy they were to have me and that I'll be a big help. I sat down, the lights were turned off, and the movie projector started.

These films were of the last Sunday game against the Colts, where the Packers blew a 10–0 lead in the last quarter and were beaten on an on-side kick recovery. It was also the game where the starting running backs were put out for the season. So everyone was very tense. Wow! I have never been through anything like it before. Marv Fleming had had a particularly bad day. I had never met Marv Fleming at this time but he was six-foot five and 245 pounds and one of the best tight ends in the game. And Lombardi was on him so bad, so much that he had Fleming about in tears. Lombardi's voice kept getting higher and higher, and it was excruciatingly painful just to know what Fleming was going through! I just could not help but think, "My God, what am I in for here?"

He got so pissed off at Fleming that he turned on the guy who was playing behind Fleming, Allen Brown, and started chewing him out. He started on Brown and Brown had not even gotten into the game. He said, "Brown, you should be ashamed of yourself, letting that man beat you out of the starting job. He's terrible and that makes you even worse!"

No one ever escaped. He'd be all over Jerry Kramer if he missed a block, even Forrest Gregg, the receivers, any and all. Except Bart. I don't think I ever heard him criticize Bart, ever, in any kind of team meetings. Maybe he did it when they had their private pregame and postgame meetings, but never before the team. Bart was sorta special to him.

It was not more than two weeks later that I made my first mistake, my first big game mistake. I was on the punting team, protecting the punter. As the up-back, I was supposed to pick up anybody who broke through on my side. This was the Rams game in Los Angeles. We had already won our division and this game meant nothing in the standings, but he told us before the game that we damn well better win. He said we were on national television and this game was for pride. He wanted the nation to see the Green Bay Packers as the best team in football. He wanted to win that game. It was a great game and we are leading with less than two minutes to go, 24–20.

The Rams rushed eleven guys and blocked a Donny Anderson punt. I made an assignment mistake and so did four or five others. Anyway, they scored and we lost.

That Monday, I went over to the locker room. In Green Bay, unlike other towns, the players would go over to the stadium, get their mail, maybe have a sauna or meet and go out for a beer. It's the off day in the players' routine and with the Packers, because we were so close, most of the players would just meet at the stadium. I was hurt a little bit and was sitting in the whirlpool and he caught me. There was no place for me to hide, and he let me have it. "Jesus Christ, Mercein, you did not hit anybody!" He berated the hell out of me, and I just kept sliding deeper and deeper into the water, hoping I'd just drown. He knew how bad I felt; I just dreaded the next day when he was going to show the films.

On Tuesday, he yelled at almost everyone on that punt team. And then, almost as an aside, he said, "Mercein, you did not get your assignment either but don't feel bad, you haven't been here that long. It wasn't your fault, it was everybody's." And he took me from being a hundred miles below the surface of the earth to feeling like a human being again. It was a super psyche job.

We played our ass off in that game when it was just for pride. The Rams had to win or the Colts would have taken the title. Next week, the Rams killed the Colts and won their division and everybody was hailing them as the team of the future, saying that we were old and through.

On my ring, the one with the three diamonds that signify the three NFL titles in a row, there is the phrase "Run to Win." Vince took that from one of St. Paul's epistles, about there being many runners in a race but there can be only one winner so "run to win." And this was the theme of the speech he gave us before the Rams playoff game in Milwaukee that year. He talked about the fact that even though we had won before and had many championships, there was still going to be only one winner that Saturday and it should be us. It was a very emotional speech.

He never overplayed his skills as an orator. He was a great orator. But he would not give you a talk every day of the week. He maybe would not say one thing for two or three days, I mean in an inspirational manner. But then, all of a sudden before practice, he'd walk in and call everybody together and he'd give us a twenty-minute speech that just knocked your eyeballs out. And that was all you needed till the game.

We never had any difficulty getting up for the games. We had the same general theme all along: that we were the best team, we had the best players, and if we did our job properly, we'd win. We knew that we would not make mistakes and that if we wanted the game enough, we would be the victors. The question of losing was almost never thought of and never mentioned. It was a very positive approach, and I felt it completely even though I'd just been there only a little while.

I never really appreciated what I was part of, because we were all so busy trying to win that third in a row. And even after I had had such a good game against Dallas and we had won the third in a row, I never was conscious of my being somewhere that special until my folks called the week after the Dallas game. They said, "Guess who is on the cover of *Sports Illustrated*?" And I said, "Who?" I never thought of Mercein; after all I was just a guy playing with all these greats. But it was me. And I thought, "Hey, wait a minute. This is a major thing." I never had even dreamed of it! There were all kinds of press going on about the Dallas game and the upcoming Super Bowl game, and that's really when I started to "pinch" myself to see if I was dreaming!

After that, everything became kinda dreamlike, for me and for the rest of the team. The Super Bowl was anticlimactic. It was not much of a game; we knew we were going to win so we really did not have that feeling as we did before the Rams game and the Dallas game. There was nothing like those two games and the weeks leading up to them.

The Rams game was something very special for all of us, especially the Coach. They were really high and they thought that they would beat us. Anyway, they came to play us and they were cocky and strutting all over the field during the warmups. There was some talk on the field between the players and the Rams seemed very confident. And so were we.

We ran the Power Sweep quite a bit that game against Deacon Jones. And I made some good blocks on him. He would look at me as if to say, "How dare you block me!" And Forrest Gregg just did a great job on Jones, just ate him up. The Rams scored early and then I fumbled deep in our territory. It could have been a big setback to us. They were very much in the game then, and what happened was that a defender made good penetration and got a hand in on the ball just as I was getting it from Bart. And as I came off the field, Coach came up and asked what happened. I told him someone got their hand in and he said, "Forget it." I wasn't benched and we took over the game, and I scored a real good touchdown on a draw play.

Being in the huddle with Bart Starr was quite an experience. He had great command and presence. He was not a dynamic person, but he was all business. There was never any talk unless one of the veterans was asked something by Bart. Not that we did not volunteer information. It was just that he had the game plan down so well and knew what he was doing all the time, so none of us questioned his selection of plays. I was thrilled to be with them. I was like a kid out there, playing with the big boys. I was aware of the greatness around me, and I tried to play up to their standards.

Footballwise, these players on the Packers were the most intelligent I had ever played with or against. You know, some of them had been in the league for ten or twelve years, and they were so knowledgeable. That was such a great offensive line. They could change blocking so easy that there was no defense that could outsmart them. The plays themselves were not complicated, and they could make adjustments in a game without any trouble.

When I joined the Packers, I knew I was with the greatest team in the history of pro football. But there was never any wild backslapping after we had won a big game. They just smiled and shook hands, and there was no mugging for the cameras or television. The first thing always after a victory, or defeat even, was a prayer. That settled you down and made you kinda remember who you were. It was always sorta combination thank you prayer for not getting hurt and for winning. It was very businesslike most of the time.

But that Rams game was something special even though it was the ninth or tenth championship or playoff game for many on the team. It was my first championship game, and the tension was different from the regular season games. You know it's all over for the year if you don't win this game, and that made the Rams game something special for me.

Now came the Dallas Cowboys and if we beat them, Vince and the Packers would have their third NFL title in a row. And yet, as we got ready that week, I kinda felt that the team was less afraid of Dallas than the Rams. After all, they had the Cowboys' number. In fact, I don't think that Tom Landry had ever beaten Lombardi or the Packers up to that game. Somehow, even though they had been great games when we had beaten them, there seemed to be a more relaxed atmosphere in the locker rooms and among the coaches. We also had two more days to prepare for them than we did against the Rams.

There were no special plays put in by coach. Unlike the prior year, when he put in that influence play for Pitts and they destroyed the Cowboys' confidence on the first play, this time there was nothing special. Of course, the big play would turn out to be the "sucker" play or the "give" play. But that had always been an adjustment play off the Sweep to stop pursuit by the defensive tackle. And Dallas had the best and quickest defensive tackle in the game in Bob Lilly.

The press coverage that week was extra heavy, but we did not really notice it. The weather turned bitter cold and I think we all were kinda glad for that. I think it gave us a psychological edge; not much of one, but an edge. In fact, I remember the Coach telling some visiting writer who was complaining about the cold that this was "Packer" weather. Everything was "Packer this or Packer that" when he talked to the writers.

After the game started, around the middle of the first quarter, I came back to the huddle and told Bart that the "give play" was there. It would work. It's going to go. Of course, I would not have the audacity to tell him to call it. But I wondered if he had forgotten it, because he had not called it the whole game.

I found out why after I caught that 19-yard pass and got down to the Dallas 11-yard line. Then Starr called the "give." What a gem of a call. He had saved it for that time, almost like he had hidden a jewel and brought it out at the last moment to save us. I carried the ball to the two. Lilly chased Gillingham on what he thought was the Sweep to the right and I took the ball from Bart and headed for the goal line. I'd have scored if I'd had better footing, because Gregg was out there blocking on the defensive back coming over to tackle me and I could not cut, so I just ran into Gregg and the tackler. But the ball was on the two. There were fifty-four seconds left in the game.

It was the perfect play but it was a "ballsy" call. I mean, forget the game if Lilly does not leave and stays home. He might have even stripped me of the ball and caused a fumble.

Looking back to that game, I remember that the first two times we had the ball, or maybe it was three times, we scored. Bart hit Boyd Dowler for two touchdown passes. Then Herb Adderley intercepted Meredith's pass and we had the ball on their 32. But they stiffened and we punted. If we had gotten at least a field goal, then it would have been all over. I remember how mad Coach was after we had to punt. I guess he knew what a missed opportunity that was. But I never thought about it that way.

And as it turned out, Willie Wood fumbled a punt — which he never did — and Dallas got a field goal and then Bart fumbled while trying to pass and they picked it up and ran it in, and we were suddenly in a ball game. We stunk out the place in the third quarter, but our defense was stopping Dallas so it was a standoff until they scored early in the fourth quarter. Now they led 17-14. And we still couldn't move the ball.

With five minutes left in the game, Dallas had to punt and we got the ball on our 32-yard line. The field conditions by this time were terrible. The temperature had been 13 below zero when the game started and it had been sunny. But as the sun went down, it became even colder and the field even more frozen.

As we got ready to go out on the field I remember thinking that it might be as cold as the radio broadcaster had said it was when I got up in the morning — 56 below zero. I had never heard of such a thing so I called the airport and they assured me it was only 20 below.

But as we ran out on the field, the cold and everything else was forgotten. I think Bart might have said one thing in the huddle, like, "Okay, we're going to go down and score" or something very positive like that. Everybody was very poised and confident. I'll never forget it. I just felt this feeling of confidence that we would score and win. I did not feel an anxious feeling that we might f— up somehow or that we would make a mistake somehow. There is a plaque in the Green Bay Hall of Fame showing the plays in the drive. We had 68 yards to go and I ended up getting about 40 of those yards.

Donny caught a swing pass for 6, I got 7 more off tackle, and then Bart hit Dowler over the middle for 13, just to keep the Dallas pass defense aware of the receivers. I remember watching Dowler getting tackled; they threw him down so hard he bounced and spun like a top on the ice. Then Donny lost 9 or 10 on a sweep, but Bart hit him in the flat for 12. I came back and told Bart I could beat the linebacker on the side because the linebacker was dropping straight back. Sure enough, Bart hit me coming out of the backfield and I went 19 yards to their 11. And the next play was "54 give," and I remember thinking, "Oh God, I hope he goes like he's been going." And Bob Lilly left and the hole was there, and I got to their 2.

Talk about pride of professionals. I met Bob Lilly in Manuche's in New York about three or four years later. Howard Cosell was there, and Howard was giving it the big mouth as he always does. "There he is fans, Chuck Mercein, up the middle for 9 yards past big Bob Lilly." Lilly looked at me and quietly said, "You know, Chuck, that was a great call and play, but you really were not my responsibility. Lee Roy [Jordon] was supposed to fill my place." But I knew that Jordon as middle linebacker would make the same move again, toward the flow of the play, and even if he did recover, I would have been through the hole and there was no way he could have stopped me, either.

Now Donny carried the ball and almost scored on the next play. But the officials marked it on the 1. It was first down, however. I knew that the next play had to be the "30 wedge." But he gave the ball to Donny on a "44 dive" which is just a straight power play over our two best blockers, Forrest and Jerry. Donny slipped going for the handoff and I almost had a stroke. How

Bart got him the ball and did not fumble is beyond me. Bart had to have given him the ball six inches off the ground. Now Bart called time-out. It was our last; there were sixteen seconds left. The ball was still on the 1.

In the huddle, there was no question that we were going to go. No one mentioned field goal to tie. We knew we could make it and that we would run it in. There was no question we all wanted to go for it.

Bart came back and simply said, "Let's get it," and he called my play, the "30 wedge." I did not worry about fumbling or anything. I just knew I was going to score. And with the snap I fired off, but I saw after two steps that Bart was keeping it and I thought to myself, "Don't assist him! God Almighty, you can't ram into him." And that's why I went over the top. It almost looked like I was signaling a touchdown. It's sort of a "hotdog" kinda move, but I was really trying to show the refs that I was not helping in any way. Bart was in and it was all over.

There was real happiness. We all were smiling and I remember looking over to the Coach and he had his arms in the air and the guys on the sidelines were jumping and grinning. It was just the warmest, greatest feeling. And then I looked at the Cowboys. Their faces were empty. I think they were in shock. They had a look of almost absolute disbelief that this had happened to them.

I never asked Bart why he kept the ball. I know why. It was a safer play, the percentages were with him. The blocks were going to be made or they weren't going to be made, and there was no sense in risking a handoff. It was typical of Starr to minimize the risks.

This time in the locker room there was a real celebration. The excitement was everywhere, and the backslapping and huge men hugging and kissing each other was something else. It was just damn exciting. We came running off the field and into the locker and the television cameras were there. I wasn't even thinking of anything except how lucky I was. I was about half-dressed when the next thing I knew, I was on national television with the Coach. Later my mother called and said that the next time I go on TV, put my teeth in.

Before Vince let everybody in, he talked to us for just a second. At times he would become so emotional that he just could not talk. And all he could say was "You were great and thank God we won and let's have a prayer." That's about all I remember. And you knew how much this meant to him and how deeply he felt for us. I always had that empathy with Coach Lombardi, because I'm Italian on my maternal side and I could understand him even when he was screaming and raving at us. It was not like an Allie Sherman. When he'd scream at you, it would be irrational; it would not make any sense. He'd go crazy and you really did not think it was deserved. But with Lombardi, you knew it was never personal, that you earned it; he had that smile, so genuine and warm, that even after he had yelled at you and he'd smile, you forgot the yelling.

I had so much respect for Lombardi. I respected his religious devotion, the way he conducted himself, his affection for his players — everything about him. And though he never said it to me, others told me that he liked me. I really did not need anyone to tell me that because I could sense he was pleased with the way I was playing and putting out.

I always felt it was a real honor to be where I was, an honor to work for him. It was a different feeling than I ever had before or since. It was just unique.

There were a few parties after the game, but the temperature dropped even more, if you can believe that, and I was home before midnight. As I said, the Packers kinda took championships in stride, even this one. I felt like I was on cloud nine but with a deep satisfaction that did not need to be boasted about. I knew I was part of something that few football players will ever know, only the forty of us who played for him and in that game. I guess that is reward enough.

Monday morning what had happened started to hit me. The papers were full of stories and there was a lot of ink about me. And I was sore. My arm was so swollen that I had twenty-five-inch biceps on the left side. And I was scraped all over. It came from the field because the cleatmarks on the field had frozen, and they were like little razor blades sticking up. And when you fell or slid on the ground, they would cut into your skin. Not deep cuts but little cuts that looked as if someone had scored your body like a piece of meat. I did not get frostbite like a lot of the guys did, especially the Cowboys. But when I walked that morning, I was hunched over like a little old man of ninety.

And then the phone calls started to come in and there was a full-page interview in the paper that afternoon, so a lot of people were finding out more about Chuck Mercein. It was very flattering and that's one of the rewards of playing on a championship team. But there were no phone calls from anybody on the Giants.

We got together Tuesday in Green Bay, and it was even more cold than on the Sunday game day. We tried to practice that day and Coach decides to practice in the stadium rather than go over to the practice fields because it's closer. That day they had the grid working.

One of the world's greatest salesmen must be the guy who convinced Vince Lombardi to put electric cables under the playing field in the stadium to keep the field from freezing and to keep it dry on wet, snowy, cold days, like they sometimes have in Green Bay. He had it installed earlier that year before the season began, and he was very proud of it, always telling visitors that nobody will ever complain again about playing in Green Bay in the cold because the field will be like new. The day of the Dallas game, the electric cables had been on for two days before and the field was just perfect for the game. Twenty minutes before we took the field to warmup, they removed the tarp. What they had not planned on was that the tarp kept the water that had condensed underneath from getting out. So when they took off the tarp, there was a flash freeze and in twenty minutes, what was a perfect field became an ice rink. This game was also the first test of the system. I was not there when Chuck Lane had to tell Coach what happened, but they said he turned livid green and then deep red as he blew his stack. And at Lane!

Anyway, the Tuesday after the Dallas game the cables were working but it was damn cold. It was ridiculous! As we went out there was two or three feet of fog covering the ground! You could lie down and nobody could see you! We were all laughing and hiding and running around and Coach was really pissed. He did not know what to say, and if we had not just won that game, he'd probably have kept us out there all day.

That day, the cold really, really affected me. I had to go in after ten minutes because my contact lenses literally froze to my eyeballs! I could not see. I think I had ice forming in my eyes. The top of my head felt like it was going to blow off. And after I got inside my contacts fogged up and I could not see or get them off until I thawed out! Within five minutes, Lombardi brought the rest of the team in. I don't know if it was because of the cold, which was about thirty below zero, or whether it was that he could not stand looking at the fog on his field. Whatever, we were off to Florida the next day.

One interesting thing that happened in the little time we were out in that fog and the cold did not seem to mean much to me at the time, but later I remembered it and I think it was my first indication that Super Bowl II would be Lombardi's final game with the Packers. I was standing behind the huddle, as backs do when they are not running in the formation, and Vince and an assistant were a little to my left and ahead of me. Travis Williams took a handoff from Bart, and for some reason, really put it into afterburner and took off. And Vince turned to the other coach and said, "You know, that kid could make me stay around." Travis had such potential, just unbelievable. Had Lombardi stayed at Green Bay, Travis Williams would have been one of the all-time greats. And as it was he had terrific years. But he needed Lombardi and the motivation Vince gave him. It's too bad.

We stayed at the Galt Ocean Mile in Ft. Lauderdale, Florida. It was a nice place but with all the reporters, the fans, the cameras, and television, it was like Disneyland. To tell you a story about being confident, Coach Lombardi, as early as the spring of 1967 before we had even started the season, had "Hawg" Hanner check out accommodations in Ft. Lauderdale for the team to stay there. He knew the Super Bowl was going to be in the Orange Bowl in Miami, and he wanted everything checked out. And that was ten months before we beat Dallas!

Coach was very, very concerned about distractions. There was no swimming in the pool, no hanging around the lobby, no breaking of curfew, and the fines were triple the normal fines if you were caught. There were so many reporters and cameramen and fans around that it was almost impossible to concentrate on the game. But we really were not worried about beating Oakland.

He was concerned that we would lose that edge of competitive fire; he wanted us to be worried about Oakland. But after what we had gone through against the Colts and the Rams and Cowboys, there really was a feeling that this game was going to be anticlimactic. Even in the film meetings, he'd try to get us up but he did not have his heart in it. I remember we saw a film of the Jets playing against the Raiders. The Jets had the ball and they had this offensive tackle who was huge. Lombardi could not resist running the film back and forth, and he and all of us were laughing because this guy was so big and so slow and so out of shape. Coach really did not have a great deal of respect for the AFL.

There was this strange feeling I had about the whole thing. It was like everybody was out of it. He was out of it. He tried to get upset and put on his act, but it was hollow and all of us, I feel, were the same way. We knew we would win and the game really had no meaning. At least that's the way I felt.

During the game at half-time, Jerry Kramer said to all of us he thought that this was going to be the last game for the "Old Man," and "let's go out and give these last thirty minutes to him." And as soon as he said it, I remembered that comment in the fog in Green Bay and I knew Jerry was right. Then, the game took on some meaning. We took the second half, marched downfield, and Donny scored. It was all over.

Afterward, in the locker room, there was no big celebration. I guess some of the guys felt elated, but there was very little show. Some of the veterans, like Fuzzy Thurston and Max McGee, might have played their last game. But nobody made a big thing out of the win. It was like we had just cleaned up some last minute small details and wanted to catch the train home from work.

Another thing that always impressed me about the Packers players was the way they divided the shares due from the championships. I've heard about other clubs where there are terrific fights about giving this guy or that trainer or that rookie a full share. Not with them. Everyone got a full share and it was a lot of money. I remember Doug Hart, one of our defensive backs, asking me after the Super Bowl what I was going to do with all the money. It was about thirty thousand! And I really did not know or care. I was sure I'd spend it. As Willie Davis said, "My creditors will take good care of it."

But what I was really excited about was that ring! I could not wait for it. It did not come and did not come, and I was going nuts. It finally came about two months later. And when I got home and it was there, I was just knocked out! I could not believe it, it was so beautiful. It meant so damn much; something nobody could ever take away from you. It showed what I'd been a part of. Only a few have this ring with the three diamonds across the top. And I was right about the money. It went real quick. But I still have the ring. Coach Lombardi designed the ring himself with the three diamonds for the three championships in a row and on the side is the inscription, "Run to Win." It is easily the most expensive ring ever given to players on a championship team, and the Packers paid for this, not the league. So he did not scrimp; he went all out to make this ring something special to all of us.

The first time I saw Coach Lombardi after he had retired was when I came back for summer camp. We only saw him from a distance. Bengston now had the team, and we'd see the coach kinda standing far off on the sidelines. It was eerie. It was like a ghost coming back and yet he had to stay out of it. He had put Phil in and he would not interfere. But almost immediately, we knew that he had to get back into coaching. He had made a terrible mistake and he knew it, and we knew it and it was only a question of time before he came back. We all wanted him back with us and talked about it, but I think we all knew he'd never do that after he gave Phil the team.

In retrospect, having him around not doing anything was more difficult for us and the coaches than if he had just packed up and left right after he quit. It was an unworkable situation. He was a lone figure, like a retired man who leaves a business but comes back just to be around. We knew he'd like to talk to us, but he just could not.

And when the season began, there was some divisiveness that was not there before. There was criticism of the new coach, and he did nothing to stop that. In fact, his speech to us before one game was to tell us how to line up when the national anthem was played. And all of a sudden, there were questions in our minds and the team starts to factionalize. It was just a complete difference and it showed itself in places where Lombardi always picked us up, the game plan, the midweek speech, and the pregame speech.

The 1968 season was a disaster for the defending World Champions. We lost our opener and then Bart got hurt and we did not seem to be able to win the close games. We still had the talent, but it just wasn't happening. I remember before that season began, Ray Nitschke, our great middle linebacker, wrote or had written a story for *Sports Illustrated* saying that the 1968 Packers would be the best Packers team of all time, and without saying it, hinted that the reason we won all those championships was not Lombardi but the players and that the players would show everybody that year who really was responsible for those winning years. And he was right. We showed everyone. We won six and lost seven and tied one! For the first time since Vince Lombardi came to Green Bay, the Packers had a losing season.

In the spring of 1969, Coach resigned as general manager of the Packers and went to Washington to rebuild the Redskins. I was in New York when I heard about it and I was very happy for him and for football to have him back. I knew the 'Skins didn't have too much, but whatever they had would be better than what they were the other years. That spring, I was playing golf at Winged Foot and Coach was there with some of his friends from New York. He saw me and waved me over and said to meet him after the golf matches and have a drink. Later, at the bar in the club, he asked me how would I like to be his fullback in Washington. And of course, I was ecstatic. He did not say he was going to trade for me, but I felt that he was going to do what he could to get me to Washington.

I did not know until I got back to Green Bay for the summer camp before the 1969 season how bitter the feeling was on the coaching staff and in the management toward Vince, and there was an unwritten rule that the Packers would not trade with Lombardi. They were still very pissed off that he left and, I have heard this rumored but don't know for a fact, made Vince promise, as part of giving their approval for him to go to Washington, that he would not trade for any Packers or try to sign any of the free agents.

As it turned out, he could not trade for me and I was still with the Packers when the season began. We opened up against the Bears and Bart was fine and we won, 17–0. We still had a great group of veterans and there seemed to be that old feeling. But an incident happened during that game that forever made me wonder what people are made of. Vince's first game was against the Saints down in New Orleans. We were at home and as is the custom around the league, during a timeout, the PA will give scores of other games. When they announced that New Orleans is leading the Redskins in the third or fourth quarter, the Packers fans cheered and some of the coaches on the sidelines started grinning. Can you imagine? They were still so bitter that he was gone that they cheered and laughed because he was losing! None of the players smiled, I'll tell you that. We all wanted him to win. As it turned out, they came from behind and won the opener.

By the tenth game, we were out of the chase and barely playing five-hundred ball. I wasn't playing much, and there was really very little to be happy about. It must have been something like the days before Lombardi, but at least the townspeople were not harassing us. One night during the week, I took my family out for a fish-fry and then met a couple of the Packers at a spot called Brothers, where a lot of the black ballplayers go. It was about eleven at night and Bengston walked in. I said hello and offered to buy him a beer. He said he was very disappointed in me and a bunch of other things. This wasn't the night before a game or summer camp curfew; there were no restrictions on our movements. So I went outside to go home and there were a couple of police cars there. It seemed Bengston was looking for another player and did not find him. I came in the next day for practice, he called me up and told me he was going to fine me for being out. I did not agree that it was a violation but I paid the $750. That week we went to Pittsburgh and Bart was the only quarterback we had who was healthy. About twenty-five minutes before the game, I finished putting my uniform on and was ready to go out to warm-up. Phil came up and said that they were going to take me off the active roster to make room for the new kid. I said okay and told him to keep me off. And I just cut my ties with no real remorse at all. Oh, I missed the players but not that organization, not what it had become without Lombardi.

I went back home with the team after the game and called the coach in Washington. Marie answered and right away she knew something was wrong. I told her and she said Vince was out but he would call as soon as he came back. He called and it was just great. He said to come on back right away. He said he'd have to make room for me and that I could not be activated right away, but to come on and he'd sign me.

I went to the Packers locker rooms on Monday to get my gear and say good-bye to the guys. It was tough because I really had so many close friends, but I did not mind because they all wished they were going with me to play for Lombardi again and they were happy for me.

He was delighted to see me when I got there, at least he seemed to be. He told me that it might cause some kind of a ruckus and that I was to check in at the Shoreham Hotel under an assumed name. He still had that secrecy thing! No problems on the contract though. Which was very nice because, being a five-year veteran, the Packers, in cutting me the way they did still had to pay me so Vince did not have to pick up my contract. But he did. I was recognized by a writer and then the word was out. As it turned out, I could not be activated because of some league rule, but I did work out with the team and travel with them and I became part of the Redskins.

Then the summer came and I went back to camp in Carlisle, Pennsylvania, and I was very excited about the upcoming season, as were all the veterans. We felt that we had a shot that year. There was another players' strike so camp did not open on time, but we worked out anyway.

Then we heard Coach was in the hospital. And then he was out. And we heard that the operation was a success. But he was back in within a month, and he never came out. And before anybody even realized it, he was gone.

I went to the hospital with Vince Promuto a couple of days before he died, and when I saw him, I knew it was all over. I was so shocked when I saw him in that condition I could not speak. He was such a strong, physical person, as well as being a strong person in morals and character. He always emitted invincible power. He had a great build, barrel-chested, powerful shoulders, and strong legs.

At first, I almost did not recognize him. He looked almost like an old grandfather. It was awful. He had lost so much weight that I don't think he weighed eighty pounds. He was all gray, with sunken cheeks. I could just barely fight off the tears, just barely. And I remember just thanking him for everything he had done, and I just said good-bye. When I got outside the room, I started to cry. And I kept crying. I knew I had lost a most important member of my family, and even though we were not close on a social basis, he was so close to me that I can't explain how I felt except to know I had lost someone I loved.

People often wonder if Lombardi would have won with the Redskins as he did with the Packers. I don't know. I think he would have. He had the basics there to make a winner, and in Sonny Jurgenson he had the greatest passer I ever saw. He had great receivers in Charley Taylor and Jerry Smith. Lombardi loved the passing game so I know that with some trades and good drafting, which he always did well, he'd have had the Redskins in the Super Bowl. And they would have won.

One of the greatest privileges I've ever had in my life was knowing and playing for Vince Lombardi. Not that it was such a pleasurable experience when I was undergoing it. At those times, I was afraid of the man and felt his anger when I screwed up. But looking back on it now, I know how important that was to me and my growth as a person. I learned a lot from him and the kind of operation he ran. I was very fortunate to have been in the right place at the right time, to have been associated with him and to still be associated with him. You cannot have played for Vince Lombardi, cannot have been around him for any time without his influence still affecting you. There are few great men who come along in one's lifetime. He was one. He is one. And I was blessed having been there with him.

And when I think about him now, as I often do, I forget the anger and the sidelines and the practices and the Tuesday films. I remember his laughter. I remember that smile that took all of us in and yet was for each one of us, individually. He had a beautiful smile.

Coach Lombardi on the Milwaukee sidelines in the game against the Rams for the Western Conference championship. *(Vernon J. Biever)*

Chuck Mercein scoring on a draw play against the Rams in the playoff game in 1967. *(Vernon J. Biever)*

One of the most famous plays in the history of pro football was Bart Starr's quarterback sneak to win the NFL championship against the Dallas Cowboys with only 13 seconds left on the game clock. (*Vernon J. Biever*)

In the final drive against the Cowboys to win the game, Chuck Mercein accounted for more than half the yardage. (*Vernon J. Biever*)

After the win and knowing he had his third NFL title in a row, Vince Lombardi meets the press and he's radiant. (Vernon J. Biever)

After Super Bowl II, Vince Lombardi and his two "stars" of the game. Don Chandler kicked four field goals and Bart Starr was named the Most Valuable Player in the game, as usual. *(Vernon J. Biever)*

Lombardi being carried off on the shoulders of his players for the last time. *(Vernon J. Biever)*

9
Washington

IN ALL the great years of the Green Bay Packers, they never played in our nation's capital. But in the year that Vince Lombardi was the general manager, they came to Washington to play the Redskins. Before the game, some boys walked around the stadium carrying a banner. It said, "S.O.S. — Save Our Skins. Hire Lombardi!" Little did they know that earlier that morning, the salvation of the Washington Redskins had begun.

The day his Packers came into training camp in the summer of 1968, Vince Lombardi knew he had made a terrible mistake in giving up his coaching job. And he knew he could not go back to the Packers. Soon, it became unbearable and he let the word out that he would consider the right job. But, it had to include an ownership position in the club.

With Peter Campbell Brown, his attorney, representing him, Vince started to put together a group to buy an NFL franchise. He was interested in the Philadelphia Eagles. Earlier he had been offered a chance to go with the Rams but had turned it down. And then the New York Jets got into the act. They wanted Lombardi and his group and the negotiations got to the point where there would be a deal if Lombardi agreed. But Vince realized it would be impossible for him to take over an AFL franchise, even though it was in New York where he wanted to be. How could he do that to the Maras and the NFL. So he passed.

At breakfast in their hotel in Washington before the Redskins game, Vince was joined by Edward Bennett Williams, president of the Redskins and an old friend from the league. In a joking way, Williams asked what it would take to get Vince to come to Washington and rebuild the Redskins. Lombardi told him to speak to Peter Campbell Brown. Williams couldn't believe it. But he spoke to Brown. They were old friends from the Truman days, when Peter was with the Justice Department. And Brown confirmed. Thus began the long process of getting Vince Lombardi to move from Green Bay to Washington. Soon the rumors that he was leaving and going somewhere filled the papers. The denials and the coverups were difficult on him, but it was the only way it could be done.

When he finally settled everything, he made his good-byes. He loved Green Bay, but he couldn't stay out of coaching and he couldn't go back to take over the team, even though everyone wanted him to.

He knew he had a hell of a job in front of him: to make those Redskins winners. But it was the challenge that he welcomed. And he was so happy to be back that those who wished he'd stay in Green Bay were happy for him.

Washington couldn't believe their luck. The S.O.S. had been answered. The greatest coach in football would be running the Redskins. The players were overjoyed and the phones between Washington and Green Bay were humming as this Redskin asks that Packer what's he really like.

There was no Super Bowl for Washington that year, but the Redskins did have a winning season; the first one in fifteen years. A few Washington players might have played for Vince in Green Bay, but only a couple — Sonny Jurgenson, Chris Hamburger, and maybe one or two others.

After the season — sometime in early February of 1970 — Vince was in town for league meetings. He came to Mike's and we met and had a drink. The place was filled with football people as well as broadcasters, writers, and fans. Vince was sitting at a table with me, Mike Manuche, Frank Gifford, and about six others. Everybody was talking, mostly about what a great job Vince had done with the Skins that year. Bill Heinz was also in town from Vermont about another writing project, and he joined us. He and Vince were very close, and he congratulated Vince on the season, saying what a heck of a back Larry Brown, his rookie running star, was. Vince smiled, and soon everyone was telling him how great Brown was. He just kept smiling and said nothing, and someone brought up the story about the hearing aid Vince had put in Brown's helmet to help him hear the snap signal.

Finally, someone asked the question. How good is Larry Brown really? Vince usually ducked these questions, but for some reason he answered this one. "He would not have been allowed on the field in Green Bay when I had the Packers." Then he qualified the statement. "Someday, Brown will be a fine back, maybe even a great one. But if he were to have been in Green Bay with my Packers as a rookie, he would not have made the cut. Of course, I'm talking about the days I had Taylor and Hornung and Moore and Pitts and others." Well, he was the coach and I guess we all just nodded, because if anybody knew how good someone was, it had to be him.

Later that same evening, the conversation got around to Sonny Jurgenson. Most knowledgeable football people put Jurgenson, as a passer, in the top five all-time passers with Tittle, Baugh, Unitas, and Van Brocklin. So when Bill Heinz asked Vince how Sonny would have done with the Packers, Vince again answered without hesitation. (I've never heard him talk so much about his players.) "If Jurgensen had played with the 1961, 1962, or 1963 teams, we probably would have scored 75 points a game and never have lost."

Now all hell broke loose because many there believed Starr was the greatest quarterback of all time. And Vince explains: "When Starr was quarterbacking those early teams, they were the greatest teams in the history of the league. And he did a great job. But he never was the pure passer Jurgenson was. And given the talent we had, Jurgenson and his ability as a passer would have been too much for any team to handle. We would have just overpowered everyone, as we did with Starr. But when we got older, Starr was much the better quarterback for us because we could not overpower teams on offense. We had to finesse them, pick them apart, capitalize on their mistakes. He was the greatest in history at taking a team apart. So there are really two Packer eras — the early sixties, where we just out-talented everyone and where Jurgenson would have been dynamite, and the teams that won three in a row, where Starr matured into a great player. His attitude and knowledge and temperament made him ideal for those teams."

Vince Promuto was one of the Redskins, a guard and one of the few good players in Washington. He looked forward to playing under Lombardi, but he decided he would not call any Packers or read any of the books by and about him beforehand. Promuto, it turned out, was a Lombardi-type player.

VINCE PROMUTO

I came from Holy Cross College. It's a small college — a hundred Jesuit priests at the time and eighteen hundred students and no fraternities. Our most famous graduate was a basketball player, Bob Cousy.

I got drafted in 1960. In fact, I was traded to the Redskins from New York. The New York Giants drafted me fourth, and I was traded for Dick Lynch and got down to the Redskins.

When I first heard that Lombardi was to be our new coach I was elated, knowing what he did in Green Bay and knowing that I had played for nine years with the Redskins and we hadn't won many games. In the early sixties we were lucky to win two or three. I figured that this was my big shot. I was a good guard. I made the Pro Bowl a couple of times. I was a good enough football player to play for Lombardi and it was a great challenge, but I also knew that we'd have great benefits out of his coaching here.

I received a letter from Coach Lombardi stating that the veterans were due at training camp on July 20, and that the rookies should come six days before that. I had told myself, when I found out Coach Lombardi was to come to Washington, that I wouldn't read any of the books. I wanted to judge him on my own.

It turned out to be a mistake because I came the twentieth, like he said. And not only that, the meeting was set for eight o'clock at night and when I walked in about ten to eight, the first thing I heard was, "Promuto, you're late! How dare you come here the day I tell you to come here. And never come here ten minutes before the meeting. You're five minutes late!"

So I found out that this was not the way he ran the time schedule. When he said eight o'clock you should be there at quarter to eight, and when he said be there the twentieth you should have enough interest to come five days ahead of time.

The first team meeting with Coach Lombardi at camp was a little tense, because we all knew what he did at Green Bay and we knew he was a great coach and we were real apprehensive to find out what he'd say. The one big thing that stuck out in my mind, outside of the few plays he gave us then, was that he asked us all to believe in what he did. It didn't seem too hard at the time, because he had done so much for Green Bay, but it got to the point where he was changing a lot of our football methods around, and it got to be where the type of football I was used to playing wasn't good enough for Vince Lombardi. It was a hard thing after playing nine years and playing good pro football. I had made the Pro Bowl a couple of times and I was confident enough in what I was doing and I didn't want to have to change to his type of football. In the beginning, when I tried to change my thinking process, I was playing poorly. I was getting yelled at every day and so I'd always remember those few weeks when he said, "You have to believe in what I say and we'll be successful." I think, if anything, that took me through those crises.

Well, I received a leg injury in doing the same type of blocking I had done for nine years. Had I listened to the type of blocking he wanted us to do I wouldn't be hurt today. There are two types of blocking: one is position blocking, which the Cleveland Browns use a great deal and are very successful with; on the other hand, Lombardi uses a straight, direct attack, where you just have to attack that man and you have to physically win over him.

For years, in particular plays, I would take a position on a man and try to create the hole. I did that one day and the halfback was running through the hole and my leg was sticking out and I tore up all my ligaments. Again, I should have listened to the Coach and I wouldn't have broken that leg. But that's a hard thing to do. Like I say, you don't want to think about what to do in a football game. It has to come second nature, and this transition was a tough thing for me in training camp.

After I got hurt, it was the day before the second exhibition game, and the coach came in and said, "Vincent, how do you feel?" I said, "Well, coach, I'm hurt. But that's the name of the game and you have to play hurt." I taped up my knee and I went out and played. One thing about Coach Lombardi is that outside of any real major injuries you had to play hurt. I think that, in a way, it's a contradiction to the American philosophy because we Americans, when we're hurt, want to sit down or lay down or go to a hospital and get the best lawyer possible.

But to play football, like Lombardi always said, it's a spartan type game where you had to sacrifice and you had to play in pain. Outside of maybe losing your leg or damaging it to an extent greater than it was already, to play for this man you had to play hurt.

If I had to contrast Coach Lombardi's training camp to the other training camps I've been in — and Coach Lombardi was my fourth coach — I'd have to say the Lombardi camps were the shortest as far as time spent on the field goes. In fact, again, I didn't read that football book *Run to Daylight!* or the book that Kramer wrote about Coach Lombardi. With the other coaches, we had two and a half hours on the football field in the morning and another two hours in the afternoon. Coach Lombardi said we'd be on the field an hour and fifteen minutes in the morning and another hour and a half in the afternoon.

I worked harder than I ever worked before. I thought this would be a pushover, because it was an hour less anyway you look at it. You have to be able to survive with an hour's shorter practice. But I was wrong. I didn't know about those ups and downs, the grass drills. I'd heard about them, but I hadn't any idea what they were. The reason why Coach Lombardi's training camps were so hard was that in the first fifteen minutes he'd completely fatigue you. You'd go through your calisthenics and then start the ups and downs. After doing forty or fifty, he'd have you sprint about a quarter of a mile, and then, without any rest at all, you'd start again with another set of fifteen-yard sprints. And he'd do them so fast that you'd sprint out those fifteen yards and by the time you got turned around, you had to go back down and do them again. He'd do about eight of those. By the time you finished that, and it only took fifteen minutes, you'd be physically exhausted. To get through the rest of the practice it took so much will power and so much mental tenacity that it just was the worst thing I've ever been through. But, like anything else, you do it for the first week, and before you know it, by the second week you've already gone past these barriers mentally and physically and it becomes easier. I think one of the great things about Coach Lombardi was that he pushed you beyond points you'd never before been pushed. He was such a disciplinarian himself — he pushed himself so far — that he didn't feel bad about pushing us. He knew it could be done.

It wasn't that he made us run twenty miles or anything like that. It was the constant pressure. The amount of work you did in such a short amount of time. The first fifteen minutes that you were on that field would have you physically whipped completely, what with the ups and downs and the running and sprinting and getting off on the ball. And by the time you started thinking about football and the plays that you had to learn, you had to force yourself mentally and physically.

Then he'd always talk about kindergarten kids, who had a concentration span of five seconds he said, and we couldn't even get three seconds. That was kind of an insult to talk about kindergarten kids and us being professional football players. But he'd always start off like that to get a little spark in us to push ourselves. And, like I say, you can't imagine it unless you've done it. To be completely exhausted physically and have to force yourself to think to get your body moving and getting around on that block on an end run.

It really was things like this that Coach Lombardi could make you do that I don't think other coaches could. Some other coaches might try to do the same thing and you'd have a mutiny on your hands, because they didn't live the standard of life that Lombardi did. He pushed himself harder than anyone else, and we all knew it. He was the only man I have ever met who had one standard. He didn't have a double standard. He lived his life trying to strive for excellence in his religion and in his personal life. He went to bed later than any of us did. He got up earlier. He worked harder than all the football players. He yelled louder than anyone else in the world. And he was there on every play.

Other coaches would look at the play at the point of attack and they'd see if there was a breakdown there, but they'd never be able to have a look at the whole offensive line. He was the first man I'd ever met who disciplined himself enough so that he could see every football player. He knew his system so well that if someone was out of position, even if he was the least important man on that particular play, he'd get yelled at. After a while, when you were running to the right and you might be a left tackle, you knew in the back of your mind that the Coach was looking right down at you just as he was at the point of attack.

Everyone had to do their job. It was really a whole new dimension in my life of football. Before he came to the Redskins, I thought you were judged more or less on your individual job, and to me, as an offensive guard, I was usually judged against the defensive tackle I played. I played against the Karrases and the Lillys and all of them. If you played good against them, kept them off the passer, got them off the line of scrimmage, well then you'd done your job.

But Coach Lombardi didn't want you only to do your job; he wanted you to do it his particular way. There was a definite reason for your doing it a particular way, so that you wouldn't put a burden on the man next to you. It was just sound, simple football that had to be done his way so that the halfback could run to daylight.

And that's what he was talking about when he'd say run to daylight. Instead of only having one hole, they call the play *and* the hole to run at. If you did it his way there were three or four possible holes to run to. He had a different philosophy, and it made a lot more sense after you got to know him. He'd give us a game speech on a Tuesday, because he believed the only way to win a football game was to work hard during the week. If you could execute and if you could work hard physically and mentally during the week, then the game was easy. It might sound like a contradiction to anybody who had never played under Lombardi, but the easiest part of playing football under Coach Lombardi was playing the game. It was a time when you had the freedom to go out there and you didn't have a whistle to stop and have him come and yell and scream. You felt like this was your big chance to get judged on the whole game's performance instead of each particular play. He strived for perfection in every single play on the practice field, so it would just be a constant pursuit for running each play better. Even though it would work well and get fifteen yards in the game, it wasn't enough in practice because it had to be done as close to perfection as possible. We were just looking forward to playing these games, because it was the only time that he was restricted to the sideline, and he couldn't get any closer to us than that.

Like I said, it was a great thing to walk in on Tuesday. All the things he had to say about football didn't really pertain to football itself. They were much more general. These things we were striving for in winning football games were things that would help us be better men. It wasn't just the victory and the job of victory, but it was the fact that we dedicated ourselves as individuals and as a team to accomplish something and to have this overflow into other things we did in life. I think it was he who was trying to tell us this.

There were a lot of changes for the veterans when Coach Lombardi came. I mean about the attitude we had playing that individual game against the man we played against and thinking that if we could play good against him we'd accomplished our job. One of the real notable changes I saw was with Sonny Jurgenson. He is a great football player. I have always felt that way, and I'm sure most people feel that way. He's very talented physically, but he had never really looked up to any one of the coaches we had at the Redskins.

In fact, he knew so much football that at times you'd wonder if he was just trying to be nice as he stood there and listened to the game plan.

It was very noticeable from the very start that Jurgenson idolized Coach Lombardi. He just couldn't wait to hear the next word he had to say, because he was finally learning more football and there was a rhyme and reason for the defensive keys he was learning. And it was working out on the football field. He was more consistent in his passing. He had a better running game than he had ever had before, and we had no real great backs. Sonny, I think, was the greatest example of a guy, an old pro, who was really enthused. He did everything we did. Before he'd stand on the sidelines and throw the ball around while we went through all the torture. Now he went through every single up and down and tried to lead us around that quarter mile and head up the starts and everything. When things really, really got bad, and I was feeling like I couldn't do the next up and down, I'd look at him and I'd look at Sam Huff, who was playing, and I'd say, "Hell, if they can do it, I can do it. I'm younger than they are and I'm a lineman." It got me through. It was a great thing to see someone like Sonny, who had gotten to the point where he was almost bored with the game, learning more about the game. To see him with Coach Lombardi, becoming like a whole newborn person, waiting for that next meeting so that he could learn some more was fantastic.

A lot of people talk about Coach Lombardi and about playing for him under a feeling of fear. I never had that feeling. I always felt that I had to prove something, because he did demand a lot. But it was never through fear. I find it hard to think of anyone playing that way. He was, again, a man who really strove for excellence and pushed us beyond all those points that we'd ever been pushed before. But it was a lot of fun to know that you could be pushed, and it was so easy that second time knowing that you could do it. He yelled at me, and I could always tell how he felt about my play in practice. If I did something wrong he wouldn't call me by my first name. He'd go, "Promuto, what the hell is going on!" If I did something good, if I got around the defensive end real quick and upfield real well, he'd just yell out, "Way to go, Vincent!" I always felt he'd never use his name in anything derogatory because we both had the same first name. So I'd be "Promuto" when I was the bad guy and "Vincent" when I was the good guy.

He had a very forceful smile. It was just a magnanimous thing. When you had him smile at you, you were like a little kid getting patted on the head for doing something good. I don't want to take it in that particular context, because we're men and we're not looking for a pat on the back, but when you got it from him it was a special thing.

And it wasn't only hard on us as football players, because he was also the general manager. It was a real exciting thing to see the front office of the Redskins change. They weren't the greatest managerial functioning team, but when he took over they really turned out to be a first-class organization. People were jumping. He made some changes in that the press had to be in a certain place, and in the rules and regulations. Not only was the team playing better, but the whole organization was better. I think to have a championship team not only do you have to have good football players, but the managerial people and the whole organization have to be working right. He put all this into perspective.

Another thing about Coach Lombardi was that he didn't have six thousand rules like we had with other coaches. We had some simple rules and they were very basic. They made a lot of sense, and you'd better not break them because shame on you if you do. They were easy to live with.

I really feel that if he'd come back and been our coach the next year, we'd have gone all the way. I feel he was very important to this country. In fact, I think that one of the big reasons he came here rather than going to New York was that Washington was the nation's capital. It is a place that had a lot of crime. It is a place that basically was a loser, where it should have been the real showplace for the nation. I really think that Coach Lombardi was thinking along these lines, and it was a real challenge not only to have a winning football team but also to have a place that all the people in the country looked to for pride and accomplishment. Maybe some of that would rub off onto the people in Washington, making them talk about something more than the ghettos and narcotics and all the crime.

When he talked to us on Tuesdays, he always talked not only about winning football games but about America and the people. He always said that people who work hard never really get in trouble; that they find a sense of accomplishment and that if you have a sense of accomplishment you live better by the rules because you have respect for yourself; and that makes you respect community rules and laws and it makes you a better person.

If he taught us anything, he taught every one of us to respect ourselves. I think a person has to respect and love himself before he can love other people. By working as hard as we did and by going through these barriers and being pushed beyond this point, we had a greater respect for ourselves individually and a greater respect for each person who worked on the team. This is the thing that brings about this love. It makes you learn the give and take of life. You don't judge a person by the particular thing he does, but by his whole person. Many times you might have read articles about Lombardi talking about love; and for some people this might sound effeminate, but that's not the type of love he was talking about. He talked about the ultimate respect — respect and love for his fellow man.

When I first heard that Coach Lombardi was sick, I did not pay too much attention. I mean, it never dawned on me that he could be sick and so I thought it was just something minor. Then I heard he had cancer. We were having another of those players' strikes and camp didn't begin on time that summer, so all the veterans in the Washington area got together and worked out until the camp opened.

We talked about the Coach and his illness, but I still never thought there would be anybody else coaching us that year. But when I heard that he had gone back into the hospital for more treatments, I knew, for the first time, it was serious. So one day after a workout, Chuck Mercein and I went over to his room at Georgetown Hospital to visit him.

He was very tired, but as sick and tired as he was, you could see how pleased he was that a couple of his boys came to see him. We only stayed a second and I remember saying to him, as he lay there, "I thank God that you came my way — at least, for a year."

To ease the pain of retirement, Vince Lombardi played as much golf as he could and still ran the Packers from the office. Sometimes even the best golfers find the rough!

(*Vernon J. Biever*)

Six months after the celebration and happiness of a great season, he sits on a blocking dummy at the end of the practice field and watches someone else coach his team. *(Vernon J. Biever)*

The only time Vince Lombardi spoke to the team in 1968 was before the game in Washington. He told them that the fans there had never seen the Green Bay Packers in person and to go out and show the nation's capital what the Packers were all about. *(Vernon J. Biever.)*

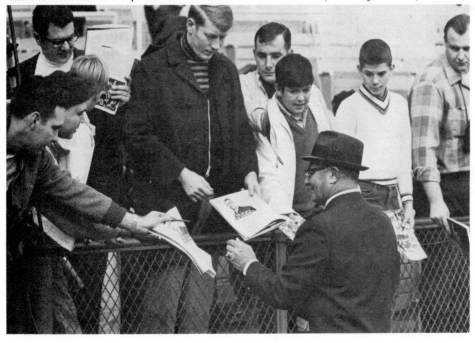

When the announcement was made in the winter of 1969 that Vince Lombardi was coming to Washington to "save the 'Skins'," all of Washington went wild. *(Copyright © 1969 by The Washingtonian Magazine. Photograph by Curt Barlow; sculpture by Charles Mendez.)*

One thing Lombardi knew he had when he took over the Redskins was the best thrower in football. For pure passing, Sonny Jurgenson ranks at the very top. *(Vernon J. Biever)*

Washingtonian

75c AUGUST 1969

The Coach
sign thee,
and keep thee:

The Coach
make his face
shine upon thee,
and be profane
unto thee:

The Coach
lift up the
NFL title
before thee,
and give thee
victory.

Win for COACH
Win for GOD
Win for TEAM

Lombardi gave the Redskins victories, and he gave them pride.
For the first time in 14 years, the
Redskins won more games than
they lost. Copyright © 1969 by The
Washingtonian Magazine. Photograph by Curt Barlow; sculpture
by Charles Mendez.

10

September 3, 1970

WHEN THE ANNOUNCEMENT was made that Vince Lombardi was dead, it was impossible to believe. We knew he had been sick, but you never thought he would ever die. I mean you knew that he would die someday but you never thought about his dying. Even in the hospital, you always thought that the next announcement would say he had recovered and would be at practice tomorrow.

And so on that day he died, millions of people who knew of him and about him and hated him or loved him and hated his Packers or loved them, all felt a terrible loss. Here was this squat Italian with the horrible temper whose teams had destroyed pro football teams everywhere. And people all over were crying. After all, he was only a football coach.

Or was he just that? Is any man just what the title says he is? If it says school teacher, is that all you are? If it says taxi driver, is that all you are? Vince Lombardi showed us all that we are and can be more than what the label says. He was more than a football coach in the same way that Michelangelo was more than just a painter. He was a man who fought for what he wanted out of life, and he never let his goals be sidetracked by adversity.

Watching his teams play, you knew that they were an extension of his personality, and as they overcame the opposition, you knew that it was his heart and his guts and his mind out there with them. It was that fire about Lombardi we all remember. He was alive in the fullest meaning of the word. Lombardi was electric. Just being with him in the same room, you could feel his power and his strength. And every year he put it on the line for all of us to watch. In effect, he said, "Here is my team. This is my creation and these are my people. If you want to be better, you'll have to beat us on the field." And watching this year after year, you could feel the challenge and the intensity as they went after him and his team.

That's what we like to see in this country. A guy stands up and says I'm the best and backs it up. Today, we have too many of the compromisers running things. Too many taking the easy way out so they won't have to solve life's problems. Lombardi never took the easy way. And we respected him for that.

Vince Lombardi loved America. He made it big in this country knowing that there is no other place on earth where a man not born to the purple could have accomplished what he did. He wanted desperately for America to continue to grow so that everyone might have a chance to do what he had done. He never understood people who had no goals in life. And he dismissed them if they ever passed his way.

"Winning isn't everything; it's the only thing." What's wrong with that? He did not mean that you had to cheat and kill to win. He meant that you gave everything you had to achieve your goals, within the rules of society. And if you sometimes failed, at least you had tried. And the next time, by trying harder, you may win. And everybody knows that winning, no matter what it is, is a hell of a lot better than losing.

Now, he is gone and yet he is still with us. You can't watch football without someone mentioning Lombardi and that's good. They should always talk about him. For he gave us a standard of excellence that everyone should try to emulate. Indeed, he was not the perfect man; he knew that better than anybody. But he fought to overcome his faults and to succeed at what he did best. And he did succeed. I wish to God he were still here to help us. But at least we still have the memories and the standard.

After he retired in Green Bay, there was a special tribute by the town and it was Vince Lombardi Day. *(Vernon J. Biever)*

VINCE LOMBARDI, 1913-1970

Shaped Packers' Dynasty

Coach Vince Lombardi Dies

By BOB VERDI

Vincent Thomas Lombardi, who shaped the Green Bay Packers pro football dynasty in the 1960s, died of cancer early yesterday in Georgetown University Hospital, Washington D.C. He was 57.

Lombardi was head coach and executive vice president of the Washington Redskins at the time of his death. His greatest triumphs were at Green Bay, however, where Lombardi won five National Football League championships and two Super Bowl titles.

Lombardi this summer underwent two operations—the first in late June. He left Georgetown Hospital on July 10, but returned for surgery again later in the month.

He had been in a coma for several days, and on Wednesday, a statement issued by his family thru the hospital ended the silence concerning his illness and confirmed that Lombardi was suffering from "an extremely virulent form of cancer."

He died at 6:12 a.m. Thursday [Chicago time].

The body will be at the Gawler Funeral Home in Washington today. Tomorrow and Sunday, the body will be at the Abbey Funeral Home, 888 Lexington Av., New York City.

On Monday, a funeral mass will be said in St. Patrick's Cathedral, New York, at 10 a. m. [Chicago time]. Cardinal ... Cook, Roman Catholic Arc... York, will conduct the mass.

Burial will follow in Moun... tery in Middletown near Red ...

Lombardi is survived by the... a son, Vincent H. of Potomac... daughter, Mrs. Susan Bickhem of Chicago Heights, Ill.

Also surviving are his parents, Mr. and Mrs. Harry Lombardi of Brooklyn, N.Y.; two sisters, two brothers and six grandchildren.

Lombardi was born June 11, 1913, in Brooklyn, to Harry and Matilda [Izzo] Lombardi. His fater, an Italian immigrant, was a wholesale meat dealer; his mother pri... marily spent time at home ... —daughters ...

... in business and distinguished himself on t... gridiron as a spunky 170-pound guard on t... renowned and feared line, the "Seven Bloc... of Granite."

Frank Leahy, the legendary Notre Dam... coach, was a line coach for Lombardi ... Fordham. Said Leahy: "He wasn't lar... physically. I don't recall ... relieved him ...

Spor...

"The right words ... come easily when I ... express my deep so... the passing of Vin... bardi," said George ... the Bears yesterday.

"All too few m... around to match his ... leadership and ...

...WS, TUESDAY, SEPTEMBER 8, 1970

Football Mourns Loss of Lo...

By DAVE BRADY

...ASHINGTON, D. C. — Green ... was Camelot to the common ... when Vincent Thomas Lom...di dwelt there.

...e eminence of that hamlet as ...rofessional football shrine was ...e secure from all the foul in...ues of designing metropolises ... his mere residence.

...ashington, D. C., was big ...ugh for President Nixon and ...bardi if the Chief Executive ... willing to move up his tele...on news conference, as ap...red to be the case when the ...sty little Signor, who died of ...cer, September 3, made his ...t grand entrance.

...he snoops of the news media ... from the White House as if ...were about to be sacked again ... the British to get to the press ...ference of the executive vice-...esident of the Redskins in the ...andeliered opulence of the ... Sheraton-Carlton Hotel.

...t was the measure of the 5-...t-8 Ghengis Kahn to tow... over mere mortals such as ...rt Starr, Daryle Lamonica and ...en Al Davis and mustachioed ...n Davis when the Green Bay ...ckers were getting ready to re...force once more their suprem...y in the Super Bowl.

A Great Non-Competitor

Never had a non-competitor ...minated a promotion of such ...agnitude, but by the unspoken ...t unanimous admission of mil...ons who would see the game ...rough the miracle of the magic ...e, he did.

It was his commitment to ex...ellence that made such an ap...eal to a populace yearning for ...mporary relief from the quiet ...esperation of everyday life.

He underwent an indoctrination ... the importance of being No. 1 ...y a godfather with established ...redentials, the famed horse train...er, Sunny Jim Fitzsimmons. They ...ere neighbors in the upper-mid...dle-class Sheepshead Bay section ...f Brooklyn.

Lombardi, the boy, melted in the ...thnic pot of the big city as a ...tudent at Cathedral and then St. ...rancis Prep. His father, Henry, ...ventually convinced Vincent that ... this life "there is no hurt; hurt ...s in the mind."

The son learned the le... ...and as an ...

bu... en... 1... ligh... feri... doc... wan... spiri... while... Lon... could... of his... traps. ...umphs ... town ... describ... executiv... ern.

Wiv...

Not a ... gratiated ... players' ... mortificati... champions... coats. The ... would have ... gain basen... all those ... lators of Lo...

Small won... fare was na... He burrowed ... ness of the ci... of the Counc... tions, was pre... Health Associ... the State Can... of Pop Warner ... man of the St... cal ...

NEWS phot...

Harry Lombardi and wife, Matilda (left, photo right) arrive at cathedral for son's ...

St. Patrick's Is Jamme... For Vince Lombardi ...

By MARTIN McLAUGHLIN

"In that last struggle with death this man won the final victo... praying for all of ... words Cardinal Cooke join... ...thedral and with sports ...

☆☆ Section 3 —3

Pepe's series ... Legend and ... e 70.

...chool's famous ... - Alex Wojcie...n, Ed Franco, ...arbartsky and ...

... most famous ...ade up the list ...ers, including ... Lombardi's ...ons — Bart ... and Willie ...

...earer

...rs were Col. ...o was head ... when Lom... tant; Tony ...acker great ...ve with the ... Williams,

president ... the presid... National ...

Many ... names w... Jerry K... Sonny J... and A l... Brown, ... Rote of ...

O...

Lom... H., se... Mass, ... patio... from ... bers ... son ... Mar... the c... att... he... Bi...

...DEX TO
...n King 39
...latters 46
...McHarry 51
...les 56
..., Children 52
...s
..., Voice
... This
...ecurity
...arket
...ylvester

CHICAGO TRIBUNE, FRIDAY, SEPTEMBER 4, 1970

...ince Lombardi, Famed Football Coach, Dies at 57

[Co...nued from first page]

...et with a woeful pro...onal team.

... talked with the bosses ...the Packers — "with our ...uctant permission," ac...rding to a Giants' official. "I knew it was time to ...ake a move, if I ever was ...going to make one," Lombardi said. "It is a challenge."

On Jan. 28, 1959, Lombardi, at age 45, accepted the challenge. He signed a five-year contract as head coach and general manager of the Packers. The Giants released him from the last year of his contract. "I'm in the unique position of being very happy to have this opportunity and very sad to be leaving the Giants," he said.

He replaced Ray [Scooter] McLean as coach and Verne Lewellen as general manager. He inherited a moribund team with a 1-10-1 record, worst in Packer history.

"I'm no miracle man," he cautioned the Packer brass time and time again. What followed was, of course, a miracle.

What followed was nine glorious years for the Packers and Green Bay—years that put the smallest town [population 63,000] in pro football on the map, and ... six division titles and ...championships. ... over,

Packer Jerry Kramer carrying Lombardi off field after Green Bay routed Oakland Raiders in 1968 Super Bowl.

Green Bay Mourns Loss of Old Friend

GREEN BAY, Wis., Sept. 3 (UPI)—It rained in Green Bay today.

It was as if the steel-gray skies were in mourning, too. Shrouds of rain obscured ... Field, the site of ... Lombardi's ...

The players grew to accept the "Lombardi Spartanism." He was very tough, but very respected.

"The best thing you can do when he is chewing you out," said one veteran, "is to just sit and be still—mighty still. Pretty soon he'll cool off and five minutes later he won't remember what he was mad about. He's just a tremendous perfectionist."

"When Mr. Lombardi says 'sit down,' I don't even bother to look for a chair," said one ...cker veteran.

... He treats us all ... grinned

...ability — you need a strong defense for morale purposes," Lombardi taught. "I can still hear Red Blaik saying 'there is nothing more discouraging to a bunch of players than sitting on the bench watching some other team run roughshod over your defense.'"

Always at Lombardi's side were his assistants. "Our coaches have no secrets from each other," said St. Vincent. "Nothing—absolutely nothing—is ever done by one of our coaches without the full knowledge of the other coaches."

Lombardi, as general manager, also kept total surveillance over the Packers' financial situation.

"He'll count those bucks sometimes like they were the last dollars in the world," observed an aide. "And then he'll turn right around and shell out a bundle for a party for the players and their wives."

And there were plenty of reasons for parties, for while the 7-5 record in '59 was a revelation, it was Lombardi's poorest season in Green Bay.

In 1960, Lombardi guided Green Bay to an 8-4 record and a Western Conference championship, but "The Pack" was defeated in the N.F.L. title game by Philadelphia, 17 to 13. Lombardi blamed himself for the loss, citing as faulty his first quarter strategy to go for a touchdown [which failed] rather than a field goal. "I made the wrong guess," he moaned.

The dynasty fully burgeoned in 1961, when the Packers won 11 of 14 regular season games and trounced the Giants, 37 to 0, for Green Bay's first league championship since 1944. ... labeled itself ... rightfully so.

TV Special on Lombardi Set Tonight

NEW YORK, Sept. 3 (UPI)—The American Broadcasting Company will televise a half-hour special tomorrow night on Vince Lombardi called "Vince Lombardi—What His Life Was All About."

The show, which will be shown from 6:30 to 7 p. m., Chicago time, will be a film tribute, utilizing exclusive ABC-TV footage of his career ... Green Bay and his first ... camp with ... last

Coach Lombardi and Quarterback Bart Starr made a celebrated winning combination for the Packers in 1965, 1966, and 1967, when the Packers won three successive NFL championships.

...skins' ultra-efficient training camp that summer. The Redskin players, who were seldom accused of shunning the good life, worked hard for Lombardi.

"I have no preconceived notions about the Washington players," Lombardi said, alluding to the tales of their nightlife. "Whatever happened in the past is in the past."

Indeed it was. The Redskins won seven games, lost only five, tied two and finished second in the Capitol Division in 1969.

"There is," Lombardi said after the season, "plenty of work to do here. There were some good points this year, and some disappointments."

During the off-season — if there was such a luxury for him — Lombardi dabbled in golf, but spent much of his time at home. A deeply religious man, he was always active in community life — near New York, Green Bay, then Washington.

During the spring, Lombardi was inducted into the Fordham Hall of Fame.

When asked recently about today's problems with youth, Lombardi replied: "I do not question the right of young people to dissent, I only question their right to destroy. I don't know what all this revolution stuff is about. I just know I don't like to hear such talk. You will not hear about any member of the Washington Redskins talking this way."

Lombardi said the charges that the violence of football parallels the violence on college campuses were "ridiculous . . . a school without football is in danger of becoming a medieval study hall."

Lombardi was involved in preparations for the upcoming season and the summer contract negotiations among N.F.L. players and owners when, on June 27, he underwent surgery in Georgetown Hospital. Doctors removed a tumor and a two-foot section from his colon. The hospital report said the tumor ... benign." It wa...

The Lombardi Credo

Following is an excerpt of a speech made by Vince Lombardi earlier this year:

"Leaders are made, they are not born; and they are made just like anything else has ever been made in this country—by hard effort. And that's the price that we all have to pay to achieve that goal, or any goal.

"And despite of what we say about being born equal, none of us really are born equal, but rather unequal. And yet the talented are no more responsible for their birthright than the underprivileged. And the measure of each should be what each does in a specific situation.

"It is becoming increasingly difficult to be tolerant of a society who has sympathy only for the misfits, only for the maladjusted, only for the criminal, ... Have sympathy for them, help them, ... for all of us to stand up for ... one who recog... who ...

World Pays Tribute to Vince

His passing away is a ...t loss, not only to foot... but also to the entire ...try."

...sewhere in the nation, ...rs joined in paying trib... to the onetime boy from ...oklyn who became a ...ter coach.

...om New Brunswick, ..., Col. Earl [Red] Blaik, ...r whom Lombardi ...ed as an assistant coach ... Army before joining the ...essional ranks, said: ...ombardi epitomized 20th ...ury America by his devotion to his family and dedication to his church and country. He was a strong-willed man whose extraordinary success in life came from a seriousness of purpose and hard work. This, coupled with a remarkable intellect, made him the peer of his profession.

"He was a volatile, sometimes gruff, loveable, loyal friend who somehow seemed indestructible."

Football Commissioner Pete Rozelle, in New York, described Lombardi as "a very rare person" and said his death was "a deep, personal loss to all in professional football, but those who will miss him the most are those who still had yet to play for him, who might have been taught by him, led by him and counseled by him."

At Green Bay, Wis., Phil Bengtson, who succeeded Lombardi as head coach and general manager of the Packers, said no one had a stronger influence on his life than his former boss.

"By example he taught the value of complete dedication to his family, his religion and his profession," Bengtson said.

Bart Starr, the Green Bay quarterback tapped for the No. 1 job by Lombardi when he took over the Packers in 1959, said at team practice:

"I told my wife before I left the house this morning that it was like losing a father . . . I felt that strongly about him."

ington Redskins are working out in preparation for an exhibition game Saturday, Wide Receiver Charlie Taylor said:

"It seems all the people I gained so much from and admired are no longer with us —John Kennedy, Martin Luther King . . . and now Coach Lombardi."

Sonny Jurgensen, veteran quarterback who had his greatest season in 1969 under Lombardi, said, "I learned to love that man. I benefitted tremendously as a football player and as a person. I hope we can go on playing the games of football and life the way he wanted them played."

Another Redskin, Wide Receiver Bob Long, said he visited the dying coach three weeks ago.

"I was on National Guard duty and got a long lunch hour to go to the hospital," he said. "I tried to thank him for all he'd d...

said he always admired Lombardi because "he brought out the best in people.

"He was a man who was kind of misunderstood by the public," Landry added. "He was looked upon as a tough, hard type, but he had a great heart and was compassionate."

In Madison, Wis., Gov. Warren Knowles said, "the citizens of Wisconsin will always remember the exciting championship years of the Green Bay Packers under Vince's leadership. He brought the Packers to the pinnacle of professional excellence and made himself and his teams a legend in their own time."

In Boston, where his team is playing the Red Sox, Manager Mayo Smith of the Detroit Tigers said:

"The sports world doesn't realize just how much they'll miss him ...

spurred us on — his determination to win. He always told us second place was nothing."

Grabowski said he had spent a lot of time thinking about Lombardi and would "always cherish the two years I played under him."

Zeke Bratkowski, the former super-sub quarterback who now is backfield coach, said the most gratifying thing about Lombardi was "being exposed to his philosophy of life."

...I wi...
your ...
will b...
that t...

He ...
at 126...
for hi...
embar...
lenge-...
ratic...
son al...

"Wa...
and ...
have ...
a foot...
said ...
role.

not c...
rappo...
the e...

Th...
whip ...
In...

Dr...
upon ...

Farewell to Vince

the swirling, emotional frenzy that ...ed the Green Bay Packers after their ...eously dramatic victory over the Cowboys in the final 13 seconds of ...67 championship playoff, the heroes interviewed endlessly. No statement with more impact than that delivered by Jerry Kramer, whose thunderous ...y touchdown.

...rry reached all the way to Camelot ...l a parallel to the one-for-all spirit ... Green Bay team. Then he spoke of ...ach, Vince Lombardi.

...is one beautiful man," said Jerry. ...was a strange choice of words, almost ...n their incongruity. Vince was one ...least beautiful of men—on the out...But Kramer was looking deeper. He ...riends, players, associates and others ...connected with him over the years ...eautiful man.

...'s why there had been so much ap...sion in sports circles for almost two ...as the whispers kept spreading that ...had been victimized by cancer. It ...be the same race-horse type that ...down five years ago another beau...an, Jack Mara of the football Gi...nie's close friend and also mine. ...ad a nobility of character although ...mbardi personality was far more ...x than Mara's.

Expert Critique

...ne could possibly have ...

Vince Lombardi
This was one beautiful ma...

left-handed tribute to the overw... strength of the man that he coul... mand such iron discipline in an er... men sneered contemptuously at au... including such once impregnable ... holds as the Army, the courts a... church.

Vince was so strong that he just c... comprehend the situation when ... was ordered to the hospital only ... ago. It was impossible, he thoug... anyone with his vigor could be ill. ... if he expected to wish i... ill power.

The Warning

...left the hospital the fir... ...owner battle was rag... ...t there was no indicati... ...settled in time to start t... ...much less the wholes... ...showed up at one sessio... ...gaunt. But the old fire... ...within him.

..." he said to the ... ...way your game to a ... ...kids."

...voice of management. ...e. It was not heede... ...panic of a quick settle... ...rdi words made a mo... ...than he thought w... ...hey are likely to be r... ...rs to come. Many c... ...ated them as if they ... ...treasured.

...thing esoteric abo... ...ught. It was straigh... ...hose two key fund... ...g and good tackli... ...well in his dema... ...fection that he ha... ...most successful coa...

HEAVY PRAISE FOR FORMER PACKER COACH

Lombardi's Death Shocks Players

By BUD LEA

They were well aware of the seriousness of his illness. Those veterans who played under Vince Lombardi at Green Bay. Yet, the announcement of Lombardi's death Thursday morning had a shocking effect on the Packers.

"I can't face the reality of it," said Willie Wood, who 11 years ago wrote Lombardi for a tryout and then became an All-Pro safety. "I always felt there was some real hope that he would recover."

From 1959 to 1968 this was Lombardi country. Titletown, if you please. The Packers un-

Football League championships.

There are only 15 Packers left on the 1970 team who wear Super Bowl rings. Those are the ones who mourn him deeply.

Quarterback Bart Starr, who knew Lombardi well, solemnly said, "I told my wife before I left the house this morning that it was like losing a father. I felt that strongly about him. Fellows who had the pleasure of playing under him are better people for it."

"One thing that was characteristic of him was the pursuit of excellence. He said the pur-

suit of excellence would make you a better person than you otherwise might be content to be. I think it was the most valuable thing he left with us.

"I know I'm a better person than I otherwise would have been."

Reserve defensive end Phil Vandersea, whom Lombardi sent to New Orleans in the expansion draft and then recalled him the next year to Green Bay, said, "I only played one year under him but it was an experience I'll never forget. I know what a great man he was."

Wide receiver Carroll Dale

was one of the key players Lombardi acquired in trades.

"I appreciate the confidence he showed in me when I came from the Rams," Dale said. "He was a great man because he was interested in the total development of a player — of becoming the best possible citizens we could be."

Donny Anderson and Jim Grabowski — the big catches in the 1966 draft — both were moved by Lombardi's death.

"It's tragic that a person that young with so much ability has to pass away," said Anderson. "As far as a person I didn't get to know him v

24   Jeter   "L..."

...wski, along with ... Lombardi three ... Col. 2

der Lombardi had built an image that nobody could beat them in the big games and they proved it by winning two Super Bowls and five National

---

Starr   Dale

...l be ...with ... the

...s, and ...her 25 ... teams, ... football ...including ... Packers, ... Redskins ... Roosevelt ... and Kyle

...mbers ...n, Vincent ...during the ...lay partici...ort passage ...ment. Mem...ncluding the ...'s widow, ...munion from

...of the family ...daughter and ...and Mrs. Paul ... his

...mbardi, Football Coach, Dies

...was Feb. 2, 1968. A year later Lombardi resigned as general manager of the Packers to become head coach of the Washington Redskins.
—Photo by Vernon J. Biever

As one of Fordham's Seven Bl... Granite in 1935, Vince Lombar... 175 pound guard. Two years le...

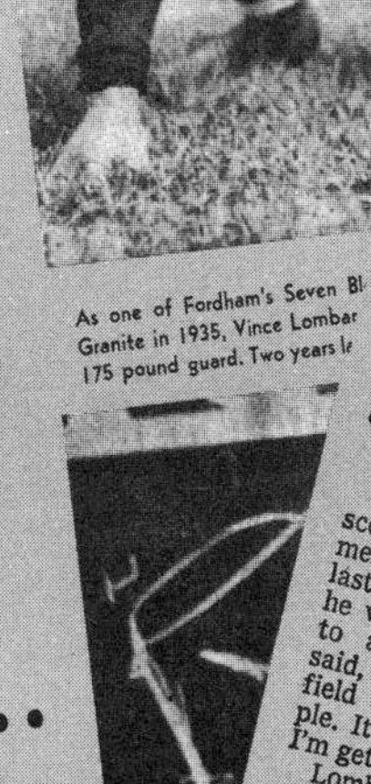

Vince Lombardi, Pro Footba...

Continued From Page 1, Col.

Sunday." Edward Bennett Williamns, president of the Redskins, early in 1969 offered Lombardi a position as coach, general manager and owner of 5 per cent of the team's stock, and the offer was quickly accepted.

"Everyone wants to own something sometime. Isn't that right?" asked Lombardi in explaining why he resigned the Packer post with five years remaining on his contract.

Lombardi was a symbol of authority.

"When he says 'Sit down,' I don't even bother to look for a chair," one of the Packer players explained.

"He's fair. He treats us all the same—like dogs," said Henry Jordan, another Packer.

"He coaches through fear," said Bill Curry, a sensitive player Lombardi let go.

Most of his athletes accepted his demanding ways and biting criticisms. His primary target was a player named Marvin Fleming, who said in reflection, "I didn't mind. When I came to him I didn't have anything. He taught me how to be a winner."

Another Packer, Jerry Kramer, said, "His whippings, his scoldings and his driving all fade; his good qualities endure."

'It's for Them'

Lombardi admitted that his scoldings sometimes were merely for effect. During his last season at Green Bay, when he was goading an aging team to another championship, he said, "I have to go on that field every day and whip people. It's for them, not just me. I'm getting to be an animal."

Lombardi was always a hard man when it came to football.

In college, at Fordham where he graduated with honors in 1937, he played guard on a famous line called the Seven Blocks of Granite. He was the smallest of the group at 5 feet 8 inches and 175 pounds. "But he hit like 250," a teammate said.

The son of an immigrant Italian butcher, Lombardi was born June 11, 1913, and grew up in the Sheepshead Bay section of Brooklyn. He went to Cathedral High School and St. Francis Preparatory School before Fordham. His ambitions to ...

Vince Lombardi demonstrating a pitchout to quarterbacks at training session in Washington. Last year, the team had its first winning season in 14 with Redskins. He was coach, general manager and part owner.
The New York Times (by Mike Lion)

President Leads T...

Many notab... yesterd...

...ssing play. He once said, "Coaches who can outline plays on a black... zen. The ones who win get inside their players and motivate them."

...son

...r Vince . . .

Robert Riger

By BUD LEA

I had been covering the Green Bay Packers for five years and was becoming quite resigned to writing about losers. During this span I had outlasted three coaches.

Being young and optimistic, I truly believed each head coach — in his own way — could have ended the drought that set in during the late 40s. After all, there was a winning tradition at Green Bay. The Packers had won six National Football League titles—all in the dark ages.

It didn't happen.

When the team hit skid row in 1958 and finished with its worst record ever, it ...sports...

...PRESSIONS

...LACE ...profes... ...who ...d dedi... ...intesti... ...George... ...hington, ... Marie, ... were at... ...ted the ... ...the pre... ... National ...nineteen... ...league...

The Redskins had long been losers. But Vincent Thomas Lombardi had never associated with losers in his 31 years as a football coach.

Last year, his first in Washington, the Redskins had their first winning record in 14 seasons.

"Winning isn't everything," Lombardi once insisted. "It is the only thing."

Under his direction the Green Bay Packers won six division titles and five national Football League championships in nine...

best winning record and Lombardi was acclaimed as the sport's best coach.

He retired from coaching after the 1967 season, when he was 53 years old. But his wife and his close friends wondered how long he could stay away from the sidelines. The answer: one year. Most pro football games are played on Sunday afternoons and during the season that Lombardi confined himself to the duties of the Packers' general mana... ger he said, "I miss the fire o...

Serve ...nkind

...of the greatest of great man with the

...ian ...born ...up in ...tion of ...Franci...fore F...tions to ...

...was ...success. ...line day... ...said. "Th... ...inside the... ...vate them."

...Lomb... ...was no... ...the
...of ...room ...coul... ...have ...Jacks ...tache

They named after him the street on which the Packer offices are located. *(Vernon J. Biever)*

Marie Lombardi makes the acceptance speech at the dedication of the Vince Lombardi Service Area on the New Jersey Turnpike *(New Jersey Turnpike Authority)*

A moment of silence in memory of Vince Lombardi before his beloved Packers take the field. #66 is Ray Nitschke, the great linebacker who was the heart of Lombardi's defense.

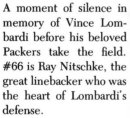

Vince Lombardi can be remembered for many things: football greatness, a towering desire for achievement, discipline, excellence, strength and fire. But to those who knew him well, who enjoyed his company and friendship, he'll be remembered for the warm laughing man he was. (*Vernon J. Biever*)

Index

Adderly, Herb, 72, 88, 99, 131, 166, 186, 190
Aechtner, Mike, 155
Allan, George, 158
American Football League (AFL), 38, 54, 86–87, 99, 113, 141, 154, 183, 194, 204
Anderson, Donny, 83, 187, 191, 195
Austin, Bill, 94, 95–96

Baltimore Colts, 11, 35, 38–39, 71, 87, 93, 151, 152, 155, 156, 166, 172, 173, 176–77, 178, 185, 187, 188, 194
Barbatsky, Al, 52
Bell, Bert, 69, 70, 82
Bengston, Phil, 75, 85, 120, 122, 123, 144, 174, 187, 195–96, 197
Bilotti, Ray and "Duds," 14, 69, 135; on Vince Lombardi, 118–24
Blackburn, Lisle, 93
Blaik, Col. Earl, 32, 50, 54, 58–60
Borden, Nate, 111
Bratkowski, Zeke, 101, 166
Breslin, Eddie, 38, 175
Brockman, Bob, 140–41
Brodie, John, 22
Brown, Allen, 187
Brown, Jimmy, 36, 87
Brown, Larry, 205
Brown, Paul, 71, 75, 82
Brown, Peter Campbell, 38, 204
Bucannan, Buck, 170, 171
Buck, Jack, 154
Buffalo Bills, 183

Cahill, Joe, 51; on Vince Lombardi, 58–62
Canadeo, Tony, 68, 119, 134, 158; on Vince Lombardi, 82–88, 151, 153
Carpenter, Lew, 104
CBS, 139, 147, 151, 154, 156, 157
Cerotti, Hooks, 43
Chandler, Don, 152, 172

Chicago Bears, 19, 75, 120, 123, 165, 172, 196
Christman, Paul, 154
Cleveland Browns, 36, 64, 68, 71, 87, 110, 155, 172–73, 184, 186, 207
Cohane, Tim, 130, 159
Cone, Fred, 93
Conerly, Charlie, 63, 64
Cosell, Howard, 191
Costello, Vince, 184
Cox, Father Ignacius, 53
Crowley, Jim, 28, 52, 54
Currie, Dan, 72, 84

Dale, Carrol, 84
Dallas Cowboys, 74, 84, 85, 146, 152, 153, 169, 173, 174, 186, 188, 189, 190–92, 193, 194
Daly, Art, 142
Danowski, Ed, 32
Davis, Willie, 69, 71, 72, 84, 87, 96, 104, 124, 147, 166, 168, 169, 175; on Vince Lombardi, 110–14
Detroit Lions, 93, 123, 131, 132, 151
Devine, Dan, 122, 123, 138, 145
Dowler, Boyd, 75, 141, 154–55, 190, 191
Dumont Network, 139

Esquire magazine, 145–46, 159–60, 173

Fink, Jim, 140
Ford, Lenny, 64
Fordham University, 13, 19, 25, 28, 29, 31–32, 50, 51, 52–53, 83, 130
Fleming, Marv, 186, 187
Forester, Bill, 72, 93
Fredrickson, Tucker, 183

Gifford, Frank, 51, 87, 205; on Vince Lombardi, 63–65
Gowdy, Curt, 154
Grabowski, Jim, 83, 185, 186
Graham, Otto, 184–85
Green Bay Packers, 9, 10, 16–17, 24, 25,

35–36, 37, 47, 52, 53, 54, 67–124 *passim*, 132, 139, 176–77, 185–93, 216; black players on, 110–11; Vince Lombardi as general manager of, 14, 37, 70, 75, 84, 113, 120, 143, 156–58, 196; Vince Lombardi becomes coach of, 10–11, 13, 17, 28, 33, 51, 62, 63, 64, 67–68, 69–70, 82, 134, 151; NFL titles and, 12, 14, 17, 19, 34, 75, 112–13, 121, 130, 131, 146, 151, 153, 156, 178, 182, 188, 190; Super Bowl and, 12, 14, 36, 37, 75, 84–85, 86–87, 99, 101, 113, 141–42, 143, 152, 154–55, 169–70, 171–72, 178, 188–89, 194–95; training camp for, 12, 95–96, 100–101, 111, 131, 173

Gregg, Forrest, 11–12, 68, 88, 104, 111, 147, 185, 187, 189, 190; on Vince Lombardi, 93–99

Gremminger, Hank, 72, 93, 99

Halas, George, 75, 120
Hamburger, Chris, 205
Hanner, Dave "Hawg," 71–72, 93, 100
Hart, Doug, 195
Hartman, Sid, 144
Hawkins, Alex, 177–78
Heinz, Bill, 17, 86, 124, 130–32, 138, 205; on Vince Lombardi, 132–35
Holeb, E. J., 171
Hornung, Paul, 11, 73, 87, 88, 93, 96, 104–105, 131, 147, 166, 167, 168, 177, 182, 205
Howell, Jim Lee, 12, 33, 54–56, 63, 82, 164
Howton, Bill, 71, 93
Huff, Sam, 87, 172, 183
Humphrey, Hubert H., 14, 15

Izenberg, Jerry, 139–40, 147, 159; on Vince Lombardi, 164–80

Johnson, Chuck, 158–59
Jones, Deacon, 189
Jordon, Henry, 71, 72, 84, 87, 124, 168
Jurgenson, Sonny, 23, 198, 205, 209–10

Kansas City Chiefs, 36, 54, 86–87, 99, 101, 141–42, 155, 160, 170, 171–72
Karras, Alex, 131, 209
Kennedy, John F., 9, 14–15, 62
Keppler, Jack, 86
Kinsel, Jim, 142
Kramer, Jerry, 11, 68, 87, 88, 143, 168, 187, 195, 207
Kramer, Ron, 87, 93

Lambeau, Curly, 83
Landry, Tom, 63, 74, 164, 190
Lane, Chuck, 138–39, 170–71, 172, 177, 193
Lilly, Bob, 190, 191, 209

Lindeman, Bard, 134
Lombardi, Beth Ann (Joe's daughter), 43
Lombardi, Betty Costanza (Joe's wife), 27, 34, 35, 38, 39; on Vince Lombardi, 41–44; marriage of, 31, 32, 43
Lombardi, Billy (Joe's son), 35
Lombardi, Claire (Vince's sister), 29
Lombardi, Dorothy (Vince's cousin), 40
Lombardi, Harold (Vince's brother), 29, 31, 32
Lombardi, Harry (Vince's father), 27, 29, 32, 33–34, 35, 37–38, 42; Vince's death and, 40–41
Lombardi, Jill (Joe Jr.'s wife), 39
Lombardi, Joe (Vince's brother), 42, 175; on Vince Lombardi, 27–41; marriage of, 31, 32, 43; on St. Cecilia's team, 29, 30, 31, 45
Lombardi, Madeline (Vince's sister), 29
Lombardi, Marie (Vince's wife), 14, 28, 29, 32, 33, 35, 37, 39, 42, 85, 118, 119, 121, 130, 131, 134, 172, 178, 197; Vince's death and, 39–41, 160
Lombardi, Matilda (Vince's mother), 27, 28, 29, 33, 34, 37, 42; Vince's death and, 40–41
Lombardi, Pete (Vince's uncle), 40–41
Lombardi, Vince, Jr. (Vince's son), 39
Los Angeles Rams, 16, 83, 85, 93, 104, 111, 156, 158, 186, 187, 188, 189–90, 194, 204

McGee, Max, 73, 75, 96, 104, 147, 154, 155, 166, 195
McHan, Lamar, 101–104
McLean, Scooter, 93, 94, 151
McPartland, Father Guy, 27, 29; on Vince Lombardi, 45–48
McPhail, Bill, 154
Manuche, Mike, 38, 39, 122, 131, 175–76, 205
Mara, Wellington, 51, 82, 170, 183; on Vince Lombardi, 52–56
Mara family, 33, 38, 39, 51, 70, 82, 164, 204
Martin, Billy, 153
Matte, Tom, 172
Mercein, Chuck, 85, 211; on Vince Lombardi, 183–98
Miami Dolphins, 123, 160
Miller, Tom, 68, 122, 140, 141, 157; on Vince Lombardi, 69–77
Minnesota Vikings, 99, 123, 140, 153, 156, 160
Moore, Tom, 166, 205
Murphy, Jack, 170
Murray, Jim, 145, 159

National Football League (NFL), 37, 38, 39, 51, 54, 86–87, 99, 101, 113, 119, 140, 141, 143, 152, 155, 170, 174, 175, 183–85, 205; draft, 122, 151, 183, 206;

title games, 11, 12, 14, 17, 19, 34, 75, 112–13, 121, 130, 131, 146, 151, 153, 155, 164, 188, 190; Western Conference titles, 16, 75, 152, 156, 177
NBC, 147, 154
New York Giants, 9, 10–11, 13, 34, 38, 39, 52, 53, 62, 71, 85, 87, 113, 131, 165, 172, 183, 186, 206; Vince Lombardi as offensive coach for, 10, 12, 25, 33, 50, 51, 56, 60, 63–66, 82, 83, 94, 153, 164–65
New York Jets, 38, 183, 194, 204; Super Bowl and, 38, 39
New York University, 28, 53
Nitschke, Ray, 17–18, 72, 88, 196
Nix, Doyle, 93
Nixon, Richard M., 14–15
Nolan, Dick, 154
Noll, Chuck, 160

Oakland Raiders, 194–95
Olejiniczak, Dominic, 82, 165
Owen, Steve, 52, 164

Palan, Andy, 29
Paquin, Leo, 28
Parkey, Reggie, 46
Philadelphia Eagles, 34, 38, 113, 151, 204
Pierce, Nat, 52
Pitts, Elijah, 153, 166, 185, 190, 205
Pittsburgh Steelers, 11, 139, 160, 184
P. J. Clark's, 39
press, Vince Lombardi and, 13, 37, 40, 70, 85, 123, 124, 132–33, 138–80 passim, 190
Price, Eddie, 63
Promuto, Vince, 198; on Vince Lombardi, 206–11
Proski, John, 142

Quinlan, Bill, 71, 72, 84, 168

Riger, Robert, 130
Robinson, Dave, 84
Robustelli, Andy, 87
Rockne, Knute, 54, 160
Rollow, Copper, 159
Rote, Kyle, 63, 87
Rote, Tobin, 93
Rozelle, Pete, 170
Run to Daylight! (Lombardi and Heinz), 10, 17, 130–32, 135, 171, 207

St. Cecilia's High School, 13, 19, 25, 27, 28, 45–47, 135; Joe Lombardi and, 29, 30, 31, 45; Vince Lombardi teaches at, 31, 42–43, 47, 50,
St. Louis Cardinals, 184, 196
San Diego Charges, 12
San Francisco 49ers, 104, 140, 154
Schecter, Leonard, 145–46, 159–60, 173

Scott, Hal, 156–57
Scott, Ray, 139, 140; on Vince Lombardi, 151–61
Seven Blocks of Granite, 28, 29, 52, 82
Sherman, Allie, 183, 184, 185, 192
Shula, Don, 84, 160
Skoronski, Bob, 93, 178
Smith, Jerry, 198
Smith, Red, 9–10, 13, 74, 87, 130, 132, 147, 159, 165
Solomon, Mars, 34
Sports Illustrated, 9, 188, 196
Starr, Bart, 11, 12, 16, 19, 22–23, 67, 68–69, 74, 75, 77, 87, 88, 93, 96, 118, 124, 131, 139, 141, 143, 144, 147, 166, 167, 168, 172, 177, 185–97 passim; on Vince Lombardi, 105–106
Stengle, Casey, 153
Summerall, Pat, 154
Super Bowl, 12, 14, 37, 75, 84–85, 120, 143, 144, 152, 160, 169, 174, 188–89, 194–95; first, 87, 99, 101, 113, 141–42, 147, 154–55, 169–70, 171–72; Jets vs. Colts, 38
Sutherland, Jock, 52

Taylor, Charley, 198
Taylor, Jim, 11, 68, 73, 82, 84, 85, 87, 88, 93, 166, 167, 172, 182, 205
television, 11, 15–16, 36, 39, 40, 75, 138, 139, 140, 151, 160, 171, 187, 192
Thurston, Fuzzy, 73, 141, 146, 169–70, 171, 195
Tittle, Y. A., 87, 183

Unitas, Johnny, 22, 87, 152, 177

Voris, Dick, 134–35

Walker, Val Joe, 93
Wallace, Bill, 165
Washington Redskins, 13, 185; Vince Lombardi as coach of, 37, 38, 39, 47, 68, 75–76, 85,–86, 100, 105, 123, 134, 174, 196–97, 198, 204–11 passim
Webster, Alex, 87
Weiss, Don, 142
West Point Academy, 13, 15–16, 25, 51, 60, 62, 82, 83, 160; Vince Lombardi becomes coach at, 31, 32, 50, 51, 58–59
Whitaker, Jack, 154
White, Billy, 46
Whittenton, Jesse, 72
Williams, Edward Bennett, 204
Williams, Travis, 186, 194
Wilson, Ben, 84–85, 186
Winter, Max, 140
Wojohowicz, Walter, 28, 54
Wood, Gary, 183, 184
Wood, Willie, 72, 101, 124, 190–91
Worty, Frank, 52